American Literary Scholarship

1963

American Literary Scholarship

An Annual / 1963

Edited by James Woodress

Essays by Walter Harding, Hyatt H. Waggoner, Willard Thorp, Sculley Bradley, John C. Gerber, B. R. McElderry, Jr., Richard P. Adams, Frederick J. Hoffman, Richard Beale Davis, Louis J. Budd, J. Albert Robbins, C. Hugh Holman, Louis D. Rubin, Jr.; Charles T. Davis, Oliver Evans, Malcolm Goldstein, Harry Finestone.

Duke University Press, Durham, North Carolina, 1965

Foreword

The idea for this book originated when I returned from a year in Europe and was overwhelmed by the quantity of scholarship produced during my absence. The MLA bibliography now lists more than 1,500 items in American literature each year. It seemed to me that there was a real need for an annual review in which various scholars would survey the past year's work in American literature within their particular areas of competence. I proposed the present project to the Advisory Council of the American Literature Group and they adopted it as a Group project. I invited the contributors represented herein to join the enterprise, and the Duke University Press agreed to publish the essays. I hope that this collection will be the first volume of an annual series.

Without being bound by many restrictions, each contributor was asked to write a brief essay summarizing the year's work in some segment of American literary scholarship. The aim was to provide a guide for scholars in areas adjacent to their own fields of specialization. Because this was the first volume in a projected series, it was agreed that the individual essays could deal, if space permitted, with the scholarship of recent years as well as the output of 1963. Some of the contributors were able to go back to 1961 or 1962; others had their hands full covering the calendar year 1963. In general, the volume edited by Floyd Stovall for the Modern Language Association, *Eight American Authors* (1956), was the model for this work. Contributors, however, were given a free hand to evaluate the scholarship under review, if they wished, and they have availed themselves of the opportunity to varying degrees. They also were allowed to be selective or inclusive in the choice of items reviewed. Some have preferred to cover as much ground as possible, discussing many articles and books briefly; others have reviewed in more detail only the items regarded as the most important. Thus it is that no effort has been made to fit all the essays into a Procrustean pattern.

The most significant difference between this work and the MLA-sponsored volume lies in the scope of the project. The essays here do not deal only with the most important individual authors. More than half of the essays cover periods, genres, combinations of both, or pairs of authors. There is also an essay treating the scholarship classified by the MLA bibliography as miscellaneous. This has been included on the grounds that these items, some of which are very important, are likely to be overlooked by scholars because they do not fit neatly into pigeonholes. The net has been cast widely enough that most of the items listed in the 1963 MLA bibliography have been reviewed.

The form of bibliographical notation used follows closely the style adopted by the MLA bibliography. In general the articles reviewed give the author of the article, the title, the journal, the volume, and the pages. It may be assumed that in every case, unless otherwise stated, the year is 1963. When articles are cited from journals that page each number separately, the number of the issue is included. The periodicals in which the articles appear are repre-sented by abbreviations or acronyms, and a key to the periodicals may be found in the front matter. Books cited are listed with author, title, place of publication, and publisher. The dates, as with journal citations, are 1963 unless otherwise noted.

I am greatly indebted to the seventeen contributors who have submitted essays for this volume. Their efforts represent a large expenditure of time and effort in the service of fellow scholars. The volume also could not have been produced without the competent assistance and encouragement of Jeanine Ianne, Marion Magee, and Roberta Woodress.

James Woodress

San Fernando Valley State College
Northridge, California

Table of Contents

Key to Abbreviations

AGR	American-German Review	CUF	Columbia University Forum
AH	American Heritage		
AI	American Imago	Cweal	Commonweal
AION-SG	Annali Istituto Universitario Orientale, Napoli, Sezione Germanica	DA	Dissertation Abstracts
		DR	Dalhousie Review
		DramS	Drama Survey (Minneapolis)
AL	American Literature		
AlaR	Alabama Review	DVLG	Deutsche Vierteljahrsschrift für Literaturwissenschaft und Geistesgeschichte
AN&Q	American Notes and Queries		
AQ	American Quarterly	E&S	Essays and Studies by Members of the English Association
AR	Antioch Review		
ASch	American Scholar		
AtM	Atlantic Monthly	EIC	Essays in Criticism (Oxford)
BA	Books Abroad		
BAASB	British Association for American Studies Bulletin	EIHC	Essex Institute Historical Collections
		EJ	English Journal
BB	Bulletin of Bibliography	ELH	Journal of English Literary History
BBr	Books at Brown		
BHPSO	Bulletin of the Historical and Philosophical Society of Ohio	ELN	English Language Notes
		ES	English Studies
		ESQ	Emerson Society Quarterly
BNYPL	Bulletin of the New York Public Library	EUQ	Emory University Quarterly
BSTCF	Ball State Teachers College Forum	Expl	Explicator
		FFC	Folklore Fellows Communications
BuR	Bucknell Review		
CB	Classical Bulletin	FN	Fitzgerald Newsletter
CE	College English	ForumH	Forum (Houston)
CH	Church History	GaHQ	Georgia Historical Quarterly
CJ	Classical Journal		
CJF	Chicago Jewish Forum	GaR	Georgia Review
CL	Comparative Literature	HJ	Hibbert Journal
CLAJ	College Language Association Journal (Morgan State Coll., Baltimore)	HMAB	Harvard Medical Alumni Bulletin
		HTR	Harvard Theological Review
ClareQ	Claremont Quarterly		
CLC	Columbia Library Columns	HudR	Hudson Review
CLQ	Colby Library Quarterly	ISHSJ	Illinois State Historical Society Journal
ColQ	Colorado Quarterly		
Com	Commentary	JA	Jahrbuch für Amerikastudien
CRAS	The Centennial Review of Arts & Science		
		JASA	Journal of the American Statistical Association
Crit	Critique: Studies in Modern Fiction		
		JEGP	Journal of English and Germanic Philology
CritQ	Critical Quarterly		

JGE	Journal of General Education
IHI	Journal of the History of Ideas
JPH	Journal of Presbyterian History
JQ	Journalism Quarterly
KR	Kenyon Review
L&P	Literature and Psychology (N.Y.)
LHUS	Literary History of the United States
LitR	Literary Review (Fairleigh Dickinson Univ., Teaneck, N.J.
MASJ	Midcontinent American Studies Journal
MD	Modern Drama
MdHM	Maryland Historical Magazine
MF	Midwest Folklore
MFS	Modern Fiction Studies
MHR	Missouri Historical Review
MidR	Midwest Review (Nebr. State Teachers Coll. at Wayne)
MissQ	Mississippi Quarterly
MLQ	Modern Language Quarterly
MLR	Modern Language Review
ModA	Modern Age (Chicago)
MP	Modern Philology
MQ	Midwest Quarterly (Kans. State Coll. at Pittsburg)
MR	Massachusetts Review
MSpr	Moderna Sprak (Stockholm)
MTJ	Mark Twain Journal
NA	Nuova antologia
NCF	Nineteenth-Century Fiction
NCHR	North Carolina Historical Review
NDQ	North Dakota Quarterly
NEQ	New England Quarterly
NOQ	Northwest Ohio Quarterly
NR	New Republic
NS	Die neueren Sprachen
NYTBR	New York Times Book Review
OUR	Ohio University Review
OW	Orient/West
PAAS	Proceedings American Antiquarian Society
PAPS	Proceedings of the American Philosophical Society
PBA	Proceedings of the British Academy

PBSA	Papers of the Bibliographical Society of America
Person	Personalist
PMASAL	Papers of the Michigan Academy of Science, Arts, and Letters
PMHB	Pennsylvania Magazine of History and Biography
PMHS	Proceedings of the Massachusetts Historical Society
PMLA	Publications of the Modern Language Association of America
PNQ	Pacific Northwest Quarterly
PolR	Polish Review
PQ	Philological Quarterly (Iowa City)
PR	Partisan Review
PrS	Prairie Schooner
QH	Quaker History: Bulletin of the Friends Historical Association
QJS	Quarterly Journal of Speech
RACHSP	Records of the American Catholic Historical Society of Philadelphia
REL	Review of English Literature (Leeds)
Ren	Renascence
RES	Review of English Studies
RHT	Revue d'histoire du théâtre
RIH	Rhode Island History
RLM	La Revue des lettres modernes
RLV	Revue des langues vivantes (Bruxelles)
RNC	Revista nacional de cultura (Caracas)
RUL	Revue de l'Université Laval (Quebec)
SatR	Saturday Review
SAQ	South Atlantic Quarterly
SB	Studies in Bibliography: Papers of the Bibliographical Society of the University of Virginia
SELit	Studies in English Literature (Eng. Lit. Soc. of Japan, Univ. of Tokyo)
SFQ	Southern Folklore Quarterly
Shen	Shenandoah
SM	Speech Monographs
SN	Studia neophilogica
SoQ	Southern Quarterly
SovLit	Soviet Literature
SQ	Shakespeare Quarterly
SR	Sewanee Review
SWR	Southwest Review

TAr	*Theater Arts*
TCL	*Twentieth Century Literature*
TDR	*Tulane Drama Review*
TFSB	*Tennessee Folklore Society Bulletin*
Thoth	(Dept. of English, Syracuse University)
THQ	*Tennessee Historical Quarterly*
TQ	*Texas Quarterly* (Univ. of Texas)
TR	*La Table ronde*
TSB	*Thoreau Society Bulletin*
TSBooklet	*Thoreau Society Booklet*
TSE	*Tulane Studies in English*
TSL	*Tennessee Studies in Literature*
TSLL	*Texas Studies in Literature and Language*
TUSAS	Twayne United States Authors Series
TWA	*Transactions of the Wisconsin Academy of Sciences, Arts, and Letters*
UKCR	*University of Kansas City Review*
UMPAW	**University of Minnesota Pamphlets on American Writers**
VC	*Virginia Cavalcade*
VMHB	*Virginia Magazine of History and Biography*
VQR	*Virginia Quarterly Review*
WF	*Western Folklore*
WHR	*Western Humanities Review*
WMH	*Wisconsin Magazine of History*
WMQ	*William and Mary Quarterly*
WSCL	*Wisconsin Studies in Contemporary Literature*
WWR	*Walt Whitman Review*
XUS	*Xavier University Studies*
YR	**Yale Review**
YULG	*Yale University Library Gazette*

Part I

Part I

1. Emerson, Thoreau, and Transcendentalism

Walter Harding

i. Transcendentalism

Transcendentalism as a movement, despite the fact that it was one of the most vital and productive in American literary history, has always been and still continues to be strangely neglected by literary scholars. There has never been an adequate history of the movement and, so far as I know, there is none in sight. Comparatively little attention has been paid to its sources and still less to its influences. It is disappointing but not surprising then to find that so little has been done in the field in the past year.

Cameron Thompson, in "John Locke and New England Transcendentalism" (*NEQ*, XXXV, 1962, 435-457), documents the fact that New England Transcendentalism was primarily a revolt against John Locke's "sensationalism," which had for more than a century dominated American philosophy and which had been largely responsible for the development of Unitarianism in America. The Transcendentalists centered their attacks chiefly on Locke's philosophy; and conservatives, such as Andrews Norton and Francis Bowen, who replied to these attacks replied primarily in Lockean terms. Paul Osborne Williams, in "The Transcendental Movement in American Poetry" (*DA*, XXIII, 1962, 1372-73), points out that the five chief Transcendental poets—Emerson, Thoreau, Jones Very, Christopher Cranch, and Ellery Channing the Younger—were the most radical American experimentalists in poetry of their time, writing verse metrically rough, varied in verse length, often colloquial, free in rhyming practices, and often highly compressed. The central theme of their poetry was the process of experimentation, but they also discussed such topics as isolation, friendship, love, and the alliance of man and natural law. Chester E. Eisinger, in "Transcendentalism: Its Effect upon American Literature and Democracy," *American Renaissance, the History of an Era: Essays and*

Interpretations (Frankfurt, Diesterweg, 1961), pp. 22-38, gives a brief but cogent history of the movement. After a recent extended visit to India, Frederic I. Carpenter, in "American Transcendentalism in India (1961)," (*ESQ*, No. 31, pp. 59-62), reports that because of a lack of adequate texts there has been surprisingly little interest in such figures as Emerson and Thoreau in the Indian universities, but through the inherited tradition of Gandhi's interest, the influence of American Transcendentalism on the political leaders of the country has been spectacular. Kenneth Walter Cameron, in *Transcendental Climate: New Resources for the Study of Emerson, Thoreau, and Their Contemporaries* (3 vols.; Hartford, Conn., Transcendental Books), has gathered together such primary source materials on Transcendentalism as the catalogues of the Hasty Pudding Library of 1838, the Boston Social Library of 1823, and the Columbian Social Library of Boston in 1815. He also includes among other items F. B. Sanborn's diary of 1854-1855, Charles Chauncey Emerson's Commencement Address, and the early records of the Concord Lyceum.

ii. Ralph Waldo Emerson

Although only a few years ago scholars were universally acknowledging an apparent decline in interest in the life and writings of the Sage of Concord and he was being dismissed in some circles as an outdated Victorian, there has recently been a resurgence of interest that belies any supposed loss of vitality.

a. **Bibliography, texts, and editions.** *The Journals and Miscellaneous Notebooks of Ralph Waldo Emerson, Vol. III, 1826-1832* (ed. William H. Gilman and Alfred R. Ferguson, Cambridge, Mass., Harvard Univ. Press: Belknap) brings the new, definitive edition up through the years of Emerson's engagement and marriage to Ellen Tucker and her death, his school-teaching, his Divinity School days, his pastorate of the Second Church in Boston, and his visit to Florida. As with the earlier volumes in this edition, we are presented with a scrupulously exact text, coming perhaps as close to the original manuscripts as can be done in a printed text.

    Emerson's "Indian Superstition," a short poem which he wrote for an exhibition at Harvard in 1821, was edited with a long introduction on his interest in Orientalism at Harvard and many annotations by Kenneth Walter Cameron in a limited edition in 1954. It has now been re-issued for more general circulation in *ESQ*, No. 32, Pt. 1. Kenneth Walter Cameron, in *Index-Concordance to Emerson's Sermons with Homiletical Papers* (2 vols.; Hartford Conn., Transcendental Books), has provided scholars with a 709-page alphabetical concordance of 150 of Emerson's unpublished sermons, plus an essay on "History and Biography in Emerson's Unpublished Sermons" (pp. 654-661), a note on "Emerson's Ideal Clergyman: Hersey Bradford Goodwin" (p. 662), a reprinting of Emerson's "Right Hand of Fellowship" (p. 663), an outline of three of his sermons (pp. 664-667), the "Homiletical Background of Emerson's 'Gnothi Seauton'" (pp. 668-693), "Emerson's Anecdote from Goethe of St. Philip Neri and the Nun" (pp. 693-694); and a checklist of "Emerson's Preaching Record, 1826-1838" (pp. 695-703). In *Transcendental Climate* he has gathered together source materials pertaining to many of Emerson's college activities such as his reading, his classes, his Bowdoin prize dissertations, and his extracurricular activities, as well as the later writing of "Uriel." And in "'Indian Superstition' and Orientalism in Emerson's Harvard" (*ESQ*, No. 33, pp. 7-15), he lists and describes the contents of some books of Oriental literature possibly available to Emerson when he was a student at Harvard.

b. **Biography.** Brad Luckingham, in "The Pioneer Lecturer in the West: A Note on the Appearance of Ralph Waldo Emerson in St. Louis, 1852-1853" (*MHR*, LVIII, 70-88), gives a very full account of Emerson's six lectures on "Conduct of Life" given in St. Louis in December, 1852, and January, 1853, and their reception. "Photographs of Literary Concord, Emerson, and His Family" (*ESQ*, No. 32, Pt. 2) is a collection of forty-one 8½" x 11" photographs of Emerson, members of his family, and Concord scenes.

c. **Criticism.** A. M. Baumgartner, in "'The Lyceum is My Pulpit': Homiletics in Emerson's Early Lectures" (*AL*, XXXIV, 477-486), believes that Emerson's early homiletical training at the Harvard Divinity School, and particularly his reading there of such authors as Jeremy Taylor and Hugh Blair, helped him to develop the techniques that made him the most popular figure in the lyceum of his day. Ray Benoit, in "Emerson on Plato: The Fire's Center" (*AL*, XXXIV, 487-498), shows that the apparent inconsistency of Emerson's being simultaneously claimed as a pragmatist and an idealist is actually a logical inconsistency that stems from his contact with Plato and that he chose neither spirit nor matter but viewed each as aspects of a ground of being higher than both. Paul Lauter, in "Emerson through Tillich" (*ESQ*, No. 31, pp. 49-55), feels that if Emerson's religious ideas and concepts are examined in the light of Paul Tillich's theology, they are revealed to be not vague, soft, and platitudinous, as many have felt, but vital and strikingly pertinent to our anxious culture today. William Magee Wynkoop, in "Three Children of the Universe: Emerson's View of Shakespeare, Bacon, and Milton" (*DA*, XXIII, 3358-59), believes that Shakespeare, Bacon, and Milton represented three stages in the development of religious awareness to Emerson; that Shakespeare, because of his deficiency of moral and religious feeling, represented Innocence; that Bacon, through his moral fall in the Essex case, suffered and became receptive to the Moral Sentiment; and that Milton was the true poet who advanced beyond the level of the Sayer to that of the Knower. Harold L. Berger, in "Emerson and Carlyle—Stylists at Odds" (*ESQ*, No. 33, pp. 61-65), feels that probably no two writers, so one at heart in their beliefs, have been more antithetical in expressing them than Emerson and Carlyle. Carlyle's prose was like a mountain torrent; Emerson's like a smooth flowing river of the plains; Carlyle was concerned with the practical and immediate; Emerson, with the speculative. But each by following his own inclination made a contribution to our literature and thought. Yukio Irie, in "Emerson and Quakerism" (*SELit*, Eng. No., pp. 63-82), demonstrates that Emerson was much more widely read in Quaker literature than is generally believed and was profoundly influenced by Mary Rotch, the New Bedford Quaker.

As to more specific criticisms of Emerson's individual works: Chadwick C. Hansen, in "Ralph Waldo Emerson's 'Nature': Gospel of Transcendentalism" (*American Renaissance*, pp. 39-51), presents a carefully worked out detailed explication of the essay, section by section. Patrick F. Quinn, in "Poe's *Eureka* and Emerson's *Nature*" (*ESQ*, No. 31, pp. 4-7), suggests that a joint reading of Emerson's first major essay and Poe's last sheds new light on both because both authors were trying to answer essentially the same questions. It also emphasizes the fact that Emerson's essay is primarily an affirmation of life while Poe's is a poem of death. And Kenneth Walter Cameron, in "Emerson's *Nature* and British Swedenborgian-

ism (1840-1841)" (*ESQ*, No. 30, pp. 11-89), reveals that David
George Goyder, in his *Biblical Assistant and Book of Practical Piety*
(London, 1841), published in its entirety Emerson's essay *Nature*,
and may thus have helped to create an audience for Emerson in England, but also stirred up a controversy among the British Sweden-
borgians about the "errors" of Emerson's doctrines. Portions of
Goyder's book, including the printing of *Nature*, are reproduced in
facsimile. Henry Nash Smith, in "The American Scholar Today"
(*SWR*, XLVIII, 191-199), states that the same type of young men to
whom Emerson addressed his "American Scholar"—those whose love
of letters and ideas placed them in opposition to society—exist today
and find in the writings of Paul Goodman and William H. Whyte
what Emerson's scholars found in his writings. And Robert H. Woodward, in "Emerson's Cinder Metaphor in 'The American Scholar'"
(*ESQ*, No. 33, p. 17), points out that Emerson's odd use of the word
"cinders" indicates he was thinking of it in the sense of coke or char-
coal and thus still capable of supporting flame. According to Dan
Vogel, in "Orville Dewey on Emerson's 'The Lord's Supper'" (*ESQ*,
No. 31, pp. 40-42), the essay "Religious Institutions" in the *Christian
Examiner* for November, 1832 (XIII, 253-272), is apparently a reply
by Emerson's kinsman Orville Dewey to his sermon on the Lord's
Supper. Clark Griffith, in "Caves and Cave Dwellers: The Study of
a Romantic Image" (*JEGP*, LXII, 551-568), indicates that caves
and cave dwellers were favorite images of Emerson as well as of
Melville, Poe, and Hawthorne; and that in his essay on "Illusions"
in particular, the cave symbolized the limitations of knowledge and
constituted a threat to values from which man must escape. John
Lydenberg, in "Emerson and the Dark Tradition" (*CritQ*, IV, 1962,
352-358), says that although Emerson is usually thought of as an
apostle of sweetness and light, in his essay on "Experience" he shows
at least an awareness of the same feelings of nightmare and horror
that characterize the writings of Poe, Melville, Faulkner, and
Hemingway. Here the few cheerful notes are all but drowned in a
tone of gloomy emptiness. For a brief moment, at least, he was as
frightened and shuddering as any of our American apostles of
darkness. Edward J. Rose, in "Emerson and King Arthur" (*ESQ*,
No. 33, pp. 49-51), cites an apparently original fable about King
Arthur that Emerson recorded in his 1822 journal as a good example
of the lasting appeal that the figure of Arthur has often had for
English and American writers.

As for Emerson's poetry: Robert L. White, in "Emerson's
'Brahma'" (*Expl.* XXI, Item 63), suggests that Emerson's most controversial poem is primarily anti-Christian but addressed to his
contemporary Christian audience in an attempt to explain his own
personal rejection of the Christian dogma that the proper end of
man is heaven. James E. White, in "Emerson's 'Hypocritic Days':
Actors or Deceivers?" (*ESQ*, No. 33, pp. 72-73), suggests that the
word "hypocritic" in Emerson's poem "Days" should be interpreted
as "acting out a part." After studying various Oriental sources available to Emerson, Kiffin Ayres Rockwell, in "Emerson's 'Hamatreya'—
Another Guess" (*ESQ*, No. 33, p. 24), suggests that Emerson might
have created the title word to mean "children of Father Sky / Mother
Earth." E. J. Rose, in "Melville, Emerson, and the Sphinx" (*NEQ*,
XXXVI, 249-258), contrasts the use of the sphinx symbol in Melville's chapter of that name in *Moby-Dick* and in Emerson's poem,
showing that it reveals Emerson's characteristic confidence in the
explicability of the "all" and Melville's skepticism. Paul O. Williams,
in "Meaning in Emerson's 'Una'" (*ESQ*, No. 31, p. 48), suggests
that Una in Emerson's poem seems to be a mental presence always
with a traveler but which disappears when one is at home.

d. **Reputation and influence.**   Richard Eberhardt, in "Emerson and
Wallace Stevens" (*LitR*, VII, 51-71), contrasting the Concord and
Hartford poets, says, "where one can secure the kernel of significance in Emerson in studying one poem, such as 'Brahma,' one
cannot get the meaning of Stevens without reading many." Emerson
he thinks relatively straightforward and simple; Stevens, complex.
You may read Emerson on your own level, but you read Stevens
to excel yourself. Joseph Marion Garrison, Jr., in "John Burroughs
as a Literary Critic: A Study Emphasizing His Treatment of Emerson, Whitman, Thoreau, Carlyle, and Arnold" (*DA*, XXIII, 3372-
73), details the record of Burroughs' personal acquaintance with
Emerson and traces, in chronological order, his changing attitude
towards Emerson's writings. Paul C. Wermuth, in "Santayana and
Emerson" (*ESQ*, No. 31, pp. 36-40), says that Santayana was more
attracted to Emerson than might be supposed and that his often
ambiguous attitude toward him might be attributed to the fact that
he resembled him in many ways. Shunsuke Kamei, in "Emerson,
Whitman, and the Japanese in the Meiji Era" (*ESQ*, No. 29, 1962,
pp. 28-32), cites a number of examples of interest in Emerson in

Japan in the Meiji era (1868-1912), including a Japanese biography published in 1894. Edith Mettke, in *Der Dichter Ralph Waldo Emerson: Mystisches Denken und poetischer Ausdruck* (*Beihefte zum JA*, No. 11, Heidelberg, Carl Winter), tries to correct the opinion of the German public that Emerson was famous only for his prose. She makes a study of his early and mature poetry and concludes that Emerson was a gifted poet of peculiar poetic and mystical insight.

iii. Henry David Thoreau

As an aftermath of the 1962 centennial commemoration of the death of Thoreau, the amount of published material on him, always large in recent years, is this year even larger. Two collections of essays— "Thoreau: A Centenary Gathering," edited for the Autumn, 1962, issue of the *Massachusetts Review* by John H. Hicks and also issued as *TSBooklet*, No. 17 and *The Western Thoreau Centenary*, edited as *Utah State University Monograph X* by J. Golden Taylor and also issued as *TS Booklet*, No. 19—add considerably to the literature for the year.

a. **Bibliography, texts, and editions.** [Leo Stoller], in "Henry David Thoreau, 1817-1862: Books, Manuscripts, and Association Items in Detroit and Ann Arbor" (*TS Booklet*, No. 18, pp. 1-13), catalogues in detail an exhibition at Wayne State University commemorating the centennial of Thoreau's death. Included are facsimiles and careful transcriptions of a number of unpublished Thoreau manuscripts. Walter Harding, in "Additions to the Thoreau Bibliography" (*TSB*, No. 82, pp. 3-4; No. 83, pp. 2-4; No. 84, pp. 3-4; No. 85, p. 3), lists and describes all current additions to the Thoreau bibliography as well as newly discovered earlier items. Joseph J. Moldenhauer, in "A New Manuscript Fragment by Thoreau" (*ESQ*, No. 33, pp. 17-21), reproduces and annotates a brief unpublished manuscript of 1859 that was apparently once a part of Thoreau's essay on "Autumnal Tints."

    Thoreau: People, Principles and Politics, ed. Milton Meltzer (New York: Hill and Wang), is a collection of Thoreau's political essays, such as "Civil Disobedience" and "Life without Principle," tied together with a series of further political comments excerpted from the letters and journal. *The River: Selections from the Journal,* arranged with notes by Dudley C. Lunt (New York: Twayne), presents in a seasonal arrangement an anthology of his journal comments on the rivers of his native Concord.

b. **Biography.** Milton Meltzer and Walter Harding, in *A Thoreau Profile* (New York: Crowell, 1962), present the first pictorial biography of Thoreau, the text a pastiche of the writings of Thoreau and his contemporaries. Carl Bode, in "The Half-Hidden Thoreau" (*MR*, IV, 1962, 68-80), applying Freudian techniques to a study of Thoreau's life, concludes that he never outgrew a mother fixation, that he constantly searched for a father-substitute, and that he willed his own death to expiate his feelings of guilt. Dorothy Nyren, in "The Concord Academic Debating Society" (*MR*, IV, 1962, 81-84), presents the official records of a debating club in which Thoreau participated as a boy of eleven or twelve. Louise Osgood Koopman, who is the ninety-nine-year-old daughter of the Ellen Sewall Thoreau once loved, in "The Thoreau Romance" (*MR*, IV, 1962, 61-67), tells some of the family traditions about Thoreau and reveals that Ellen Sewall reciprocated Thoreau's interest much more than has been suspected. Paul Schwaber, in "Thoreau's Development in *Walden*" (*Criticism*, V, 64-77), feels that Thoreau matured greatly as an individual during the writing of *Walden* and though he was still at odds with the habitual and wrong attitudes and institutions of men, he was not nearly as prickly as he had been. Raymona E. Hull, in "Hawthorne's Efforts to Help Thoreau" (*ESQ*, No. 33, pp. 24-28), traces Hawthorne's efforts to aid Thoreau's career as a writer and suggests that he was much ahead of his time in recognizing Thoreau's genius. Robert W. Bradford, in "Thoreau and Therien" (*AL*, XXXIV, 499-506), investigates the "dark and muddy" problem of Thoreau's attitude toward Alek Therien, the French-Canadian woodchopper of *Walden*, and concludes that while Thoreau first hailed him as a "Homeric" man, he became bitterly disillusioned with him when Therien became an alcoholic. Harriet M. Sweetland, in "The Significance of Thoreau's Trip to the Upper Mississippi in 1861" (*TWA*, LI, 1962, 267-286), makes the first systematic study of Thoreau's western journey, pointing out the value of his abbreviated notes as an historical record of early Minnesota, stressing the influence the journey must have had on Thoreau's companion, the seventeen-year-old Horace Mann, Jr., and pointing out that Thoreau cut his plans for the trip short because of his rapidly fading health. Kenneth Walter Cameron, in *Transcendental Climate*, has gathered together source materials pertaining to Thoreau's journey to Canada, his surveying (including all his field notes), his lecturing in Concord, and his reading.

c. **Criticism.** Reginald L. Cook, in "Think of This, Yankees" (*MR*, IV, 1962, 44-52), feels that the trait which defines the special quality of Thoreau is the relentless exercise of moral will in pursuit of a goal and that if he were alive he would be standing up to be counted on the major moral issues of our day. J. Golden Taylor, in "Thoreau and the Integrity of the Individual" (*TSBooklet*, No. 19, pp. 16-28), believes that the heart of Thoreau's philosophy is a belief in the integrity of the individual and that those individuals who follow their heart's desire based on self-knowledge make the most valuable contributions to society. Paul Lauter, in "Thoreau's Prophetic Testimony" (*MR*, IV, 1962, 111-123), argues that all of Thoreau's writings are prophetic, in the Biblical sense, in that they are "an embodiment of a man's search to incarnate his ultimate values in his actions and the final means by which that man would attempt to move others toward their own testimonies to such values." William Drake, on the other hand, in "Spiritual Ideals and Scientific Fact: Thoreau's Search for Reality" (*TSBooklet*, No. 19, pp. 54-62), believes that because Thoreau's "search for reality" led him away from mankind and into solitude, it resulted in a barrenness of imagination and final unfulfilment. Robert S. Dickens, in "Thoreau and the 'Other Great Tradition'" (*ESQ*, No. 29, 1962, pp. 26-28), asserts that Thoreau's statements about God classify him as a panentheist who views God as "Eternal-Temporal Consciousness, Knowing and Including the World in His Own Actuality." Willard H. Bonner, in "Mariners and Terreners: Some Aspects of Nautical Imagery in Thoreau" (*AL*, XXXIV, 507-519), points out that many of Thoreau's most vivid images in his writing are associated with the sea or the seashore, that the sea symbolized spiritual existence for Thoreau, but that since not all of life is spiritual, Thoreau thought man can live the most vital existence on the shore between the marine (spiritual) and terrene (material) worlds. Edward J. Rose, in "'A World with Full and Fair Proportions': The Aesthetics and the Politics of Vision" (*TSBooklet*, No. 19, pp. 45-53), says that Thoreau's politics, like his aesthetics, is born of the vision of one who in striving for perfection becomes a work of infinite art, one with the totality of all things because he is at one with himself. Richard Drinnon, in "Thoreau's Politics of the Upright Man" (MR, IV, 1962, 126-138), points out that while it is a matter of definition as to whether or not Thoreau is termed an anarchist, through such writings as "Civil Disobedience" he made a major contribution to radical politics today, while Richard M. Weaver, in "Two Types of American Individualism" (ModA, VII, 119-134), contrasts the philosophies of Thoreau and John Randolph of Roanoke and concludes that Thoreau's is anarchic and subversive while Randolph's should be cultivated today.

As to more specific comments on Thoreau's individual works: Fred Erisman, in "Thoreau and the Texas Colonel" (ESQ, No. 31, pp. 48-49), suggests that when Thoreau refers to "Fanning" in A Week, he probably meant James Walker Fannin [sic], a colonel in the Texas revolutionary army. William White, in "A Week in the Feinberg Collection" (TSB, No. 85, p. 2), describes Whitman's copy of Thoreau's first book as well as a copy that Thoreau corrected for a Miss Caroline C. Andrews. Koh Kasegawa, in "Thoreau's Walden: A Nature-Myth" (SELit, XXXIX, 213-240), feels that Walden should be read as Thoreau's nature-myth, "symbolic of his own and man's everlasting quest for the unity of his spiritual dualism—an existential and aesthetic unity of the conscious with the unconscious, Spirit and Nature, Self and World." Walter Harding, in "Five Ways of Looking at Walden" (MR, IV, 1962, 149-162), points out that Thoreau's masterpiece may be approached as a nature book, a guide to the simple life, a satirical criticism of modern life, an example of good writing, and a guidebook to a higher spiritual life. Lee A. Pederson, in "Thoreau's Rhetoric and Carew's Lines" (TSB, No. 82, p. 1), suggests that Thoreau included Carew's lines on "The Pretensions of Poverty" at the end of the "Economy" chapter of Walden in mocking deference to those who did not agree with his opinions. Paul O. Williams, in "The Borrowed Axe: A Biblical Echo in Walden?" (TSB, No. 83, p. 2), suggests that Thoreau might have been thinking of II Kings 6:1-7 when he spoke in Walden of dropping his borrowed axe into the pond. Martin Leonard Pops, in "An Analysis of Thoreau's Cape Cod" (BNYPL, LXVII, 419-428), is the first to give serious critical attention to Thoreau's account of his excursions to Cape Cod and finds that while it lacks economy, intensity, and wholeness, it does have commendable character analysis, descriptive passages and humor that give us a different viewpoint of the author from that provided in some of his better-known works. For many years Fanny Eckstorm's "Thoreau's *Maine Woods*" (*AtM*, CII, 1908, 16-18, 242-250) has been considered the authoritative discussion of the book, but Mary P. Sherwood, a trained naturalist, in "Fanny Eckstorm's Bias" (*MR*, IV, 1962, 139-147), has checked over Mrs. Eckstorm's statements and concludes that most of her criticisms of Thoreau as a woodsman are the result of a personal bias against out-of-staters and that actually Thoreau was remarkably adept in the woods.

d. **Reputation and influence.** Edgar L. McCormick, in "Thoreau and Higginson" (*ESQ*, No. 31, pp. 75-78), points out that Thomas Wentworth Higginson, now almost completely forgotten as a critic, was one of the earliest to recognize Thoreau's genius and that his reviews of Thoreau's books did much to keep interest in Thoreau alive through the latter years of the nineteenth century. Richard Bridgman, in "Holmes, Thoreau, and Ponds" (*TSB*, No. 83, pp. 1-2), suggests that Oliver Wendell Holmes was satirizing Thoreau when he spoke about the vagabonds at Wuinnepeg Pond in *Elsie Venner*. And Joseph Marion Garrison, Jr., in "John Burroughs as a Literary Critic: A Study Emphasizing His Treatment of Emerson, Whitman, Thoreau, Carlyle, and Arnold" (*DA*, XXIII, 3372-73), traces, in chronological order, Burroughs' changing attitude towards the writings of Thoreau.

George Hendrick, in "Thoreau in the Twentieth Century" (*American Renaissance*, pp. 89-96), stresses that Thoreau's ideas are as pertinent today as in his own day and cites his influence on Gandhi as an example. Stanley Edgar Hyman, in "Henry Thoreau Once More" (*MR*, IV, 1962, 163-170), after reading six recent books on Thoreau—Henry Beetle Hough's *Thoreau of Walden*, Leo Stoller's *After Walden*, Sherman Paul's *The Shores of America*, Perry Miller's *Consciousness in Concord*, Walter Harding's *Thoreau Handbook*, and Mark Van Doren's *Henry David Thoreau*—feels that contemporary critics tend to overlook Thoreau's cantankerousness and to forget that he was primarily a writer rather than a reformer or a naturalist, and that they overemphasize the influence of Transcendentalism as a movement on him. Gladys E. H. Hosmer, in "Remarks on Thoreau, Concord, and Walden" (*TSBooklet*, No. 19, pp. 9-15), describes the current interest in Thoreau in his native town and gives the history of the recent campaign by the Thoreau Society to save Walden Pond's woods from the axe, while Theodore Baird, in "Corn Grows in the Night" (*MR*, IV, 1962, 93-103), feels that despite Thoreau's values, there has been a cult growing around him which refuses to admit any of his weaknesses. Walter Harding, in "The Influence of Civil Disobedience" (*TSBooklet*, No. 19, pp. 29-44), points out the wide influence Thoreau's essay has had on Gandhi, the Danish anti-Nazis, the Reverend Martin Luther King, and various American radicals. Willard Uphaus, who at the height of the McCarthy hysteria of a decade ago was queried by the Attorney General of New Hampshire and sent to jail for one year for contempt of court for refusing to reveal the names of guests at his World Fellowship Center, in "Conscience and Disobedience" (*MR*, IV, 1962, 104-108), says he based his refusal on the same principles which Thoreau endorsed in "Civil Disobedience." William Stuart Nelson, in "Thoreau and American Non-Violent Resistance" (*MR*, IV, 1962, 56-60), points out that all the current participants in sit-ins, freedom rides, and other forms of non-violent resistance are deeply indebted to Thoreau for the principles he set forth in his essay on "Civil Disobedience." Leo Stoller, in "Civil Disobedience: Principle and Politics" (*MR*, IV, 1962, 85-88), says that Thoreau's essay is experiencing a renaissance of influence because those fighting to end segregation for the Negro see conditions that dictate the use of non-violent resistance in order to be successful.

Thornton H. Parsons, in "Thoreau, Frost, and the American Humanist Tradition" (*ESQ*, No. 33, pp. 33-43), suggests that Thoreau was a precursor of Irving Babbitt and Frost, who has carried the humanist tradition on since Babbitt's time, and that the three men present surprisingly close philosophies. D. Gordon Rohman, in "*Walden I* and *Walden II*" (*PMASAL*, XLVIII, 639-648), contrasts Thoreau's *Walden* with the *Walden Two* of the contemporary psychologist B. F. Skinner and concludes that the two books have nothing in common, for Thoreau concerns himself with producing better men through developing individual integrity while Skinner concerns himself with developing a better material world through group action. Mordecai Marcus, in "Eugene O'Neill's Debt to Thoreau in *A Touch of the Poet*" (*JEGP*, LXII, 270-279), suggests that O'Neill based the character of Cornelius Melody on Hugh Quoil, the drunken Irishman of Thoreau's *Walden*, and Simon Harford on Thoreau himself. W. Stephen Thomas, in "Thoughts of Martin Buber on Henry Thoreau" (*TSB*, No. 85, p. 1), reports on a personal interview with the Jewish philosopher in which Buber spoke of his high regard for Thoreau's writings. Sholom J. Kahn, in "Thoreau in Israel" (*TSB*, No. 85, pp. 1-2), describes current Hebrew translations of Thoreau, now available in Israel, including an edition of *Walden*.

iv. The Minor Transcendentalists

Unfortunately, as is the case so often in literary research, there continues to be an overemphasis on the major figures with studies being done and redone *ad nauseum* while the minor figures, who have their own importance of a particular type, are thoroughly neglected. The year 1963 was no exception. Thirty-five books and articles appeared on Emerson and forty-seven on Thoreau. Yet for all the remaining members of the movement there were only ten.

H. Burnell Pannill, in "Bronson Alcott: Emerson's 'Tedious Archangel'" (*A Miscellany of American Christianity: Essays in Honor of H. Shelton Smith*, ed. Stuart C. Henry, Durham, N. C., Duke Univ. Press, pp. 225-247), says that if the one clear-cut mark of a Transcendentalist was that he believed in intuitive knowledge and rejected the Lockean claim that all knowledge is limited to that of external sensory perception, then Alcott was the arch-Transcendentalist of them all.

William R. Hutchinson, in "'To Heaven in a Swing': The Transcendentalism of Cyrus Bartol" (*HTR*, LVI, 275-295), points out that although many of his contemporaries thought of Cyrus Bartol (1813-1900) as "the model Transcendentalist," he is now almost completely forgotten. For fifty-two years he was pastor of the West Church in Boston and active in both Transcendentalist and Unitarian affairs, although he was often critical of the more radical Transcendentalists.

The Reverend James P. Haningan, S. J., in "Orestes Brownson and the Election of 1840" (*RACHSP*, LXXIII, 1962, 45-50), states that while Brownson, holding political office through the Democratic party, entered the campaign of 1840 with enthusiasm and wrote for it his essay on "The Laboring Classes," which through its radicalism only served to give ammunition to the Whigs, he became completely disillusioned when Van Buren was defeated, rejected social radicalism, and turned to Catholicism. Orestes Brownson's seminal pamphlet *New Views of Christianity, Society and the Church* (Boston, Munroe, 1836), which is thought by many to have had a profound effect on some of the younger Transcendentalists such as Thoreau and which has been virtually unobtainable for many, many years, has been reproduced in its entirety in facsimile in *ESQ* (No. 32, Pt. 3).

Warren Sylvester Smith, in " 'The Imperceptible Arrows of Quakerism': Moncure Conway at Sandy Spring" (*QH*, LII, 19-26), points out that Conway was started on his way towards Transcendentalism and liberal religion when as a Methodist circuit rider he became acquainted at Sandy Spring, Maryland, with Roger Brooke and other Quakers who first led him to question his orthodox beliefs in both religion and politics.

W. S. Tryon, in *Parnassus Corner: A Life of James T. Fields, Publisher to the Victorians* (Boston, Houghton Mifflin), adds much to our knowledge of the reception of the writings of the major Transcendentalists through his scholarly biography of their favorite publisher.

Perry Miller, in *Margaret Fuller, American Romantic: A Selection from Her Writings and Correspondence* (Garden City, N.Y., Doubleday), through a pastiche of her writings has created a vivid biography of Margaret Fuller. Included are not only generous samples from her letters, but also large selections from *Summer on the Lakes, Woman in the Nineteenth Century*, her book reviews, and her reports on the Italian Revolution. She emerges as one of the most thoroughly alive of the Transcendentalists.

Leo Stoller, in "Christopher A. Greene: Rhode Island Transcendentalist" (*RIH*, XXII, 97-116), gives a biographical sketch of a little-known follower of Emerson who participated in an even lesser-known community experiment, Holly Home, just outside Providence.

[Kenneth Walter Cameron], in "Two Harvard Essays by Jones Very" (*ESQ*, No. 29, 1962, pp. 32-40), publishes for the first time two of Very's undergraduate essays at Harvard, one on "The Heroic Character" of May 3, 1836, and one on "Individuality" of August 31, 1836.

We need more articles like Professor Stoller's, resurrecting the forgotten minor figures. There is still no biography available of Ellery Channing nor, to my knowledge, even an article on George Partridge Bradford, Abby Morton Diaz, O. B. Frothingham, or Samuel G. Ward, to name only a few at random. William Henry Channing's reform activities have been ignored, as has Frederick Goddard Tuckerman's poetry. Beginning scholars might do well to turn their attention to some of these figures and thus make some real contributions to our knowledge of Transcendentalism.

2. Hawthorne

Hyatt H. Waggoner

Like American literary scholarship in general, Hawthorne scholarship today is in a period of rapid transition. Historical, textual, and bibliographical studies flourish and biographical criticism leading to total re-interpretations of the man and the work provides a much larger share of the important items demanding discussion in such a review of scholarship as this than it would have, say, ten years ago.

Meanwhile criticism in the strict modern sense, the sense in which we have learned to use it in the last quarter-century, falls more and more into the hands of immature scholars and the pages of the lesser magazines. No doubt, one reminds oneself, *really* good criticism is as rare in any period as really good scholarship; but my impression that the critical impulse, the impulse to pure explication and image analysis, has, for the time being at least, almost exhausted itself remains and will not be argued away. When we look beyond the limits of 1963—a lean year in every sort of Hawthorne study— and survey the more important books of the last several years, the impression is strengthened.

i. Editions

Like it or not—and a good many who think of themselves as critics rather than scholars, in terms of the old dichotomy, do not—textual scholarship and the higher bibliography have occupied the center of the stage for the last several years. The establishment of the MLA's Center for American Editions and the undertaking of a Centenary Edition of Hawthorne by Ohio State University are expressions of the growing feeling that it is intolerable that we should have to get along with incomplete, inaccurate, and sometimes hard-to-obtain editions of our writers.

Our texts should fully reflect the advances of modern scholarship. We want no more "soiled fish" for unwary critics to explicate with metaphysical subtlety. That the Riverside Edition constantly varies from Hawthorne's text has long been clear, and though we may suspect that the overwhelming majority of the variants are minor matters of punctuation, we cannot be sure of this—without personally examining all the existing manuscripts—until all the volumes of the Centenary are out. The separate volumes are likely to provide the chief events for Hawthorne students in the years in which they appear.

Responsible critics are not likely to dispute the importance of having a good text, but differences of opinion do arise when we are asked to give absolute priority to textual study. Some scholars wonder whether the Dead Sea Scrolls and the works of a modern writer are really in the same case. But though one frequently hears such doubts as this expressed, the doubters would, I believe, only qualify, not reject the claim for the importance of textual study recently made by Fredson Bowers, textual editor of the Centenary Edition of Hawthorne, writing as an official spokesman for the MLA:

> The recovery of the initial purity of an author's text and of its revision (insofar as this is possible from the preserved documents), and the preservation of this purity despite the usual corrupting process of reprint transmission, is the aim of textual criticism. Hence the discipline lies at the base of all intellectual endeavor in our cultural heritage. (In James Thorpe, ed., *The Aims and Methods of Scholarship in Modern Languages and Literatures*, Modern Language Association, 1963.)

The attempt to establish an accurate text of *The Scarlet Letter*, with no manuscript in existence, began with Harry Levin's new Riverside Edition in 1960; continued with Bradley, Beatty, and Long's controversial corrected version of the University of Pennsylvania copy of the first edition in the revised edition of their Norton anthology in 1961 and in a separate printing in a Norton paperback in 1962; and culminated, for our time certainly, in the publication of the Centenary Edition in 1962. This version of the text will almost certainly be the standard edition, replacing the old Riverside of 1883, for the foreseeable future. It is presumably as accurate a "recovery of the initial purity" of Hawthorne's text as can be achieved.

It is noteworthy, though, that the editorial committee, even with the aid of the Hinman Collating Machine and teams of graduate students checking each other, did not uncover any "soiled fish" in the texts we have had to make do with in the past. As one reviewer with a pro-critical bias put it, no emendation in the new edition made any *critical* difference. That is not *quite* true, but very nearly. Probably the most important emendation—important for interpretation and evaluation of the work—is the change from "concentrated" to "concentred" in the first scaffold scene, when all eyes are "concentred," Hawthorne wrote, on Hester's bosom. "Concentred" is preferable, clearly, since it reinforces Hawthrone's circle imagery, not only in this scene but throughout the novel. But it is an added richness, not, by any stretch of the imagination, a possible basis for a new interpretation. In this sense, the *critical* difference it makes to a reader of the novel is very slight indeed.

The fact that the Centenary Edition excludes literary criticism, although richly equipped with historical and textual introductions and notes, raises the largest questions involved in what I have called the transitional character of present scholarship. The editorial committee's decision to put all criticism relating to the individual works, and to Hawthorne in general, into a separate, easily revised or replaced, volume was based, apparently, on their belief that criticism dates, needing to be redone with every major shift in the *Zeitgeist*, while the kind of exact scholarship that went into the production of this text will *not* have to be redone.

That there is something—a good deal indeed—to this point of view seems too clear to need discussion. Yet one still wonders, a little uneasily perhaps, about the larger implications of the committee's decision to segregate criticism. Critics are not likely to find this version of the "separate but equal" doctrine entirely satisfying. The *Hawthorne Centenary Essays*, which is now (1964) out, containing all the criticism the editors of the Centenary Edition intend to print, is a handsome and impressive volume, but does not its very existence as a separate work imply that criticism is not only ephemeral but somehow inferior? "Separate but equal" always seems to mean, in the end, *not* equal. One wonders how consciously the new historicists intend the implication that scholarship is for the ages, criticism for the moment.

The test of the desirability of this separation of scholarship and criticism, fact and value, evidence and interpretation of evidence, will come when the later volumes appear. With no *Scarlet Letter* manuscript available, the only way a scholar could decide whether the editorial decisions represented in the Centenary text are the best possible or not would be to repeat the whole process that has produced this text—presumably with the aid of his own collating machine and his own teams of graduate students. With the books to come, based on existing manuscripts, which it would be possible to inspect for oneself, one would expect both that the new texts will contain more interesting and important variations from the old Riverside text, and also that the new texts will be more open to negative criticism. When these later works come out, it may become apparent to anyone who takes the trouble to check the manuscript that textual scholarship and literary criticism cannot, at the level where decisions become acutely problematic, be so sharply separated.

Interpretation of what an author *intended*, where there are several possibilities, is as much a "critical" (*literary* critical) problem as it is a "scholarly" one. Attempting, for example, to decipher an unclearly written word in the manuscript, or to supply a word the author inadvertently left out, demands an understanding of the work as a whole, and of all the works; and this understanding rests in part on an ability to respond appropriately and adequately to the work as a work of art, on the imagination and the emotions in short. Even the more crucial decisions about punctuation may involve such *critical* judgment. If we equate scholarship with *fact* (it does not change) and criticism with *value* (subjective, changeable), then it is clear that at the point where crucial decisions are made, fact and value merge in a unitary *critical* decision based on all the *scholarly* evidence.

One wonders therefore whether the editors will in the volumes to come openly acknowledge the significance of criticism by reversing the earlier decision and including avowedly critical justifications of their editorial decisions as well as critical discussions of the significance of their discoveries, or whether they will bring the criticism in covertly under some other name. Surely it will have to be there in some form, whether so labeled or not, if the new texts vary in important ways from the existing ones. Fallible and subjective though the critics' intuitions and judgments may be, there is no way to get along without them so long as literature remains a humane study.

ii. Bibliographies

The most useful recent contribution to Hawthorne bibliography is to be found where one might never think to look, in one of the paperback "casebooks" that grow ever more numerous. Seymour L. Gross included in his *A "Scarlet Letter" Handbook* (San Francisco, Wadsworth, 1960) the best annotated selective bibliography of work on *The Scarlet Letter* that has yet appeared. Both the selection and the summary comments demonstrate critical judgment, once again revealing that a "scholar"—in this case the purest, least subjective, most "scientific" sort of scholar, a bibliographer—cannot afford to be content not to try to be a critic.

More complete than Gross's listing, but in a significant sense less useful because without annotation, is Robert S. Phillips' "The Scarlet Letter: A Selected Checklist of Criticism," *BB*, XXIII, 1962, 213-216. Kenneth Cameron's "Inventory of Hawthorne's Manuscripts, Part I," in the *ESQ*, No. 29 (1962), pp. 5-20, is good to have. Matthew Bruccoli is said to be in process of compiling complete Hawthorne bibliographies at Ohio State in connection with his work on the Centenary Edition. A bibliography doing for all of Hawthorne's works what Gross has done for *The Scarlet Letter* would be welcome.

iii. Biographical and Miscellaneous Studies

In the last several years (but not in 1963) two books and several articles have made significant contributions to Hawthorne biography. The books have in common that they are both "critical" biographies, in the sense of combining interpretation of the man with interpretation of the work; that both find the clue to interpretation of the work outside the work, in the life; that both normalize and unify Hawthorne in reaction against both those interpreters who see him as characterized by ambivalence and those who, following Melville's lead, emphasize the "blackness" in him; and, finally, that both are explicitly anti-New Critical, anti-psychoanalytic, anti-mythological, and anti-existential.

The importance of Edward Wagenknecht's *Nathaniel Hawthorne: Man and Writer* (New York, Oxford, 1961) lies in its attempt to rescue Hawthorne from those who have seen him, Wagenknecht believes, in their own image, as constantly ironic, ambiguous, tortured, skeptical, and dark. Wagenknecht shows us a Hawthorne as "normal" and ordinary as the Hawthorne Stewart presented some years ago. But whereas Stewart kept to the facts of the outward life and to the stated views without attempting to solve the mysteries that have troubled most biographers of this very complex man, without pretending to have found the "real" Hawthorne behind the various masks, Wagenknecht thinks he has disposed of mystery. The real Hawthorne, he believes, was confident, reverent, and affirmative, more a man of his own time than we have seen fit to recognize, and more unified. "He had happy relations with birds and animals," we are told, with the implication that this fact—and it *was* a fact, *sometimes*—disposes of the majority of Hawthorne's critics since Melville and Matthiessen.

Wagenknecht is angry at critics—the present writer explicitly included—who find in Hawthorne a sensibility very like our own. His is a "no nonsense" approach that explicitly rejects "psychological lingo" on what he calls "common sense" grounds and New Critical jargon because it needlessly mystifies, refusing to take Hawthorne at his stated word. Myth criticism he finds equally suspect. What he offers instead is an essentially nineteenth-century interpretation of a nineteenth-century writer.

Nevertheless, the book does have a certain limited value as a sympathetic presentation of Hawthorne the man from what is surely closer to Hawthorne's own consciously held point of view than is the point of view from which most contemporary critics have viewed him. At its best, the book represents an achievement in the realm of the historical imagination: like the book about to be discussed, it gives us an "inward" view of its subject. Necessarily, such a book must strike us as often uncritical, since its very aim makes it eschew the perspectives that make criticism possible.

Not surprisingly, the best chapter is the last, "God's Child," on Hawthorne's religion. Though there is not much that is new in the way of evidence here, the evidence is put together and interpreted in a way that, on the whole, carries conviction and has the value of throwing into relief a side of Hawthorne that has too often been ignored or even denied. There is no doubt at all, for example, that Hawthorne *did* believe in immortality: his statements show it; his works show it.

Wagenknecht properly emphasizes this fact. But it is equally true—and this he ignores—that Hawthorne was capable of entertaining every sort of doubt, even doubts he found self-destructive. Wagenknecht's summary of the *beliefs* Hawthorne held is balanced and sound, but—even without considering the degree to which works of art, including Hawthorne's, spring, in part at least, from something deeper in the mind than belief—surely one should make a distinction, a *religious* distinction, between professed belief and operative faith. One of the results of Wagenknecht's rejection of the insights made available by psychoanalysis is that he refuses even to recognize, much less to probe, the complexities of his subject. In biography no less than in literary criticism, "common sense" is not enough.

Hubert H. Hoeltje's *Inward Sky: The Mind and Heart of Nathaniel Hawthorne* (Durham, N.C., Duke Univ. Press, 1962) is a more significant book, despite unfavorable reaction by many reviewers. Where Stewart left the man and the work so distinct that it was difficult to see how *this* man could have created *this* work, and Wagenknecht generally interprets the work in terms of what he believes the man must have intended, Hoeltje reads the man not into but out of his work. His guiding question, in effect, is, if he wrote these works, what kind of a man must he have been?

In terms of the amount of preparation behind it, the amount of serious and original thought in it, the degree of freedom from reliance on earlier secondary works, and the determination to present all the evidence, this is a book to be taken seriously. Clearly, it is a labor of love as well as of scholarship. The job needed to be done, and we may be grateful to Hoeltje for having devoted so much of himself to it.

Still, it is likely to leave most scholars dissatisfied on a number of counts. Perhaps most damaging is the critical naïveté. If one misinterprets a literary work, or is incapable of evaluating it, and then reads the man out of the work, how much *biographical* distortion will result? Examples of what I mean by critical naïveté: the author treats Longfellow's "Psalm of Life" very respectfully as a poem, and holds that, the mystery-making New Critics to the contrary notwithstanding, "My Kinsman, Major Molineux" is simply a *funny* story.

More irritating, though probably in the long run less damaging, is the author's habit of not using quotation marks or any other means of distinguishing between his own words and Hawthorne's or telling us where he found Hawthorne's words if they are his.

Without the freshest possible memory of all of Hawthorne's works, it is impossible to check on anything that Hoeltje says.

But this way of writing, which the author must have adopted deliberately, to symbolize the *inwardness* of the narrative, is only a symptom of a greater defect. Refusing ever to stand off from his subject and view him from a distance, to *judge* him, in short, Hoeltje offers us in the end only so much understanding of Hawthorne as Hawthorne had of himself. Hawthorne understood himself unusually well, but of course not perfectly; so that the result of Hoeltje's refusal ever to analyze Hawthorne's self-portrayal is not simply lack of clarification but, quite frequently, positive error.

If the reader starts with these caveats in mind, he will find much that is of lasting value here. The emphasis on the Hawthorne-Longfellow relationship, both personal and literary, is fresh and significant. The insistence on the kinship, again both personal and literary, between Hawthorne and Emerson, though probably overdone, and though for several of the most emphatic assertions no evidence is offered, still usefully corrects the tendency to see the two men as polar opposites in everything. The treatment of Hawthorne's religion, agreeing in general with Wagenknecht's, seems sound.

The over-all interpretation of Hawthorne offered is intended to invalidate almost all of the Hawthorne criticism produced in the "Hawthorne critical revival" of the past fifteen or so years. Summarizing, the author writes on his last page, "In a review of Hawthorne's life and writings, nothing is more prominent than a quiet, deeply joyful affirmation." "Serenity," we have repeatedly been told earlier, is the key equally to Hawthorne's personality and to his work. If this is so, then of course Melville, Matthiessen, Fogle, Waggoner, Male, Levin and the others who have seen and emphasized Hawthorne's irony, ambivalence, and constant awareness of the darkness must be simply wrong. I doubt it, but neither is Hoeltje simply wrong. He is over-correcting. (Compare the view of Wagenknecht and Hoeltje on this matter with that of Folsom's book, discussed below.)

Two articles directly in conflict with the interpretation of Hawthorne's psyche offered in the two books just treated deserve mention at this time. In the Summer, 1962, issue of *HMAB*, Dr. John H. Lamont of the Harvard Medical School and Massachusetts General Hospital, writing on "Hawthorne's Unfinished Works," and attempting to find the reason for their failure, finds evidence in the late romances of some degree of psychological breakdown connected with the Oedipal situation. In his late novels, Hawthorne "too directly assigned his hero this [his own] problem, without any resolution in mind; hero and author were too close together, and both could make no progress." Potential biographers who, unlike the authors of the two books just discussed, do not dogmatically reject psychiatry, would do well to look into this piece, which has significant implications too for the literary critics. A longer version of it in 1962 won the Deutsch Prize given by The Boston Psychoanalytic Society for the best scientific paper submitted during the academic year.

Pursuing a similar psychological approach, Louis B. Salmon in "Hawthorne and His Father: A Conjecture," in *L&P*, XIII, 12-17, argues that the theme of "filial impiety" is frequently to be found in Hawthorne's work. Certain of his stories "constitute a sort of expiatory ritual whereby Hawthorne strove to say *Rest, rest, perturbed spirit* to the ghost of his sailor-father." The conjecture seems a likely one, but unlike Dr. Lamont's more limited and specific inquiry, tends to remain merely conjecture, and conjecture, furthermore, without very clear implications for literary criticism.

In 1962 Millicent Bell's *Hawthorne's View of the Artist* (Albany, State Univ. of New York) surveyed Hawthorne's stated and simplified opinions on the subject of the artist and related them to the artists in his fiction. Finally there are four articles with which I shall conclude this part of my survey. James D. Hart's "Hawthorne's Italian Diary" in *AL*, XXXIV, 562-567, describes the newly rediscovered diary Hawthorne carried with him in Italy and on which he later based his Italian Notebooks. Among other things, this diary establishes the fact that, contrary to Julian's statement, Hawthorne *did* work at his writing during Una's Roman illness (Nov. 3–Dec. 31, when there are no entries in the Notebook). The diary is in the Rare Book Room of the General Library at the University of California.

Three articles in the *ESQ* (No. 19, 1960, p. 25; No. 33, pp. 57-61; pp. 24-28) make significant, if limited, contributions to a factual knowledge of Hawthorne's life. J. Lashley Dameron in the earlier issue shows that "Hawthorne had opportunity to acquaint himself with the whole of Part One of *Faust* . . . before 1828," not that he tried to read it then but that he may have read a summarizing

review-article in *Blackwood's Edinburgh Magazine* for 1820 which
his Aunt Mary withdrew from the Salem Atheneum in 1827. Joseph
T. Gordon in the later issue sifts the evidence on Hawthorne's relation to Brook Farm, in fact and fiction, and comes to the by now
quite standard conclusions that Hawthorne's relation to the Farm
was practical rather than idealistic and that *The Blithedale Romance* is what Hawthorne said it was, romance, not autobiography
or history. (For a different view of Hawthorne's reasons for joining
the experiment, suggesting that his motives were at least in part
idealistic, see Hoeltje, above.) Also in the 1963 issue, Ramona E.
Hull documents Hawthorne's attempts to promote Thoreau as a
writer.

iv. Criticism

Of literary criticism, which has so far received only sidewise glances,
there is not so much that needs to be said. In 1961 Daniel Hoffman's *Form and Fable in American Fiction* (New York, Oxford)
appeared, with a chapter exploring Hawthorne's use of folklore
that I found very rewarding. Less imaginative but thorough and
sound, and successfully achieving the purpose announced in its
title, was Arlin Turner's *Nathaniel Hawthorne: An Introduction and
Interpretation* (New York, Barnes and Noble, 1961). In 1963 my
own *Hawthorne, A Critical Study* (Cambridge, Mass., Harvard
Univ. Press, 1955 and 1963) came out in a revised and expanded
edition, and James K. Folsom published the only completely new
book-length piece of critical analysis of the year, *Man's Accidents
and God's Purposes: Multiplicity in Hawthorne's Fiction* (New
Haven, College and Univ. Press, 1963). Folsom's over-all interpretation of Hawthorne is sharply at odds with that of Wagenknecht.
Studying the ways in which Hawthorne's "philosophical beliefs"
are revealed by his fiction leads the author to the conclusion that
Hawthorne was a "heretical" Platonist who was more interested in
the world of Becoming than in the world of Being, in the Apparent
than in the Real. A philosophical approach shows that "multiplicity"
(contradiction without resolution) is so central in Hawthorne's view
of the Apparent world that "to discuss Hawthorne at all, the critic
must simplify him to a point where he becomes unrecognizable . . .
Hawthorne's world is not amenable to order." It would seem to
follow from this, as I see it, not only that all past interpretations of

the meanings of Hawthorne's works are invalid, but that all future attempts to find a figure in the carpet are equally doomed to inanity—a conclusion I find dispiriting.

The most important article on Hawthorne listed in the *PMLA* bibliography for 1963 is Martin Green's "The Hawthorne Myth: A Protest," in *E&S*, XVI, 16-36. Mr. Green argues that Hawthorne was neither a good writer nor an intelligent or cultivated man, and that critical enthusiasm for him in recent years was a mere passing fad, easily accounted for by (1) our inability to accept Emerson's optimism and idealism; (2) our general tendency, especially on the part of the New Critics, to see life as characterized by paradox, ambiguity, and multiplicity; (3) our tendency—for which, again, the New Critics are chiefly at fault—to read the works in isolation, without looking from them back to the man who wrote them, who was most definitely not a thinker. In a curious way, the argument of this article overlaps widely with the arguments developed by Hoeltje and Wagenknecht, with the important difference that the latter two continue to like Hawthorne for many of the same reasons that Green gives for disliking him.

Of the remaining recent articles on Hawthorne, the following seem the most significant: William Gibson, "The Art of Nathaniel Hawthorne: An Examination of *The Scarlet Letter*," *American Renaissance, the History of an Era: Essays and Interpretations* (Frankfurt, Diesterweg, 1961), pp. 97-106. Aimed at German high school teachers, the essay constitutes in effect a summary of the consensus of modern criticism of the work; it is Hester's novel and Dimmesdale does rise in the end, though not wholly convincingly; cf. Davidson, below. Joseph Schwartz, "Three Aspects of Hawthorne's Puritanism," *NEQ*, XXXVI, 192-208; Edward H. Davidson, "Dimmesdale's Fall," *NEQ*, XXXVI, 358-370 (the book is *his* book, and he does *not* rise at the end); Clark Griffiith, "Caves and Cave Dwellers: The Study of a Romantic Image, *JEGP*, LXII, 551-568 (emphasizes the contrast, contra Hoeltje, between Emerson and Hawthorne in their use of the cave image; also treats Poe and Melville); E. Arthur Robinson, "The Vision of Goodman Brown: A Source and an Interpretation," *AL*, XXXV, 218-225 (as a source, Mather's *Magnalia* points toward something like Male's sexual interpretation of the story: "Brown's ordeal is to learn that his sinful longings belong to the pattern of his race, and that none are exempt, not even women"); Sister Jane Marie Luecke, "Villains and Non-

Villains in Hawthorne's Fiction," *PMLA*, LXXVIII, 551-558 (seen
in the light of traditional thinking on good and evil, most of Hawthorne's "villains"—those who knowingly choose evil—are not villains
at all but victims or imperfect men; Chillingworth and Judge
Pyncheon are his most successful villains; Hawthorne had trouble
with his villains; either they ceased to seem villains, or they ceased
to seem real human beings); and Allen Austin, "Hester Prynne's
Plan of Escape: The Moral Problem," *UKCR*, XXVIII (1962), 317-
318 (F. I. Carpenter's "Scarlet A Minus" argument, while not true
for the book as a whole, *is* true for the forest episode, in which
Hawthorne timidly draws back from granting approval to Hester).

Almost without exception, these critical books and articles offer
interpretations, or proceed in terms of assumptions, that run coun-
ter to those recommended by Wagenknecht and Hoeltje, and that
in effect continue the explorations begun for our time by Matthiessen. Thus it is the critics who are now the "conservatives," the
scholars who are the "radicals," reversing the situation of thirty
years ago. One of the unfortunate effects of the current transitional
state of Hawthorne study is the new sharpening of the distinction
between "critic" and "scholar" that ideally, I think, should not exist
at all, except perhaps as a relative matter of personal preference and
emphasis.

3. Melville

Willard Thorp

i. Scholarship Between 1960 and 1962

Before turning to the Melville scholarship produced in 1963, we should cast a backward glance at the important books which appeared in the years 1960, 1961, and 1962. To the amazement of some of our colleagues scholarly writing about Melville continues unabated in the 1960's. There are good reasons why this is so. Melville is a major writer. He was "discovered" only forty years ago. Problems and questions still abound.

The most extensive recent Melville bibliography was prepared by Maurice Beebe, Harrison Hayford, and Gordon Roper—"Criticism of Herman Melville: A Selected Checklist" (*MFS*, VIII, 1962, 312-346. Also in 1962 Tyrus Hillway and Hershel Parker prepared for the Melville Society a *Directory of Melville Dissertations*, offering a brief synopsis of each work listed.

Three important editorial tasks were completed in the early 1960's. Though Merrell R. Davis and William H. Gilman's *The Letters of Herman Melville* (New Haven, Yale Univ. Press, 1960) assembles 271 letters, the sad fact is that 145 letters known to have been written by Melville cannot be located and presumably were destroyed. Of the letters here printed 42 are new and 55 are published in full for the first time. In preparing their texts the editors aimed to present "only the characteristics within Melville's intention that seem important to the reading and understanding of the letters, reserving all the particular idiosyncrasies of Melville's hand for the textual notes."

Walter E. Bezanson's edition of *Clarel* (New York, Hendricks House, 1960) had been long-awaited. It is the sixth volume in the slow-moving Hendricks House edition of the complete works. Mr. Bezanson provides an Introduction of 117 pages, two maps, and a useful critical index to the characters. The explanatory notes fill pages 550-643. These notes, together with the Introduction, give us insight into Melville's thinking about the religious and intellectual problems of his time and help to fill up gaps in the story of Melville's inner life during "the silent years."

The edition of *Billy Budd* prepared by Harrison Hayford and Merton Sealts, Jr. (Chicago, Univ. of Chicago Press, 1962) is another major achievement. As the critical acclaim of this final work by Melville has grown, so has uneasiness about the earlier texts, the two prepared by Raymond Weaver (1924 and 1928) and the H. Barron Freeman text of 1948. Scholars who examined the manuscript were aware that the editorial problems it presents are far more difficult than Weaver or Freeman believed. The present editors decided to present two texts, a reading text and a genetic text which would record every deletion, insertion, cancellation, erasure, etc. Their reading text does not, in truth, differ in many remarkable ways from the earlier texts. The title is now *Billy Budd, Sailor* because *Billy Budd, Foretopman* was Mrs. Melville's proposal. The former "Preface" (on the Revolutionary Spirit at Spithead) and the Freeman Chapter XII ("Lawyers, Experts, Clergy") have not been used, because Melville had evidently intended to discard them. The *Indomitable* now becomes the *Bellipotent,* a renaming found in the late stages of composition.

In preparing the genetic text the editors have discovered many fascinating facts about the composition of *Billy Budd*. Here are the chief ones. (1) There are nine major stages of inscription with many substages. (2) In its inception the story was to tell of an older Billy who was guilty of mutiny. Claggart enters in a second stage and Vere in a third. (3) In perspective of the story's genesis, the theory that Melville *began* with the *Somers* case becomes untenable. (4) Weaver and Freeman mistook Mrs. Melville's hand for Melville's and in consequence accepted her suggestions and queries as Melville's own. (5) The editors find no evidence to support Freeman's belief that imbedded in the manuscript is an early form of the story, which he printed as *Baby Budd, Sailor*. Anticipating further study of the story (which will be based on their work), the editors devote sixteen pages to "Perspectives for Criticism." The "Notes and Commentary" are very detailed (pp. 133-202).

Two biographies must be mentioned: Leon Howard's *Herman Melville,* No. 13 (1961) in the University of Minnesota Pamphlets on American Writers and Lewis Mumford's *Herman Melville: A Study of His Life and Vision* (New York, Harcourt, Brace and World, 1962). Like the other pamphlets in the series Mr. Howard's study is brief (48 pages) but it is well balanced. It is certain to be widely used. The Mumford biography is a revised edition of his 1929 *Herman Melville*, a book which has become a classic and deserved to be brought into print again. Mr. Mumford wisely chose to make only minor revisions except for a few instances where he had originally gone wide of the truth.

Four book-length special studies appeared during these years: Merlin Bowen's *The Long Encounter: Self and Experience in the Writings of Herman Melville* (Chicago, Univ. of Chicago Press, 1960); Hugh W. Hetherington's *Melville's Reviewers, British and American, 1846-1891* (Chapel Hill, Univ. of North Carolina Press, 1961); Dorothee Metlitsky Finkelstein's *Melville's Orienda* (New Haven, Yale Univ. Press, 1961); and Janez Stanonik's *Moby Dick: The Myth and the Symbol* (Ljubljana, Yugoslavia, Ljubljana Univ. Press, 1962). Mr. Bowen contends that in most of Melville's works "we find ourselves looking on at the pitting, in some sense, of the single individual against the universe." In Part I he studies the protagonists and antagonists in these encounters. Part II, "The Meeting," moves from the problem of perception and judgment to the problem of action. The strategies employed in the actions Mr. Bowen identifies as three in number: defiance (the way of tragic heroism); submission (the way of weakness); and armed neutrality (the way of wisdom). In general this highly schematized approach works well. Occasionally there is forcing, as when Captain Vere is placed among the "compromisers" who submit and so turns up in the company of Falsgrave and Plinlimmon.

Mr. Hetherington's *Melville's Reviewers* grew from his dissertation of 1933, the first to be written on Melville. It is no ordinary "reputation of" study. It gives a remarkably detailed account of the public response to Melville's work, book by book, and explains the biases of many of the reviewers. Each section is furnished with a Conclusion which attempts to put the puzzle together and to some extent places the early criticism against present-day judgments.

Mrs. Finkelstein's *Melville's Orienda* demonstrates again how much is still to be learned about Melville's sources and his use of them. The ore brought to the surface is Melville's reading in the literature of the Near East, everything from Egyptology to the Persian poets. The impress of "Orienda" is found in nearly all his work but is particularly strong in *Mardi*, the Fedallah scenes in *Moby-Dick*, and in *Clarel*. Mrs. Finklestein's richest strike is her reading of *Mardi* as an "Oriental romance," a genre which was still popular in the 1840's.

Janez Stanonik's *Moby Dick: The Myth and the Symbol* posits the existence of an Ur-*Moby-Dick* in the form of a folk-tale known to Melville but now lost. The argument rests chiefly on certain details in a French account, "Le Cachalot blanc," published by Jules Lecomte in 1837 and on three novels about whale-hunts by Charles M. Newell. The best one can say for this study is that it is ingenious. The documentation is slight and too much is conjectured.

The most impressive critical study to appear in these three years is Warner Berthoff's *The Example of Melville* (Princeton, Princeton Univ. Press, 1962). The author is impatient with the studies of Melville's "mind" and the way in which he wrote his convictions into his novels. He wishes to redress the balance by talking about him as an *exemplary* writer who worked his way to the kind of writing he could do best. And his best writing, Mr. Berthoff believes, is to be classed with what the French call the *récit*, the "personal adventure chronicle, the recital, the confession," a form that was congenial to other American writers of the time. *The Example of Melville* is a thoughtful, perceptive book which demands close reading.

Richard H. Fogle's *Melville's Shorter Tales* (Norman, Univ. of Oklahoma Press, 1960) might well have been a longer work. Some of the chapters are so brief as to suggest the author was bored with his subject. The best chapters (of the ten) are those which originally appeared in periodicals: II ("Bartleby"); IX ("The Encantadas"); and X ("Benito Cereno"). The introductory chapter, "Melville's Tales," though short, has some excellent things to say about the "immeasurable and mysterious" world which Melville tried to fathom in his fiction.

In James E. Miller, Jr.'s, *A Reader's Guide to Herman Melville* (New York, Farrar, Straus and Cudahy, 1962) the thesis crowds the criticism. Mr. Miller sorts Melville's characters into three categories: those who wear masks (either nefariously or innocently); the "maskless men"; and the seekers who must "decide with what face to confront the world." For the reader of this study, trying to decide in which category a character belongs becomes a guessing game. Mr. Miller rides his thesis too hard.

A. R. Humphreys' *Melville* (Edinburgh, 1962) is a short critical study (120 pages) which will have wide currency because it is good and is in the company of other good critical studies in Oliver and Boyd's Writers and Critics series.

Though this review of the scholarship produced in 1960-1962 has considered only books, mention should be made of two excellent symposia of essays on Melville: the "Herman Melville Special Number" of *MFS*, VIII (Autumn, 1962) and the "Melville Supplement" of *ESQ* (No. 28, Pt. 3, 1962).

ii. Books of 1963

Turning now to the scholarship of 1963, we have first to consider four books: an edition of *Battle-Pieces*, a biography, and two special studies.

Hennig Cohen's *The* Battle-Pieces *of Herman Melville* (New York, Yoseloff) is handsomely printed and is embellished with Civil War drawings, many of which were prepared for *Harper's Weekly* by two English artists, Alfred and William Waud. These are not, of course, directly associated with the poems but they further vivify some of the scenes which Melville himself made vivid. Mr. Cohen's Introduction takes into account several matters: the impulses which produced the poems; the ways in which Melville used his sources; his attitude towards the war, its leaders, and the men who fought. Of special interest is his suggestion that the annual exhibition of the National Academy of Design which Melville saw in April, 1865, influenced in several ways the writing of the poems. Mr. Cohen writes perceptively about the calculated arrangement of the poems, the interrelation of themes, and the reason for the choice of particular stanzaic forms. The preparation of the text seems to have presented no formidable problems. There was only the one edition, a copy of which Melville used to enter some revisions. The five poems which appeared in *Harper's New Monthly Magazine* before book publication offer some variant readings.

The one biography of the year, Tyrus Hillway's *Herman Melville* (New York), is in Twayne's United States Authors Series. It is a neat, compact job, up-to-date in its scholarship and generally sensible in its critical judgments. The necessity for compression forces the author into such tight condensations that the point of an episode may occasionally be lost to the uninitiated reader. There are also some errors in the synopses. Ahab, in "The Symphony" chapter, does not yield to Starbuck's importunings and agree, even momentarily,

"to relinquish forever his passion for vengeance on Moby Dick."
Benito Cereno does not, after his leap overboard, swim "towards
Captain Delano's boat."

It was inevitable that sooner or later a scholar would produce
a study of the possible influence on Melville's fiction of the Gothic
novel. And here we have it: Heinz Kosok's *Die Bedeutung der
Gothic Novel für das Erzählwerk Herman Melvilles* (Hamburg,
Cram, de Gruyter). As Henry Pochmann points out in his review
in *AL* (XXXVI, 1964, 224), Mr. Kosok casts his nets far and wide
and hauls up not just the strictly Gothic novels but as well the
" 'Novel of Suspense, Novel of Terror, Supernatural Novel, Schauer-
roman, Sensationsroman, Gruselroman, Roman noir,' with the Gothic
drama, Gothic short story, and Gothic poem thrown in for good
measure." This all-inclusiveness should yield something! But Mr.
Kosok's study is grounded in fact. Melville owned, through gift
or purchase, several Gothic romances and there are many references
to Gothic fiction in his novels. The author finds the Gothic influence
chiefly in the "haunted forecastles," in descriptions of landscape
(e.g., the countryside around the house where Isabel is first seen),
and in such villains as Claggart, who may owe something to Mrs.
Radcliffe's Schedoni in *The Italian*. The organization of Mr. Kosok's
study is mechanical, and compels us to run through Melville's work
several times in pursuit of "typische Züge der Gothic Novel" under
four categories.

H. Bruce Franklin's *The Wake of the Gods: Melville's Mythology*
(Stanford, Stanford Univ. Press) is concerned with Melville's knowledge of myths around the world, his use of them, and his own myth
making. Nothing else counts and so those works in which the use
of myth is slight are either omitted from consideration or given
perfunctory treatment. To my mind the most revelatory chapters
are those on *Mardi* and *Moby-Dick*, but those on *Pierre* and *The
Confidence-Man*, where Mr. Franklin has to strain to make his points
(and possibly does not make them), are worth pondering.

The central premise is certainly valid, that the battles over the
findings of the comparative mythologists were hottest during Melville's most productive years and Melville was fully aware of the
implications of these controversies. The study aims to show, therefore, how "Melville uses the language, the theories, the knowledge,
and the techniques of both the Christian and the skeptical mythologists to explore the relations between man and his gods."

Mardi is the novel which is most closely related to the contemporary controversies. Sir William Jones's famous essay "On the Gods of Greece, Italy, and India" is seen as probably suggesting to Melville the myth-making characters in *Mardi* as well as such products" of myth as Media, the royal deity, and Taji, the astronomical deity. Mr. Franklin's contribution is his view of the novel as a well-planned romance to which coherence was given by Melville's delighted playing with the concepts of the mythologists. The chapter adds a great deal to the Mardian explorations of Merrell Davis and Dorothee Finkelstein. Mr. Franklin believes that the central myth in *Moby-Dick* is Egyptian, the struggle between Ahab in the role of Osiris (sun-god, infernal god, and the savior of man, the dragon slayer, hunter of the gliding demon of the seas of life) and Typhon, the Egyptian Leviathan. The arguments are persuasive.

Mr. Franklin seems to be most excited by his attempted solution of the baffling problems of interpretation which *The Confidence-Man* presents. We have all been off the track in seeking for ironic answers in Christian ethics. The solution is simple: look in another place. "Melville made the shape-shifting-struggles and the ultimate identity of Vishnu and Siva into the central structural fact of *The Confidence-Man*." Perhaps. I find it harder to believe that Billy Budd's death is a Druidic sacrifice.

iii. Articles Published in 1963

In considering the articles published during 1963 it will possibly be most useful to group them under the works to which they are related. A discussion of general articles will then follow and a listing of dissertations completed in 1963. A few items from 1962 will be included.

a. Typee. G. Thomas Tanselle has discovered what he considers to be "The First Review of *Typee*" (*AL*, XXXIV, 567-571). It appeared in the short-lived New York *Weekly News* on March 21, 1846. Aside from its "firstness," it is important because it is extensive, does not raise the question of credibility (an issue in later reviews), and praises the book on the grounds of its dramatic story and its style.

b. Redburn. As his title suggests, Gustaaf Van Cromphout's "Her-

man Melville's *Redburn* Considered in the Light of the Elder
Henry James's *The Nature of Evil*" (*RLV*, XXIX, 117-126) is a comparative study. As such, it does not have much point since there
can be no question of influence. (*The Nature of Evil* appeared in
1855.) It does contain, however, a good summary of Melville's
view of the nature of evil at the time of writing *Redburn*.

c. Moby-Dick. Jack Jay Boies's "*The Whale* without Epilogue"
(*MLQ*, XXIV, 172-176) raises again the question why the Epilogue
to *Moby-Dick* is missing in the English edition. He contends that
as the novel progressed Melville lost interest in Ishmael, to the
extent, it seems, of forgetting to save him at the end. "There was
simply no reason for him to survive." Mr. Boies ignores the possi-
bility that the Epilogue got lost somewhere in transit.

Robert Shulman's "Melville's Thomas Fuller: An Outline for
Starbuck and an Instance of the Creator as Critic" (*MLQ*, XXIII,
1962, 337-352) shows that Fuller's *Holy and Profane State*, which
Melville read in April, 1849, helped in shaping *Moby-Dick*. Fuller's
section on "The Good Soldier" supplied hints for the character of
Starbuck as he appears in "Knights and Squires." Suggestions for
the chapter on "Brit" came from Fuller's "The Good Sea Captain."
This article is a good piece of detective work.

In "William Starbuck Mayo and Herman Melville" (*NEQ*, XXXV,
1962, 515-520) Cecil D. Eby, Jr., makes two points. Mayo, author of
Kaloolah, did not wish to be thought of as following in the wake
of Melville. He sets his readers straight in the fourth-edition preface
to his novel. Mr. Eby's second point argues cogently for at least one
important influence of *Kaloolah* on *Moby-Dick*. In both novels the
damaged ship sinks in front of the eyes of the crew; in Owen
Chase's *Narrative* the crew casts off from the vessel before it goes
to the bottom.

In "Ishmael the Ironist: The Anti-Salvation Theme in *Moby-
Dick*" (*ESQ*, No. 31, pp. 71-75) T. W. Weissbuck and Bruce Stil-
lians seek a middle position between the "salvationists" who assert
that the theme of the novel is death and rebirth and those who
would agree with Lawrance Thompson in seeing Ishmael as a fugitive and escapist who feigns a Godlike indifference in the Epilogue.
The authors view Ishmael as an ironist who "emerges as an unre-
deemed Everyman, an uncommitted narrator and messenger." R.
Dilworth Rust, in "Vision in *Moby-Dick*" (*ESQ*, No. 33, pp. 73-75)

comes to a very different conclusion: "If Ahab's destruction can be seen in terms of his increasing blindness (both physical and spiritual), Ishmael's salvation can be traced to his increasing vision." Two articles study the socio-political implications of *Moby-Dick*. David H. Hirsch, in "The Dilemma of the Liberal Intellectual: Melville's Ishmael" (*TSLL*, V, 169-188), advances the view that Ishmael (and, by implication, Melville) found it possible to fuse a Biblical world-view with the liberalism of the Enlightenment through fraternal love. Alan Heimert's "*Moby-Dick* and American Political Symbolism" (*AQ*, XV, 498-534) begins with the hypothesis that since *Moby-Dick* was written at the time of the great controversy over the Compromise of 1850, we should expect to find reflections of that debate in the novel. Mr. Heimert has found them in abundance. I shall cite three. In some sense the dangers encountered by the *Pequod* resemble the perils surrounding the Ship of State, a trope which was used constantly at the time, in sermons, orations, and tracts. The American invasion of the rights of other nations (Mexico and Canada) was frequently compared to the aggressiveness of the Biblical Ahab. And the Ahab of the novel is made "to act and even look like the demonic, yet admirable, Senator [Calhoun] who to many Americans seemed an incarnation of Ahab of Old." Mr. Heimert does not attempt to make the novel into political allegory. He stays by the political symbols which would have struck readers in 1851.

John Halverson's "The Shadow in *Moby-Dick*" (*AQ*, XV, 436-446) makes judicious use of Jung's archetype of the shadow which, with acceptance "reveals itself as a helpful friend, helping bring up to consciousness those elements of the unconscious, especially Eros, necessary to the wholeness and health of the self." Mr. Halverson works towards this conclusion. "Pip, who knows his master is not a whole man, touches the center of Ahab's humanity. His influence is not enough to save Ahab; it is enough to transform demonic obsession into tragic agony. Ishmael is a whole man, and Queequeg is the accredited agent of his humanity and salvation."

In "*Moby-Dick*: One Way to Cut In" (*Carrell*, III, ii, 1962, 1-12) Lawrance Thompson ingeniously studies the Ahab plot and the Ishmael plot separately and then compares what each man thought he saw happening. Each is obsessively preoccupied with religious disillusionment. "The major difference is that Ahab's religious disillusionment is represented as finding expression in very bold acts of metaphysical rebellion and defiance, while Ishmael's religious disillusionment finds expression in metaphysical protests which are merely verbal." Melville's sympathetic probings of related elements in the two plots "could possibly reflect some aspects of Melville's own obsessive disillusionment."

One comparative study should be noticed: Maurice Friedman's "The Modern Job: On Melville, Dostoievsky, and Kafka" (*Judaism*, XII, 436-455). The intricate argument is well summarized by Mr. Friedman. "Ahab and Ivan [*The Brothers Karamazov*] echo Job's protest against innocent suffering and an existence deprived of meaning. Yet both remain essentially Modern Prometheans, seeking to affirm the self and man through destroying or denying the reality that confronts them. K., in contrast, not only contends but affirms. . . . The question of trust in existence which is at the heart of Job's dialogue with God is equally at the heart of K.'s dialogue with the absurd."

d. The Confidence-Man. Hershel Parker's "The Metaphysics of Indian-Hating" (*NCF*, XVIII, 165-173) takes issue with the various readings of the Indian-hater section of the novel offered by John W. Shroeder, Roy Harvey Pearce, and Elizabeth Foster. Moredock should be seen as a "Devil-hating Christian." The outrageous irony that has escaped notice is that "when Moredock is murdering Indians he is Christian and when he is enjoying the comforts of domestic life he is apostatizing."

In "Timothy Flint's 'Wicked River' and *The Confidence-Man*" (*PMLA*, LXXVIII, 75-79) John D. Seelye argues convincingly that Melville made use of Flint's *Recollections of the Last Ten Years* (1826) and his *History and Geography of the Mississippi Valley* (1828) in writing the description of the river which he evidently intended to use in the novel but discarded.

e. Billy Budd. Ray B. Browne's "*Billy Budd*: Gospel of Democracy" (*NCF*, XVII, 321-337) takes the extreme position that Vere talks Burke in the trial scene to the point of madness. A rejoinder by Bernard Suits (*NCF*, XVIII, 288-291) asks the pertinent question whether the ideas of Paine and Burke are demonstrably present in the story. Philip W. London's "The Military Necessity: *Billy Budd* and Vigny" (*CL*, XIV, 1962, 174-186) finds remarkable similarities in theme between *Billy Budd* and the three tales of Vigny which

make up his *Servitude et grandeur militaires* (1835). The question
of Vigny's influence on Melville is probably not involved though
Melville could have known the stories in English translations of
1844 and 1847.

f. **Tales.** Robert L. Gale's "Bartleby—Melville's Father-in-Law"
(*AION-SG*, V, 1962, 57-72) concludes that Melville wrote into the
story his feelings about his ever-helpful father-in-law, with Judge
Shaw in the role of the Wall Street lawyer. William M. Gibson,
in "Herman Melville's 'Bartleby the Scrivener' and 'Benito Cereno' "
(*American Renaissance, the History of an Era: Essays and Interpretations*, ed. George Hendrick, Frankfurt, Diesterweg, 1961,
pp. 107-116) discusses the interesting parallels between the "dead-
wall" confronting Bartleby, the "dead, impregnable, uninjurable
wall" of Moby Dick's immense head, and the impenetrable blackness
at the center of "Benito Cereno."

g. **General.** Hennig Cohen's "Wordplay on Personal Names in the
Writings of Herman Melville" (*TSL*, VIII, 85-97) adds to our
knowledge of Melville delight in playing with language. E. J.
Rose's "Melville, Emerson, and the Sphinx" (*NEQ*, XXXVI, 249-
258) points up the differences between Melville's thought and
Emerson's by comparing Chapter LXX of *Moby-Dick* (Ahab's mono-
logue on the sperm-whale's head) and Emerson's poem "The Sphinx."
Joseph A. Ward's "Melville and Failure" (*ESQ*, No. 33, pp. 43-48)
deserves mention for its suggestiveness. It is much too short, however, to cover so comprehensive a subject. The gist of Allen Gutt-
mann's "From *Typee* to *Moby-Dick*: Melville's Allusive Art" (*MLQ*,
XXIV, 237-244) will be found in these sentences. "The allusions
of *Moby-Dick*, unlike those of the earlier romances, are fully woven
into the fabric of the work.... The allusions expand into complex
metaphors. Even casual references are, for the most part, pertinent."
   Jack Jay Boies's "Melville's Quarrel with Anglicanism" (*ESQ*,
No. 33, pp. 75-79) first examines the life-records to discover the
connections between members of the Melville and Gansevoort families and various church groups. Mr. Boies finds no evidence that
either Melville's father or mother was a staunch Calvinist. Turning
to the fiction, he concludes that Melville appears "to have been
more directly affected by Anglicanism than by any other sect or

order." The article would be more helpful if there were some speculation on *why* Melville satirized Episcopalians.

José de Onís contends in "Melville y el mundo hispánico" (*Cua-
dernos*, No. 70, pp. 53-60) that *Moby-Dick* makes subtle use of one
of the principal early myths of the North Americans, the belief that
we were a chosen race, destined to dislodge Spain from its rightful
place in history. In his view the White Whale is Catholic evil, still
a threat to the liberal revolution. The Spanish doubloon is the talis-
man of Moby-Dick, more tangible, but symbolizing the same thing,
"el mundo hispánico." Stated thus briefly the contentions of this
article may seem far fetched. I find them very much worth pondering. De Onís does not believe, of course, that Melville was a hot
advocate of Manifest Destiny and he cites, appositely, the passage
in *Clarel* about the Anglo-Saxons (read *norte americanos*) as

> These Pirates of the sphere! Grave looters
> Who in the name of Christ and Trade . . .
> Deflower the world's last sylvan glade.

So far as I can determine six doctoral dissertations on Melville
were completed in 1963: Barbara Ruth Nieweg Blansett, "Melville
and Emersonian Transcendentalism" (Texas); Paul Brodtkorb, Jr.,
"Melville's Symbology" (Yale); Bruce L. Grenberg, "Thomas Carlyle and Herman Melville: Parallels, Obliques, and Perpendiculars"
(North Carolina); Thomas E. Lucas, "Herman Melville as Literary
Theorist" (Denver); Robert J. Packard, "A Study of Melville's
Clarel" (Columbia); Michael P. Zimmermann, "Herman Melville in
the 1920's" (Columbia). Only the Blansett and Grenberg dissertations have thus far been recorded in *Dissertation Abstracts* (XXIV,
2904, 3323). Blansett discusses Melville's early attraction to Transcendentalist ideals as they are seen in *Mardi*. The transition to the
anti-Transcendentalism of *Pierre* is traced. Pierre is "a doomed transcendental man, motivated by a desire to follow absolute truth."
Grenberg examines the possible influences of Carlyle on Melville's
writing from *Typee* through *Pierre*. Although the dissertation is
directed essentially to ideological similarities, basic parallels in style
are considered.

4. Whitman

Sculley Bradley

i. Bibliography

The "Annual Bibliography for 1963" appeared in *PMLA*, LXXIX (1964), 88-375. Whitman entries (pp. 199-200) include bound volumes and articles through November, 1963, and also those publications which appeared too late to be included in 1962.

"Articles on American Literature Appearing in Current Periodicals." A cumulative listing compiled by the Committee on Bibliography of the American Literature Group of the Modern Language Association. For 1963 see *AL*, XXXV, 427-428; 586.

"Articles in American Studies, 1963," *AQ*, XVI, 264-325.

"Whitman: A Current Bibliography." By William White. *WWR*, IX, 21-22, 45-46, 70-71, 93-94.

Eight American Authors: A Review of Research and Criticism. Floyd Stovall, ed. (New York, Modern Language Association, 1956). This was up-dated by a supplement (1955-1962) and reprinted in paperback (New York, W. W. Norton, 1963). Willard Thorp's "Whitman" (pp. 270-318) and the "Supplement," (pp. 445-451) are excellent.

ii. Editions and Textual Notes

Prose Works, 1892: Volume I, Specimen Days, was edited by Floyd Stovall (New York: New York Univ. Press). A second volume by the same editor, including *Collect* and the remainder of Whitman's *Complete Prose Works,* 1892, became available in 1964. In the same series, Thomas L. Brasher edited *The Early Poems and the Fiction,* the first complete edition, further distinguished by the annotation of all variants now identified, by the dating of the poems and by an able essay on the "publication history" of the fiction. These volumes are part of *The Collected Writings of Walt Whitman* (Gay W. Allen and Sculley Bradley, eds.) which included seven volumes by the end of 1964 with the addition of the third volume of *The*

Correspondence and the "Reader's Comprehensive Edition" of
Leaves of Grass. "The Reception of Whitman's Correspondence,"
an article by F. DeWolfe Miller (*WWR*, IX, 27-30), analyzes
twenty-four reviews of *The Correspondence*, Vols. I and II; the
majority found Whitman's letters worthy of a massive edition, and
almost all of them praised the editorial work and the editor. With
reference to the entire Whitman publication project, Gay W. Allen
published a noteworthy article, "Editing the Writings of Walt Whitman: A Million Dollar Project without a Million Dollars" (*A&S*, I,
Winter, 1962-1963, 7-12), emphasizing that co-operative research
in the humanities, though desperately needing foundation and government support, can still depend upon a large measure of sacrifice
by dedicated scholars and some financial assistance from over-
burdened institutional budgets and presses.

Henry M. Christman's "Brooklyniana" sketches—*Walt Whitman's
New York from Manhattan to Montauk*, New York, Macmillan—are
not, as the dust jacket declares, "here collected for the first time,"
since the same papers appear in Emory Holloway's *The Uncollected
Poetry and Prose of Walt Whitman*, Vol. II (1921). Mr. Christman
does not acknowledge the earlier collection in his introduction;
however, he says that his text is printed from manuscript. Whitman
in fact listed a manuscript of "Brooklyniana" among his literary
remains, but Holloway's earnest efforts did not bring it to light and
it has not since been reported. Holloway printed what Whitman
published in the Brooklyn weekly *Standard* intermittently from
June 8, 1861, to November 1, 1862. Manuscript variants observed
in spot-checking are not of prime importance unless a definitive
edition is proposed.

In "A Thousand and One MSS by Walt Whitman" (*OW*, VIII,
iv, 69-80), William White describes the massive Feinberg Collection (Detroit) and in a familiar vein illustrates the use of MS
evidence in solving crucial textual and biographical problems. Indeed it was not until a half-dozen private collections like Charles
Feinberg's were made available to Whitman research during the
last fifteen years that definitive work could be accomplished. A
small but important document (Feinberg) is described by William
White: "The First (1855) *Leaves of Grass*: How many Copies?"
(*PBSA*, LVII, 352-354), describing the bookbinder's bill to Whitman for 795 copies in three variant bindings. *The Correspondence*
reports only one letter for 1850 and only seven extant for previous

years. Now one has appeared, dated June 17, 1850 (Feinberg), in which Whitman offers the New York *Sun* serial rights to an unknown work, "The Sleeptalker," condensed and adapted from the Danish Bernhard Severin Ingeman, whom he calls "a better writer, even, than Miss Bremer"; see William White, "Whitman's First 'Literary' Letter" (*AL*, XXXV, 83-85). The same author reports, in "Some Uncollected Whitman Journalism" (*ESQ*, No. 33, pp. 84-90), four more of these elusive writings in clippings, MSS, and proof sheets (Feinberg).

Arthur Golden makes available a unique MS source in transcribing the corrections and comments with which Whitman loaded the pages of his famous "blue book" copy of the 1860 *Leaves* (Berg-Lion collection); some of these alterations survived in 1867, but those which did not are sometimes more suggestive. See "A Glimpse into the Workshop: A Critical Evaluation and Diplomatic Transcription of the 'Blue Book' ..." (*DA*, XXIV, 743).

The only foreign edition in English reported in 1963 is *Leaves of Grass*. With an Introduction by Shiv K. Kumar. New Delhi, India, Eurasia Publishing House.

iii. Biography

The bulk of the biographical commentary in 1963 adduced new materials from 1876 to 1891. One very curious coincidence is noted for the year 1860. Florence B. Freedman, in "Whitman's *Leaves* and O'Connor's *Harrington*: An 1860 Review" (*WWR*, IX, 63-65), notes that during the year of their first meeting as authors of Thayer and Eldridge, Whitman and O'Connor were linked as writers of "sensation books" and "trash" by an anonymous reviewer who defended slavery and deplored sex.

In his Introduction to the handsome facsimile edition of *Memoranda during the War* (Bloomington, Indiana Univ. Press, 1962), Roy P. Basler notes that Whitman's manifest anxiety to publish this work was heightened by his recent paralysis. His awareness of death, reflected in his poems, was also evidenced by his unsigned "puffs" for this book, which F. DeWolfe Miller describes in "A Note on *Memoranda*" (*WWR*, IX, 67-68). Two of Whitman's anonymous previews appeared in newspapers, one in New York, one in Philadelphia, simultaneously on February 19, 1876. On March 11, presumably the publication date of the two-volume Centennial Edition

of which *Two Rivulets* contained the "Memoranda," another unsigned Whitman review of the edition, in a Philadelphia paper,
made a point of the new pieces on the war.

However, Whitman's life of decent frugality seemed pretty much
the common lot to his neighbors in Camden and the farmlands and
hamlets to the east. Surviving records "do not emphasize the poverty
or monotony we sometimes hear about," reports F. DeWolfe Miller
in "New Glimpses of Walt Whitman in 1886" (*TSL*, VIII, 71-80).
Source materials supporting this statement were in the Feinberg
Collection—clippings and manuscript, including an unpublished
diary of Bill Ducket, a teen-ager who drove Whitman's carriage.
That the poet could afford in 1886 to contribute lectures to charity
is further sustained by Roy S. Azanoff's extensive report, "Walt Whitman's Lecture on Lincoln in Haddonfield" (*WWR*, IX, 65-66). In
1882 he was indulging his passion for being photographed, but with
more than the usual satisfaction, as Marchal E. Landgren shows
in "George C. Coxe: Whitman's Photographer" (*WWR*, IX, 11-15).
One of Coxe's clients, the sculptor St. Gaudens, wanted to make a
bust of the poet; and his friends Richard W. and Jeannette Gilder,
who had given Whitman much space in *The Century*, brought
Coxe and Whitman together in New York. The photograph that
Whitman called "The Laughing Philosopher" and sent to Tennyson
in 1887 was the most striking; but Coxe quietly sold many copies
of Whitman portraits to friends and gave the entire proceeds to
the poet. William White reports new information gleaned from the
Feinberg Collection in "Whitman's Poem on the Johnstown Flood"
(*ESQ*, No. 33, pp. 79-84). The flood at Johnstown, Pennsylvania,
occurred on May 31, 1889. On June 5 Julius Chambers of the New
York *World* telegraphed a Philadelphia representative to commission a poem from Whitman overnight for $25.00. The poem, "A
Voice from Death," appeared in the *World* on June 7 and was collected in *Good-Bye, My Fancy* (1891) with a few alterations shown
in this article. Two items are reported concerning the Whitman
circle. Joseph Marion Garrison, Jr., in "John Burroughs as a Literary
Critic: . . . of Emerson, Whitman, Thoreau, Carlyle, and Arnold"
(*DA*, XXIII, 3372-73), finds the naturalist a good impressionistic
critic, best with Whitman, one of his "comrades." The renewed
interest in Bucke is reflected in a twenty-page catalogue: *Richard
Maurice Bucke: Catalogue to the Exposition. June 10-14, 1963*
(Toronto, Univ. Toronto Press). A recent candidate for a place

among Whitman's personal friends is Folger McKinsey, a young newspaper man who sought the poet's friendship in the early eighties. Atcheson L. Hench, in "Walt Whitman Recollected" (*AN&Q*, I, 1962, 22) thinks that McKinsey's contributions (1886-1950) to the newspapers he names may be useful.

iv. Criticism

a. **Ideas and sources.** The effort to find a rationale for Whitman's thought as a whole occupied four of the critical articles reported. James T. F. Tanner, in "The Lamarckian Theory of Progress in *Leaves of Grass*" (*WWR*, IX, 3-11), thanks that Darwin, because potentially deterministic, was less influential than Lamarck on Whitman's theory of progress, because in Lamarck's "purposeful" universe the animal can choose among wants which develop hereditable characteristics, hence conducive to betterment. Whitman anticipated Bergson's *élan vital* in his variety of humanism. Robert Detweiler, in "The Concrete Universal in *Democratic Vistas*" (*WWR*, IX, 40-41), asserts that this work has a metaphysical objective—the poet's characteristic concern with the aspects of being and the relationships among them. When Whitman speaks of the "All," this functions as a "concrete universal," comprising in "Mankind" both the man and the mass. Marion Harris finds the key to Whitman's philosophy of knowledge in his concept of the relations between "the me" and "the not me": see "Nature and Materialism: Fundamentals in Whitman's Epistemology" (*WWR*, IX, 85-88). Cognition of "the me" results both from sensory experience (cf. Hartley's associational psychology and Coleridge) and from affective experience—for Whitman meaning intuitional idealism mounting to the level of ecstasy. "The Quality of Being" said Whitman, "is the lesson of Nature"; hence the moral law is available to all because the microcosm recapitulates the macrocosm. However, the mortal limit of the law of succession is a "Religious Democracy" in which "the not me" serves "the me." Edmund Reiss, in "Whitman's Debt to Animal Magnetism" (*PMLA*, LXXVIII, 80-88), illustrates Whitman's interest in the popular behavioral theories of his day—phrenology, mesmerism or hypnotism, clairvoyance, and especially animal magnetism. Whether Whitman accepted these hypotheses or not, their ideas and terminology supported his concepts of the seer or prophet; of the force of the attraction of sex, of comradeship, of spiritual

love; of the projection of individualistic personality; and of the
absolute cosmic cohesion.

Concepts of nationalism are treated in several articles and notes.
That Whitman's linking of nationalism with literature, especially
poetry, was influenced by ideas expressed by Johann Gottfried von
Herder is explored by Gene Bluestein in a substantial article, "The
Advantages of Barbarism: Herder and Whitman's Nationalism"
(*JHI*, XXIV, 115-126). Whitman's ideas of poetry and its sources
resemble Herder's conception that primitive communities, and folk
art, contain the energy and originality upon which great national
literature is developed. Whitman superimposed the democratic
culture and its bard. Herder conceived that a great national culture,
rooted in folk art, is compatible with other national cultures from
the same sources, and so did Whitman in his dream of the Democratic world. In "Nationalism: Unpublished Whitman" (*AN&Q*, I,
67-68) William White reproduces a Whitman MS fragment (Feinberg Collection) which he suggests may be part of a whole,
since the words follow the note, "winding up"; as follows: "The
great [cancelled] most important requisite now is a great, fervid,
emotional passionate Nationality. Though there are today but few
signs of it, I have no doubt it will come—nay, I think it is now
rapidly forming." Professor White also contributed a related comment on the national poets: "Whitman on American Poets: An
Uncollected Piece" (*ELN*, I, 42-43). In a newspaper clipping, unsigned, but inscribed by Whitman, "Advertiser, July 1st 1885"
(Feinberg), Whitman ranks Bryant first among American poets,
and Emerson, Whittier, and Longfellow in that order. In *Specimen
Days*, under the date of April 16, [1881], in "My Tribute to Four
Poets" he assigned first place to Emerson, and names the others
without ranking them. Walter Lowenfels, in "Whitman on Bruno"
(*WWR*, IX, 42-43), refers to Whitman's "Inscription for a Little
Book on Giordano Bruno." Whitman saw Bruno as one of the "Old
World martyrs" who were "beacons" for "America's mental courage";
a recent "little book" of Bruno's writings (*Cause, Principle, and
Unity*, trans. by Jack Lindsay, London, 1962) may substantiate
Whitman's evaluation.

Mordecai Marcus makes an astute general comparison of two
authors in "Walt Whitman and Emily Dickinson" (*Person*, XLIII,
1962, 497-514). Both were entranced by time and death and each
had a special attitude toward poetry. They are seen as similar in

psychological characteristics, frustrations, and certain factors of experience. Each sought mystical and immortal fulfilment, and was at once non-conformist and religious zealot. Such characteristics are illustrated in this article.

Esther Shephard, in "Whitman's Copy of George Sand's *Consuelo*" (*WWR*, IX, 34-36), identifies the five volumes of *Consuelo* and *The Countess of Rudolstadt* in the Feinberg Collection as those which Whitman told Traubel he had treasured for many years (cf. Esther Shephard, *Walt Whitman's Pose*, 1937). This was the second American edition, published by William H. Graham, New York, 1847-1848. They contain only three marked passages and no marginalia. Not reported among his books at his death, they were missing for many years.

Pierre Michel, in "Whitman Revisited" (*RLV*, XXIX, 79-83), asserts that Whitman's poetry failed as prophecy, as an expression of mystical experience, and as the poetry of democracy *en masse*. Essential in the well-organized defense of this position is the point that the poet projects a world to which he stands as *maker*, not one to which he stands as *witness*.

b. **Reputation and influence.** Three articles published in 1963 deal with Whitman's influence abroad. A persuasively argued "introduction" as the author says, to a subject on which there has been some prior speculation is Don Summerhayes's "Joyce's *Ulysses* and Whitman's 'Self': A Query" (*WSCL*, IV, 216-224), which suggests that a reading of Whitman seems "to make several aspects of *Ulysses* less inscrutable and to add a dimension to the character of Leopold Bloom." *Ulysses* contains at least four direct allusions to Whitman's poetry and several echoes and oblique references. *Finnegans Wake* and *Portrait of the Artist* contain Whitman allusions also. Parallels to Whitman's lines lead toward a deeper understanding of Bloom's central function in the novel. Bloom is an *affluent man*, as Whitman defines him in the 1855 Preface to *Leaves of Grass*: "he that confronts all the shows he sees by equivalents out of the stronger wealth of himself." "Song of Myself" and *Ulysses* both portray the development of individuals who think of themselves as "this particular man." Once achieving identification with total humanity, the individuals—Whitman's "self," Bloom and Stephen of *Ulysses*—discover their identity with the spirit of God. Martin Kanes gives a useful account of the Bazalgette-Gide controversy in "Whitman, Gide, and

Bazalgette: An International Encounter" (*CL*, XIV [1962], 341-355). Gide's translations of *Leaves of Grass* poems (1918) challenged the romanticism of Bazalgette's translations and biography a decade earlier. The debate, involving theories of translation and poetry, linguistic comparison, Whitman's alleged homoeroticism, and the conflict between aesthetic and sociological interpretation, distracted postwar readers in France from poetic values of *Leaves of Grass.*

Claire Paxton, in "Unamuno's Indebtedness to Whitman" (*WWR*, IX, 16-19), discusses Unamuno's acknowledgment of Whitman's influence, as reflected in his struggle for a sense of personal immortality (cf. *The Tragic Sense of Life*, 1913). There are also similarities of thematic structure between the two. Henry Miller (*Stand Still Like the Hummingbird*, New York, New Directions, 1962) finds an essential difference between the rationalism of the "brooding existentialist," Unamuno, and Whitman's "exalted vision," which transcends reason and pierces beyond the frontiers of knowledge.

William White, in a critical commentary, "Robinson Jeffers's Space" (*Person*, XLIV, 175-179), recalls the fact that Whitman's poetic line influenced that of Jeffers; but he adds the original observation, illustrated at length, that both poets figuratively annihilated time and space, for different reasons: "Whitman [to embrace] all humanity past and present"; Jeffers to deny and reject mankind in the mass. Florence B. Freedman, in "A Motion Picture 'First' for Whitman: O'Connor's 'The Carpenter'" (*WWR*, IX, 31-33), calls attention to the filming of the short story, in which the "Carpenter" of the title, as in the original publication by William Douglas O'Connor (1868), and in his essay *The Good Gray Poet* (1886), gave Whitman a mortal resemblance, at least, to Jesus of Nazareth. Vitagraph made the film, which was released and reviewed (July 10, 1910). Its production history is not given and only one frame of the film has been identified (Feinberg Collection).

c. Commentary. In what may be the first part of a longer study, K. A. Preuschen's "Zur Entstehung der neuen Lyrik in Amerika: Walt Whitman: 'Song of Myself'" extensively studies the proposition that this poem in 1855 represented the genesis of a "new lyric in the United States" (*JA*, VIII, 148-170). Acknowledging the intensely subjective background he finds this not inconsistent with the origin of the "first personal 'I' " in epic sources, and this again coincides with the poet's "pantheistic nature philosophy." In this basic perspective, Preuschen examines the lyric factors of vocabulary, rhythm, imagery, syntax, thematic structure, and stylistic unity. On a smaller scale than Preuschen, Chadwick C. Hansen, in a symposium some months earlier, also declared that "Song of Myself" resembled the epic in its "first personal" narrator, in cataloguing aspects of national scenery, history and myth, and in the association of its prophecy with the national struggle: see Mr. Hansen's "Walt Whitman's 'Song of Myself': Democratic Epic," in *American Renaissance, the History of an Era: Essays and Interpretations.* George Hendrick, ed. Frankfurt, Diesterweg, 1961, pp. 77-88.

Stephen D. Malin's commentary, " 'A Boston Ballad' and the Boston Riot" (*WWR*, IX, 51-57), ingeniously based on newspaper sources, points up Whitman's use of the archaic language and setting of the Revolution in conjunction with actual events of the "Boston Slave Riot" of 1854. "A Boston Ballad" is a satire of the fugitive slave laws, and it identifies Daniel Webster as the "Yankee" who had made the "cute . . . bargains" (1850) which permitted the arrest of Anthony Burns, the escaped slave, and his return to his "master" by "the President's Marshal"—the military parade to the ship involved an estimated 10,000 military personnel.

David Daiches, in a review of Geoffry Dutton's *Walt Whitman,* makes a critical observation of general interest. In summary of his own critical estimate of Whitman's value, he asserts that "the only way to confront Whitman adequately [is to] really enter into the poetry, participate in its special kinds of awareness, and learn that . . . 'who touches this touches a man.' " He believes that Dutton successfully applies this critical principle; "he sees the poems as invitations to explore experience through Whitman's awareness" but his book suffers by discursive "shadow-boxing" with Freudian critics and narrow-gauged scholarship (see Geoffry Dutton, *Walt Whitman,* Writers' and Critics' Series, Edinburgh and London; New York, Grove Press, 1961).

Frank Harris makes fourteen references to Whitman in *My Life and Loves* (John F. Gallagher, ed., five volumes in one, New York, Grove Press). He reports at some length Whitman's lecture on Paine "in 1875 or 1876" in Philadelphia, and his conversation with the poet. He found both Swinburne and the "Song of Songs" to be more erotic than Whitman's poems. His early reservations concerning

Whitman's value are evident, but in retrospect he wrote: "I could die happy if I could believe that America's influence would be anything like as true and clear-eyed as Whitman's in guiding mankind." V. K. Chari (Benaras Hindu University), in "Structure and Poetic Growth in *Leaves of Grass*" (*WWR*, IX, 58-63), argues that efforts to substantiate a topical division have been "artificial," because "the whole of Whitman's poetry proceeds from a central unity of experience" and "expresses an integrated vision" of themes complexly "interfused." He discusses the periodicity of certain "modes" with reference to a chart of major poems.

Sister Miriam Clare Roesler's "The Sea and Death in Walt Whitman's *Leaves of Grass*" (*DA*, XXIV, 1606) ably opposed the interpretation of Whitman's sea-death images as representing dichotomous opposites. The sea merges all aspects of fertility, life, death, and rebirth in "a vast similitude" of spiritual meaning.

d. **Textual analysis and explication.** The amount of intensive criticism reported was somewhat less than that which used the wider lens. Two papers on "Crossing Brooklyn Ferry" at least manifest a diverse interest. John E. Byron, in discussing the cabalistic "Significance of T, I, and O in 'Crossing Brooklyn Ferry'" (*WWR*, IX, 89-90), gives a useful list of these transliterations in ancient occult mysteries and sorcery, and especially in early Christian symbolism; he gives frequency counts but they are not comparative, and he makes no effort to persuade us that Whitman had knowledge of this lore. James W. Gargano seems to express an impression widely felt, in his "Technique in 'Crossing Brooklyn Ferry': The Everlasting Moment" (*JEGP*, LXII, 262-269). He asserts that the enigma that most readers admit finding in this poem has been present in our minds as we read, long before we find the poet's words in the penultimate stanza: "What I promised without mentioning it, have you not accepted?" The writer suggests that each, in crossing his own "Brooklyn Ferry" is offered "the moment of apotheosis," in Whitman's poem imaged in the figure of "the fine centrifugal spokes of light round the shape of my head."

William White reports "An Unpublished Notebook for 'Lilacs'" (Feinberg) in which Whitman's writing suggests hasty recording (*MLQ*, XXIV, 177-180). Its substance recalls a Burroughs letter reported in Clara Barrus's *Whitman and Burroughs, Comrades:* "[Whitman] is deeply interested in what I tell him of the Hermit-

Thrush, and says he has used largely the information I have given him." Whitman had written the thrush music of "When Lilacs Last in the Dooryard Bloom'd" soon after Lincoln's death the previous spring, according with the past tense of this letter.

An unusual analytic technique is demonstrated by Bernard De Koven and Sholom J. Kahn in "A 'Symphonic' Arrangement of Two Whitman Poems" (*WWR*, IX, 37-40). Duet arrangements of "I Hear America Singing" and "I Sit and Look Out" are facilitated by Whitman's use of reiterative cadences, phrasing and thematic references, which provide naturally for antiphonal recomposition.

Milton Hindus, in "Notes Toward the Definition of a Typical Poetic Line in Whitman" (*WWR*, IX, 75-81), suggests that what now "beckons to pioneers" of Whitman studies "is the field of technical analysis." Hindus illustrates briefly but with penetration: in language, showing that Whitman used the word "drift" with four distinct connotations; in meter, by extending de Selincourt's observation of a three-stress norm in "When Lilacs Last in the Dooryard Bloom'd"—actually the hexameter is basic but divides and recombines in threes, sixes, and nines; and in imagery, showing how this poem reiterates three triads of images.

Two explications similar in method were reported. Wilton Eckley, in "Whitman's 'A Noiseless Patient Spider' " (*Expl*, XXII, Item 20), shows how the bipartite form of the poem emphasizes the metaphors of the creators and the created object. Eckley finds a parallel, perhaps a source, for Whitman's idea in two related passages of Emerson's "The Poet," which establish the same dualism. Robert J. Griffin, in "Whitman's 'This Compost' " (*Expl*, XXI, Item 68), finds that the cyclical form in each stanza permits a sort of "play-back" in the second of materials introduced in the first— except that "life-forms" are now substituted for "death-forms."

Two analytical studies of the *Drum-Taps* volume may be thought to supplement each other. "Thematic Unfolding in Whitman's *Drum-Taps*," by Edward E. Sullivan, Jr., (*ESQ*, No. 31, pp. 42-45) summarizes a program for the explication of the *Drum-Taps* volume as a whole. It conceives a graduated emotional intensity as the involvement in the war progresses, and brings into focus a correspondingly greater panorama of the American people, the American land. Supporting themes are the role of the national poet and the expression of the nation's identity. In this broad perspective, *Drum-Taps* has a sort of epic equality or function. Sam Toperoff's "Reconciliation of Polarity in Whitman's *Drum-Taps*" (*ESQ*, No. 31, pp. 45-47) emphasizes primarily the interaction of war and peace as opposite poles in the entire volume. The use of this technique in the analysis of individual poems is extended by using elements of less emphatic polarity that are, however, operative, e.g., life-death; urban-rural; past-present, etc. Such polarities may be expressed in philosophical, psychological, or social terms; or such terms may apply collectively, as in "Song of the Banner at Day-break."

Joseph M. DeFalco, in "The Narrative Shift in Whitman's 'Song of Myself'" (*WWR*, IX, 82-84), ascribes an important function to Section 24, which he believes is intended to influence the poem as a whole. The sudden shift from the impersonal "I" to the identifiable "Walt Whitman" culminates the preparative and empirical attitudes toward Nature and sensory experience; it alters the dramatic situation by identifying a human individual spirit.

5. Mark Twain

John C. Gerber

i. Texts and Editions

Probably the most influential work presently being done on Mark Twain is in editing rather than in historical scholarship or critical evaluation. As work continues at Berkeley on the unpublished papers and at Iowa and elsewhere on a new edition of the published works, separate collections and editions of single works continue to appear.

Of the collections containing hitherto unpublished material, the most widely advertised in recent years came out in 1962: *Letters from the Earth* (New York, Harper and Row). Originally edited by Bernard DeVoto in 1939, the material was withheld from publication until Clara Clemens Samossoud, shortly before her death, finally consented to its being issued. Before sending it to the printer, Henry Nash Smith added a short preface but otherwise left it almost exactly as DeVoto had prepared it. The volume, therefore, represents an attempt to get the DeVoto version into print and not an attempt to put out an uncorrupted text. The new selections in *Letters* are the title piece, most of "Papers of the Adam Family," parts of "The Great Dark," and over a dozen minor pieces. While these strengthen our admiration for Twain's inventiveness, they offer few new insights into the nature of his mind. "Letters from the Earth" is easily the most interesting selection. The persona of Satan, even though Twain mishandles it, is brilliantly conceived. And the writing has almost all of the strengths and weaknesses of his journalism of the sixties, the same exuberance and outrageous irreverence on the one hand and the same coarseness and silliness on the other.

Edited by the indefatigable Charles Neider, "Reflections on Religion" (*HudR*, XVI, 329-352) presents five sections of the unpublished autobiography dictated by Twain in June, 1906. This also is material that Clara Clemens Samossoud withheld from publication until shortly before her death. As a matter of fact, Twain himself said that it was "not to be exposed to any eye until the edition of

A.D. 2406." Maybe it shouldn't have been. It is primarily vitupera-
tion without the ingenuity of "Letters from the Earth." The subject
matter of his other blasphemies is here, but not the drama or the
sublimely idiotic images. If any further proof were needed that
Twain required a persona to energize his imagination, these pages
will provide it. Nevertheless, they add further evidence of the
lengths to which his skepticism went in those late years.

By far the best editing of manuscript material reported here is
to be found in Franklin R. Rogers' edition of *Simon Wheeler, Detective* (New York, New York Public Library). With only minor
changes, all of them noted, the text as printed follows the manuscript
housed in the Berg Collection in the New York Public Library.
Textual notes—twenty-four pages of them—enable the reader to
recapture such revisions as Twain made in the manuscript. In
addition, Rogers reprints thirteen sheets of Twain's working notes
and a letter to Dr. John Brown of Edinburgh in which Twain describes a runaway at Quarry Farm that he later uses as an incident
in the narrative. The result of all this is an attractive and authoritative volume. Written in the winter of 1877-1878, the narrative covers
half of the action described in the play version of the story finished
in July, 1877. As it stands, the narrative is a ludicrous attack on
Southern chivalry, the Allan Pinkerton detective stories, and the
Belford Brothers, the notorious Canadian publishers who had
pirated *Tom Sawyer*. Rogers is almost too kind when he says that
none of the subtlety and restraint of the treatment in *Huckleberry
Finn* can be found in *Simon Wheeler, Detective*. At best it is a
welter of slapstick, burlesque, and melodrama.

Two relatively unimportant letters, hitherto unpublished, appear
on the cover of *SWR* (XLVIII, Autumn) and in *MHR* (LVII, 398-
399). The former, dated December 21, is an apology to Howells
for not inviting Howells and Aldrich to "hide" with him. The latter,
dated March 4, 1894, is a regret addressed to Walter Williams,
editor of the *Columbia Missouri Herald*. Martin Bucco adds a helpful note to this one.

In one of two collections of newspaper writings, Bernard Taper
assembles in *Mark Twain's San Francisco* (New York, McGraw-
Hill) eighty-three of the pieces Twain originally wrote for Nevada
and California newspapers, 1863-1866. Some of these items have
not been reprinted before, and others not in book form. Suggesting
something of the life of San Francisco at the time, the selections

are still readable for their almost incredible buoyancy. As Taper himself admits, however, his primary reason for including these particular selections is that these are the ones he has especially enjoyed. So we have only a vague idea of how exhaustive the volume is. Furthermore, although the place and date of original publication follow each selection, there are no textual notes. In short, if we are to have texts of this Western material in which we can have confidence, Taper's work will have to be done over. Pleasantly written, Taper's biographical introduction has already been reprinted in *AH* (XIV, Aug., 50-53, 90-94) and *The Twainian* (Nov.-Dec., 1963, and Jan.-Feb., 1964).

Henry Duskis imbeds a great deal that Twain wrote for the Buffalo *Express*, 1869-1871, in a work he entitles *The Forgotten Writings of Mark Twain* (New York, Philosophical Library). Some of these *Express* pieces Twain himself reprinted in 1875, but according to Duskis he "forgot" the others, and they are now revealed for the first time. Reading this revelation is a frustrating experience. The book is the old-type scissors-and-paste job with the selections lightly glued together by the author's transitions. One never knows how much of a selection has been included. Nor in some instances is one quite sure he is reading a selection really written by Twain. Had Duskis simply reprinted the Twain material with brief notes about each selection, this would have been a fascinating volume.

Of the reprinted texts the most interesting is a facsimile of the first American edition of *A Connecticut Yankee in King Arthur's Court*, edited with a helpful introduction by Hamlin Hill (San Francisco, Chandler). The name of Mark Twain is deleted in order to avoid difficulties over the trademark. Charles Neider edits what he calls *The Complete Essays of Mark Twain* (Garden City, N.Y., Doubleday). And brief selections from Twain bearing on his Western years appear in a casebook entitled *Mark Twain's Frontier* (New York, Holt, Rinehart, and Winston) edited by James E. Camp and X. J. Kennedy. A paperback, the work also includes some interesting memoirs and tales by contemporaries of Twain, and the inevitable selections from Brooks and DeVoto.

ii. Biography

Only one work of biography included here can be called a major one, and that was published in 1962. The works of 1963 fill in

chinks. Some are interesting and perceptive; more are routine. For
Mark Twain biography it is not a vintage year.

Two articles tell something of Twain's ability as a dancer and as
a lecturer. In "Twain Could Mark the Beat" (*MASJ*, IV, i, 39-44),
Louis J. Budd assembles references extending from 1850 to 1894 to
indicate that Twain enjoyed dancing and, indeed, found deep release in it. Hamlin Garland's reaction to a Twain lecture appears in
James B. Stronks' "Mark Twain's Boston Stage Debut as Seen by
Hamlin Garland" (*NEQ*, XXXVI, 85-86). Garland remarks especially upon Twain's easy style; his "raspy, dry 'rosen' voice; his
habit of coughing drily and sighing deeply."

Twain's visit to the Orient is the subject of two articles, both of
them by Coleman O. Parsons. In "Mark Twain: Sightseer in India"
(*MissQ*, XVI, 76-93), Parsons traces Twain's activities from his
arrival in Bombay January 18, 1896, until his departure from Cal-
cutta March 27. In "Mark Twain in Ceylon" (*The Twainian*, Jan.-
Feb., March-Apr.), he reports on Twain's two short visits to Colombo
in January and April, 1896. For source material Parsons uses not
only *Following the Equator* and A. B. Paine's biography but also
the appropriate Indian and Ceylonese newspapers in the British
Museum. For the basic facts of Twain's visits to the two countries,
therefore, Parsons is likely to be more accurate than either Twain
or Paine.

Other articles focus upon Twain's friendships. A portion of
Finley Peter Dunne's memoirs, readied for the press by his son
Philip, carries the title "Mr. Dooley's Friends: Teddy Roosevelt and
Mark Twain" (*AtM*, CCXII, Sept., 77-99). Amiably written, Dunne's
memoirs in the main simply reinforce what we already know about
Twain, his explosive profanity, his love for cigars, his passion for
an audience. It is interesting to discover, however, that Dunne
considered Twain a conservative who thought too poorly of the
human race to be a socialist or communist. In "Howells and Twain:
The World in Midwestern Eyes" (*BSTCF*, III, 3-8), Edwin H.
Cady offers another look at the forty-year-old friendship of Twain
and Howells, and finds the basis for it in their Midwestern heritage.
It is Cady's argument that the penetration of the vision of both men
sprang from their sense of strangeness and isolation as they stood
between the Middle West and the otherwise civilized world. And
it was to the Midwestern village that they both returned for many
of their profoundest insights.

The title of Thomas Andersson's "Mark Twain's Views on Politics, Religion, and Morals" (*MSpr*, LVII, 283-289) suggests that it covers the field lightly, and it does. Andersson catches many of Twain's dominant attitudes in these areas, but he deals almost wholly in broad generalizations. Twain's humanitarianism is the main thesis of Chris Kanellakou in "Mark Twain and the Chinese" (*MTJ*, XII, i, 7-9, 20). For a comprehensive treatment of Twain's social thought we must turn back a year to Louis J. Budd's *Mark Twain, Social Philosopher* (Bloomington, Univ. of Indiana Press, 1962). Budd's richly detailed and tightly written volume follows Twain's political and economic pronouncements from his sophomoric columns in Orion's Hannibal *Journal* to his gibes at the protectionists in the days just before his death. Pushing through the epigrams and quips, Budd finds Twain to be a reasonably consistent and optimistic Manchester Liberal who found in property rights the foundation for the happiest society. Despite the fact that Twain was clearly guilty of vacillation (partly because his Liberalism did not readily accommodate itself to his humanitarian impulses or to the profound social changes of his time), one comes away from Budd's book with the feeling that Twain had a firmer set of social principles than he is often given credit for.

As always, the Twain psyche is a matter of interest. In "Twain's Ordeal in Retrospect" (*SWR*, XLVIII, 338-348), E. Hudson Long reviews the history of the Great Debate begun by Brooks and Bernard DeVoto. "Mark Twain's Seven Lively Sins" (*TQ*, VI, iii, 92-97) by C. Merton Babcock offers a list of sins Twain would have us believe he was guilty of: stealing, gambling, laziness, smoking, drinking, swearing, and lying. Babcock is not impressed though; he thinks Twain had "a damned good moral character." A more serious study is Bradford Smith's "Mark Twain and the Mystery of Identity" (*CE*, XXIV, 425-430). Smith argues that Twain's quest for identity was central to both his writing and his personality. The fact that Twain constantly raises the question of identity in his works through the use of disguises, twins, people who look alike, assumed names, and other such devices would indicate that it is a subject that he converts into humor to make endurable. The matter of identity is also a concern of James M. Cox in "The Muse of Samuel Clemens" (*MR*, V, 127-141). In what is the most probing analysis yet of the relation between Twain and Olivia Clemens, Cox sees Olivia as a censor that Twain himself created. Thus any censorship of hers did not constitute an alien authority, for it was really his own. She was his "self-created muse," a portion of his identity as writer. And why all this? Cox's answer is that Twain's comic genius required such a resistance in order to achieve expression.

Earl Schenck Miers' *Mark Twain on the Mississippi* (New York, Collier Books) is a fictionalized biography (paperback) for boys designed to show that the young Sam Clemens was just as rip-snorting as the boys he writes about. The events described in the book have a basis in fact, but the talk of the Clemens family sounds as though it came out of a Toby and Susie show. Douglas Grant's *Mark Twain* (New York, Grove Press, 1962) is as good a medium-length introduction to the life and works of Twain as we have. Making use of the most recent historical scholarship, Grant includes most of the salient facts. He is better on the early life than the later, and better as a biographer than as a critic, but his paperback is well worth recommending to a non-specialist. It is worth noting, too, that DeLancey Ferguson's fine biography, first published in 1943, is now available in an attractive Charter Book, *Mark Twain: Man and Legend* (Indianapolis, Bobbs-Merrill).

iii. Criticism

No critical work dealing with Twain's prose as a whole appeared in 1963, though two were published the previous year. Henry Nash Smith's *Mark Twain: The Development of a Writer* (Cambridge, Mass., Harvard Univ. Press, Belknap, 1962) is an especially illuminating treatment of Twain as a craftsman and thinker. Smith shows Twain inextricably caught between the ideal and the fact, between gentility and vulgarity. Caught thus, he vacillates in style between elevated rhetoric and colloquial speech, in thought between the values of the established culture and the impulses originating in common experience. Having defined Twain's basic dichotomy, Smith then proceeds to trace manifestations of it in nine of the principal works. Not unexpectedly, he finds that Twain resolved his problem best in *Huckleberry Finn*, where, by placing the conflict between accepted values and vernacular protest within a single mind, he for once does justice to its moral depth. If Smith's thesis tends to oversimplify Twain's moral and artistic dilemmas, it clearly proves a useful instrument for separating the meretricious from the meritorious. In *Mark Twain's Humor* (Dallas, Southern Methodist Univ.

Press, 1962), Pascal Covici, Jr., argues that Twain's strategies with humor are extraordinarily successful in directing the reader's attention to the heart of the great predicaments of his time, and of all time. Though many of Covici's analyses are provocative, his judgments frequently seem overgenerous.

The criticism appearing in 1963 is marked more by its variety than by its profundity. One especially informative article, though, is Hamlin Hill's "Mark Twain: Audience and Artistry" (*AQ*, XV, 25-40). In it Hill argues that Twain constructed his books with the demands of the highly successful subscription houses in mind: the books should be large, informative, and topical. Furthermore, they should blend the moral and the sensational. In another treatment of influences, "Mark Twain and the Boy-Book in 19th Century America" (*CE*, XXIV, 430-438), Jim Hunter suggests that the Romantic belief in the innate goodness of the child lay at the heart of the boy-books in America, including those by Twain. Huck, however, is not the typical hero of the boy-book, for he remains uncommitted, unattached, and unprepared to enter society.

Of the essays dealing with individual works, one of the most unusual is by Claude S. Brinegar: "Mark Twain and the Quintus Curtius Snodgrass Letters: A Statistical Test of Authorship" (*JASA*, LVIII, 85-96). By a statistical analysis of the language, Brinegar concludes that Twain did not write the "Letters." Happily for him, Allan Bates has since discovered who did (*AL*, XXXVI, 31-37, 1964).

In "The 'Jumping Frog' as a Comedian's First Virtue" (*MP*, LX, 192-200), Paul Baender argues that the story is an attempt by Twain to carry out his own dictum, announced in 1864, that the first virtue of a comedian is "to do funny things with grave decorum and without seeming to know they are funny." Baender's essay is a substantial refutation of the contention that the "Jumping Frog" is a parable illustrating cultural antagonisms between the frontier and the East. Hennig Cohen in "Twain's Jumping Frog: Folktale to Literature to Folktale" (*WF*, XXII, 17-18) reports on a tale which appeared in the San Francisco *Evening Bulletin* two years after the appearance of the "Jumping Frog." Involving a gamecock fed rifle balls, the tale includes a reference to Twain's story.

Mark Twain, the Innocent in *Innocents Abroad*, may have been at least a partial source for Christopher Newman in James' *The American*. At least this is the interesting contention of Richard Van

Der Beets in "A Note on Henry James' 'Western Barbarian'" (*WHR*, XVII, 175-178).

In "The Road to Reality: Burlesque Travel Literature and Mark Twain's *Roughing It*" (*BNYPL*, LXVII, 155-168), Franklin R. Rogers argues persuasively that *Roughing It* is the culmination of a seventy-year tradition of burlesque travel literature. Rogers indicates that in developing the narrative of *Roughing It* Twain combined the stock sentimentalist and the stock realist of burlesque travel literature into a single character who starts out as the sentimentalist (the tenderfoot) and emerges as the realist (the old-timer). The result, Rogers believes, is not only a new firmness of point of view but the creation of an almost archetypal post-Civil War American who, nurtured in one culture, suddenly finds himself having to adjust to another. In "Rough Spots in *Roughing It*" (*MissQ*, XVI, 94-96), Kathryn Whitford turns upon Twain the guns he had aimed at Fenimore Cooper. Miss Whitford finds Twain and Ollendorff and Ballou so thoroughly stupid in handling themselves in a snowstorm that she can conclude only that they died during the night and that all the subsequent writings attributed to Twain are a hoax. Robert L. Gale's "*The Prince and the Pauper* and *King Lear*" (*MTJ*, XII, i, 14-17) discloses parallels in the two works in both character and event.

As one would guess, the bulk of the articles about particular works focus upon *Huckleberry Finn*. In "The Beginning of *Huckleberry Finn*" (*AS*, XXXVIII, 196-201), Robert J. Lowenherz contends that in the first paragraph of 108 words Twain manages to establish the vernacular, characterize Huck, create a major theme (truth *vs.* lying), provide a frame of reference for future action, and slip in some advertising for *Tom Sawyer*. Chadwick Hansen, in "The Character of Jim and the Ending of *Huckleberry Finn*" (*MR*, V, 45-66), finds that Jim is five different types: the comic stage Negro, Mr. Bones of the minstrel show, the kindly old colored mammy, the sentimental family man, and the natural man. The last two lines suggest not only escape for Huck, Hansen believes, but at the mythic level an escape for Jim too. Levi A. Olan stresses the meaninglessness of Huck's escape. Identifying Twain with Kafka, Salinger, and others in "The Voice of the Lonesome: Alienation from Huck Finn to Holden Caulfield" (*SWR*, XLVIII, 143-150), Olan asserts that Huck has no place to return to or to look forward to. Running has become an end in itself. All he knows is that he is escaping into nothing. Roy Harvey Pearce contends that Huck knows very well where he is going. In "'The End, Yours Truly, Huck Finn': Postscript" (*MLQ*, XXIV, 253-256), Pearce contends that Huck in his desire to light out for the territory "ahead of the rest" demonstrates again his uncommon prescience. Read in the light of the times, the phrase just quoted indicates Huck's realization that even if he gets to the territory he will be only a step ahead of the Boomers; Tom Sawyer's civilization will quickly overtake him.

A. N. Kaul, in *The American Vision: Actual and Ideal Society in Nineteenth-Century Fiction* (New Haven, Yale Univ. Press), sees *Huckleberry Finn* giving new vitality to the idealism that had figured in the works of Cooper, Hawthorne, and Melville. In it are polarized, as they were in the works of the earlier writers, the existing social order and the ideal social construct. Although this opposition, dramatized by shore and raft, is hardly an original idea with Kaul, his treatment of the theme is more illuminating than most because he explores the contrast as a particular manifestation of a general response to the socio-moral meaning of America. Also suggesting the opposition of the river and shore is the remarkable twelve-page letter Twain wrote in 1880 to a twelve-year-old boy who had asked him whether he would like to be a boy again. Tony Tanner in "Mark Twain and Wattie Bowser" (*MTJ*, XII, i, 1-6), points out that Twain's instinctive response to the question is no, but on second thought he gives a yes provided that he can remain on the river as a pilot with only short stays in port. Since *Huckleberry Finn* was on the boards at the time Twain wrote to Wattie, Tanner believes the letter is in part a discussion of the dilemma of boyhood *vs.* maturity Twain was facing in working with Huck.

Nancy Dew Taylor (*MissQ*, XVI, 191-199) uses the same opposition between river and shore to point up parallels between *Huckleberry Finn* and Faulkner's "Old Man"; however, she stresses the interesting difference that whereas Huck and Jim seek the river for freedom, Faulkner's tall convict, terrified by it, retreats to the security of the land. Also comparing Twain and Faulkner, an unsigned article "*The Bear* and *Huckleberry Finn*: Heroic Quests for Moral Liberation" (*MTJ*, XII, i, 12-13, 21) finds many resemblances in the experiences of Huck and Ike McCaslin. It also finds both stories rich in such mythical elements as substitute fathers, withdrawal, temptation, initiation rites, and growth toward moral consciousness. For those who are tired of such mythical interpretations William Higgins in "I Try to Do It Another Way and Am Sorry" (*BSTCF*, III, 13-14), has Huck and Jim on a handcar discussing present-day critics.

Sideswiping Leslie Fieldler, John J. McAleer, in "Noble Innocents in *Huckleberry Finn*" (*BSTCF*, III, 9-12), suggests that though Twain realized that man can be in a state of naked innocence, he also realized that nakedness does not automatically put him in that state, *vide* the Royal Nonesuch. The theme of innocence appears also in Colin Macinnes' "Everything on Our Raft" (*New Statesman*, June 21). Macinnes asserts that *Huckleberry Finn* pins us in a moment of history when America lost its innocence but was still filled with hope and promise. According to Paul C. Wermuth in "Santayana and *Huckleberry Finn*" (*NEQ*, XXXVI, 79-82), Santayana found Tom more interesting than Huck. But then Santayana probably cared little for Twain. Generally he found the mockery and skepticism of humorists poor substitutes for spirit.

Henry B. Chapin praises *Pudd'nhead Wilson* as a study of the ironies implicit in a slave-holding society: "Twain's *Pudd'nhead Wilson*, Chapter VI" (*Expl*, XXI, Item 61). The twins, Chapin contends, especially emphasize the theme that free men are themselves almost slaves in a slave-holding society. Robert A. Wiggins finds nothing so profound in the book. His "*Pudd'nhead Wilson*: 'A Literary Caesarean Operation'" (*CE*, XXV, 182-186) enumerates the work's inconsistencies, oversights, and missed opportunities. In his dissertation entitled "Mark Twain's *Joan of Arc*: Origins, Purposes, and Accomplishments" (*DA*, XXIII, 4358), Joseph G. Jurich (Illinois) calls *Joan of Arc* a key to Twain's thought of the time since it is the result not only of a long-standing interest but also of immediate political and social preoccupations.

The most rigorous piece of textual criticism published during the year is undoubtedly John S. Tuckey's *Mark Twain and Little Satan* (West Lafayette, Ind., Purdue Univ. Studies). Studying *The Mysterious Stranger* manuscripts carefully, Tuckey concludes that the chronology of composition was as follows: (1) the pre-Eseldorf story, written probably in October, 1897, and laid in America, (2) the Eseldorf story, written in three parts from November, 1897, to August, 1900, and laid in Austria, (3) the Hannibal version, written in November and December of 1898 and laid in Hannibal, (4) the Print Shop version, written in five periods between November, 1902, and September, 1908, and laid in Austria, and (5) a

Tom-and-Huck story intended possibly as another version of *The Mysterious Stranger* with an American setting, written in 1902 but destroyed by Twain. Tuckey's detective work with ink, paper, and handwriting is so thorough that the case of the mysterious Mysterious Stranger would seem to be solved. What we have been calling *The Mysterious Stranger* has been a construct of A. B. Paine and Frederick A. Duneka, general manager of Harpers. It consists of the Eseldorf version plus the last chapter of the Print Shop version. More than that, in the character of the astrologer it contains a creation of Paine and Duneka, not Twain. Obviously, Tuckey's investigation destroys DeVoto's notion that the Eseldorf version was the last and therefore the one that broke Twain's psychological block and brought him "back from the edge of insanity." In another piece of textual criticism, "*The Innocents Adrift* Edited by Mark Twain's Official Biographer" (*PMLA*, LXXVIII, 230-237), Arthur L. Scott details Paine's incredible manhandling of another Twain manuscript. Preparing "Down The Rhone" for *Europe and Elsewhere*, Paine cut over 45 per cent of the original narrative, eliminating almost all the dialogue, humor, and spontaneity.

That interest in Twain in foreign countries remains high is spelled out by two articles, Shunsuke Kamei's "Mark Twain in Japan" (*MTJ*, XII, i, 10-11, 20) and Boris Gilenson's "Mark Twain—an Accuser" (*SovLit*, No. 11).

Two collections of critical essays will be helpful to students of Twain. *Mark Twain: A Collection of Critical Essays* (Englewood Cliffs, N.J., Prentice-Hall) is edited by Henry Nash Smith. His useful introductory essay traces the changing emphases in Mark Twain criticism from Twain's own time to the present. Edited by Guy Cardwell, *Discussions of Mark Twain* (Boston, D. C. Heath) is intended primarily for undergraduates. In his introduction Cardwell argues that Twain's literary reputation cannot be considered settled.

6. Henry James

B. R. McElderry, Jr.

i. Bibliography, Texts, Manuscripts

Reissue of the New York Edition (New York, Scribners) proceeded in 1963 through Volumes X (*The Spoils of Poynton*) and XI (*The Awkward Age*). Leon Edel added Volumes V through VIII of his *Complete Tales of Henry James* (Philadelphia, Lippincott), including stories of 1892 in the latest volume. In reviewing this project, Herbert Ruhm (*SR*, LXXI, 675-680) commented on the importance of revisions that supplement early editions: "Until a variorum edition is completed . . . all editions will ultimately prove ignorant." Morris Shapira edited *Selected Literary Criticism* (London, Heinemann), twenty-three pieces from the review of Whitman's *Drum Taps* in 1865 to "The New Novel" in 1914. No annotation is provided, though in an introduction F. R. Leavis makes some characteristic reservations on James's critical views, particularly in the Prefaces to the New York Edition.

George Monteiro, using John Hay materials at Brown University, published (*TSLL*, IV, 1962, 639-695) thirty-six letters from James to Hay and two to Mrs. Hay. Monteiro's full account of the association of James and Hay appeared in *BBr* (XIX, 69-88) and in the same issue seven letters from Hay to James and two from Mrs. Hay to James were given. A letter from James to Henry Adams was also published by Monteiro (*N&Q*, X, 143-144). A further note by Monteiro (*AN&Q*, I, 68-69) printed an exchange of letters between Hay and James in 1890, indicating that at Hay's request the manuscript of *The Tragic Muse* was sent to Hay. The manuscript of this novel is not among Hay's papers, however, and thus far has not been traced.

ii. Biography

Publication of the second and third volumes of Leon Edel's biography of James in 1962 (*The Conquest of London, 1870-1881* and

The Middle Years, 1882-1895 [Philadelphia, Lippincott] called forth the same high praise given to the first volume (*The Untried Years, 1843-1870*, published 1953). Critics cool to James have naturally objected to the scale of this biography, but in general Professor Edel's meticulous scholarship, his lucid style, and his perceptive account of James in relation to the various societies in which he moved have been recognized and justly praised. Frederick J. Hoffman's "The Expense of Power and Greatness: An Essay on Leon Edel's James" (*VQR*, XXXIX, 518-528) and Christof Wegelin's "Jamesian Biography" (*NCF*, XVIII, 283-287) both remark on the creative, imaginative blend of biography and criticism in Edel's account.

iii. Criticism: General

Maxwell Geismar's iconoclastic *Henry James and the Jacobites* (Boston, Houghton Mifflin) was well advertised by publication of several sections in journals of 1962. His objections to James are: desertion of his native country; a snobbish worship of things European; ignorance and fear of sex; a preposterous overvaluation of style and form in the attempt to conceal a lack of substance. These are old charges, badly argued by Mr. Geismar, since he persists in discussing James as if he were a novelist of the mid-twentieth century. Geismar's objections to the Jacobites—James's sometimes overworshipful disciples—have more point. The James cult, it is argued, is essentially a retreat from important social concerns to safe formalist discussion. The truth of this charge is frequently illustrated by critics who discuss the master wholly in his own terms, seeking to justify his every comma and image rather than to weigh judiciously the profit and loss of his strategy. Even when Geismar has something of value to say, however, his shrill tone detracts. *The Ambassadors* he calls "perhaps the silliest novel ever to be taken seriously in world literature." His rhetorical questions are pert. His comments on such critics as Edmund Wilson, F. O. Matthiessen, and F. W. Dupee seem spiteful and contemptuous.

James is treated as one of the *Eight Modern Writers* in J. I. M. Stewart's Volume XII of *The Oxford History of English Literature* (Oxford, Oxford Univ. Press). In his fifty-page chapter, Stewart is necessarily selective, treating thirty-five of James's one hundred and thirty-five fictional works. He gives a disparaging paragraph to

James's dramatic efforts, and brief mention to a few critical works. While accepting James's technical brilliance, Stewart repeatedly objects (as vigorously, but more politely than Geismar) to his reticence, his overvaluation of moral dignity and "style," and the "exhibitionism" of the complex later works. "The Turn of the Screw" and *The Sacred Fount* he dismisses as "insusceptible of any assured interpretation." Judgments of James's major novels are deft balances of merits and objections. It is apparent that Mr. Stewart thinks the James revival has gone quite far enough. A selective bibliography is supplied by Mr. Howell Daniels.

The doubts of Geismar and Stewart about the stature of James do not affect Sister M. Corona Sharp's *The Confidante in Henry James: Evolution and Moral Value of a Fictive Character* (Notre Dame, Ind., Univ. of Notre Dame Press). From the early novels to the later, Sister Corona finds a growing sensitivity and resourcefulness in developing the role of James's confidantes. They are used to heighten the consciousness of the central figure, and to emphasize the element of choice. Fidelity, James's cardinal virtue, is illustrated by confidantes as diverse as Henrietta Stackpole in *The Portrait of a Lady* and Maria Gostrey in *The Ambassadors*. Betrayal, the corresponding vice, is shown boldly in Madame Merle in *The Portrait*, subtly in Fanny Assingham of *The Golden Bowl*. A study which might well have been an academic compilation has been turned to critical account by thoughtful consideration of the technical problems involved in the use of a single character type.

Joseph Wiesenfarth's *Henry James and the Dramatic Analogy: A Study of the Major Novels of the Middle Period* (New York, Fordham Univ. Press), focuses attention on the intensity, economy, and objectivity of the "dramatic" novels of 1896-1901: *The Spoils of Poynton, What Maisie Knew, The Awkward Age,* and *The Sacred Fount.* Brother Joseph considers these novels important in their own substance and technique, but essential as well in understanding how James achieved the powers displayed in the three great novels of "the major phase" which followed.

Christof Wegelin, "The Rise of the International Novel" (*PMLA,* LXXVII, 1962, 305-310), dissents from Oscar Cargill's views (*PMLA,* LXXIII, 1958, 418-425), finding that James was anticipated in this fictional genre by the experiments of Willis, Hawthorne, and Motley. George Monteiro, "The New York *Tribune* on Henry James, 1881-1882" (*BNYPL,* LXVII, 71-81), studies in detail the interrelations

of John Hay's review of *The Portrait of a Lady*, Howells's article in
the *Century*, with praise of James and strictures on Dickens and
Thackeray, and attacks on James as a leader of the "new school"
and as an expatriate. Clara M. Kirk, " 'The Brighter Side' of Fiction—
According to Howells and James" (*CE*, XXIV, 463-464), cites
several passages to show that James concurred with Howells's emphasis on "the more smiling aspects of life."
   William T. Stafford, "Literary Allusions in James's Prefaces"
(*AL*, XXXV, 60-70), finds many and varied references that testify
to James's wide reading. Few, however, are drawn from American
literature. Lawrence E. Scanlon, "Henry James's 'Compositional
Resource and Value Intrinsic' " (*Forum H*, IV, i, 13-19), argues
that James's architectural sense of form, as expressed in the Prefaces,
owes something to Greenough's theories, which were restated by
Louis Sullivan, a Chicago architect of James's later years; at least,
James's discussion of form shows interesting parallels to ideas found
in Greenough, and earlier in Coleridge. C. F. Burgess, "The Seeds
of Art: Henry James's *Donnée*" (*L&P*, XIII, 67-73), studies the
recurrent pattern in James of a conscious external *donnée*, often an
anecdote, followed by unconscious enrichment over a long period
of time before composition. Donald M. Murray, "Henry James in
Advanced Composition" (*CE*, XXV, 26-30) describes his successful
use of "The Art of Fiction" and other James criticism as guidance
for students writing fiction. Alan Holder, "The Lesson of the Master: Ezra Pound and Henry James" (*AL*, XXXV, 71-79), draws on
unpublished material to show that Pound was an early appreciative
critic of James, though sometimes given to strained interpretations.
   Two dissertation abstracts deal with general topics. Naomi Le-
bowitz, "Henry James and the Moral Imperative of Relationship"
(*DA*, XXIV, 300), sees D. H. Lawrence as an ally of James, and
Mailer and Bellow as inheritors. Howard E. Salisbury, "Wish-Fulfill-
ment as Moral Crisis in the Fiction of Henry James" (*DA*, XXIV,
304), compares leading characters who are "outsiders" to show the
disparity between wish and reality. Quentin G. Kraft's dissertation,
"A Study of Point of View in Selected Short Stories of Henry
James," is reported as completed at Duke University.

iv. Criticism: Individual Novels

J. A. Ward, "The Double Structure of *Watch and Ward*" (*TSLL*, IV,
613-624) finds the plan of the central character to bring up a young

ward to be an appropriate wife for himself is not well combined
with the greater interest of the ward's own psychological development. Viola Hopkins, "Gloriani and the Tides of Taste" (*NCF*,
XVIII, 65-71), traces differences in the character of Gloriani as
he appears in *Roderick Hudson, The Ambassadors,* and "The Velvet
Glove." James's original conception was probably founded on the
careers of the artists Barye and Carpeaux, which James reviewed
when still strongly under the influence of Ruskin: Gloriani represents the artist with a worldly motive. In revising *Roderick Hudson*
for the New York Edition, James modified the conception of Gloriani
to bring it closer to that in *The Ambassadors*—a loss, so far as the
earlier novel is concerned. William T. Stafford, "The Ending of
James's *The American*: A Defense of the Early Version" (*NCF*,
XVIII, 86-89), rejects Floyd Watkins' support for James's revision
(*NCF*, 1957, XII, 85-88), finding that Mrs. Tristram's remarks in
the later version detract from the comic tone. George Levine, "Isabel, Gwendolen, and Dorothea" (*ELH*, XXX, 244-257), finds a closer
parallel between James's heroine in *The Portrait of a Lady* and
Dorothea Casaubon in George Eliot's *Middlemarch* than with
Gwendolen Harleth in Eliot's *Daniel Deronda*, previously mentioned
by F. R. Leavis. George Monteiro, "John Hay's Review of *The Portrait of a Lady*" (*BBr*, XIX, 95-104), draws attention to Hay's very
favorable review in the New York Daily *Tribune*. Sister Jane M.
Luecke, "*The Princess Casamassima*: Hyacinth's Fallible Consciousness" (*MP*, LX, 274-280), shows that Hyacinth, overvaluing Paul
Muniment, commits suicide under false assumptions. Hyacinth's
"ideals," in short, were more "real" than reality itself.

Besides the extended comments of Geismar and Wiesenfarth,
whose books are mentioned above, six articles attempt to explain
James's most baffling novel, *The Sacred Fount*. Geismar sees this
novel as "a kind of disguised, and even deliberately obfuscated
spiritual autobiography, which in typically Jamesian manner, both
displayed and hid its real content." Wiesenfarth sees the structure
of *The Sacred Fount* as "quite intelligible in a comparison with
that of a double fugue." It is an extreme example of the dramatic
method by which the focus shifts from the event to consciousness
of the event. The point of the novel is its ultimate ambiguity: the
impossibility of deciding between the narrator's view of events and
that of Grace Brissenden, who tells the narrator he is "crazy."
Robert J. Andreach, "Henry James's *The Sacred Fount*: The Exis-

tential Predicament" (*NCF*, XVII, 1962, 197-216), sees a conflict
between logic and experience in the narrator, and thus an anticipa-
tion of Kafka, Joyce, and Camus. Tony Tanner, "Henry James's
Subjective Adventurer: *The Sacred Fount*" (*E&S*, XVI, 37-55),
points to analogies of comically exaggerated speculation in James's
two short stories "In the Cage" and "Patagonia." Tanner suggests
that the narrator stands for the artist type, Shaftesbury's "second
maker" whose lies may be better than truth. Parker Tyler, "*The
Sacred Fount*: 'The Actuality Pretentious and Vain' vs. 'The Case
Rich and Edifying'" (*MFS*, IX, 127-138), interprets the narrator
as James, and Mrs. Brissenden as a typical woman reader, fascinated
but skeptical. Cynthia Ozick, "The Jamesian Parable: *The Sacred
Fount*" (*BuR*, XI, iii, 55-70), insists that the novel is not a parody,
but a parable ("not universally applicable, but inevitable in its own
case"). The meaning of the parable is that the person who attempts
"to become what he is not . . . negates the integrity . . . of his personality." Jean Frantz Blackall, "*The Sacred Fount* as a Comedy
of the Limited Observer" (*PMLA*, LXXVIII, 384-393), ignoring
James's own derogatory remarks on the novel, finds it "high comedy
wonderfully well sustained." Julian B. Kaye, "*The Awkward Age,
The Sacred Fount,* and *The Ambassadors*: Another Figure in the
Carpet" (*NCF*, XVII, 339-351), links these three novels by the fact
that in each the central character is an unmarried man, an outsider,
and that in each a woman of forty is in love with a younger man.
In the earlier novels the outsider struggles unsuccessfully against a
predatory world. In *The Ambassadors*, Strether has a measure of
success in a similar struggle.

All of these interpretations of *The Sacred Fount* are open to
objection. Collectively, however, they have the useful effect of
bringing the novel into more understandable relationship to the
general body of James's work, especially in technique.

Elizabeth Owen, "'The Given Appearance' of Charlotte Verver"
(*EIC*, XIII, 364-374), points out that the scheming duplicity of
Charlotte (in *The Golden Bowl*) requires the aggressive and un-
pleasant actions of Maggie. Lotus Snow, "'A Story of Cabinets and
Chairs and Tables': Images of Morality in *The Spoils of Poynton* and
The Golden Bowl" (*ELH*, XXX, 413-435), concludes from the im-
agery that there is an "absolute unity of art and morality." Fleda
Vetch, whose motives have been adversely criticized, appears from
the imagery describing her to be intended as morally better than her

associates. If the title image in *The Golden Bowl* is derived from Ecclesiastes 12:6, as is suggested, Maggie's innocence may be the flaw symbolized by the bowl. David W. Beams, "Consciousness in James's *The Sense of the Past*" (*Criticism*, V, 148-172), points to parallels in "The Beast in the Jungle" and "The Jolly Corner." He sees in this incomplete novel an illustration of "the artist who makes life by making awareness of it."

v. Criticism: Short Stories

Oscar Cargill, "*The Turn of the Screw* and Alice James" (*PMLA*, LXXVIII, 238-249), repudiates the article he published in the *Chicago Review* (1956), later included in Gerald Willen's *Casebook* (1960). Cargill retains and expands the parallels between the governess of the story, the novelist's sister, Alice James, and Freud's early case study of "Lucy R." Mark Spilka, "Turning the Freudian Screw: How Not to Do It" (*L&P*, XIII, 105-111), attacks Robert Heilman's interpretation of the story as "general evil." The evil, Spilka thinks, is sexual, and James, like many Victorians, followed the pattern of representing sex as evil and affection as the whole of love. Without the use of Freudian principles, Spilka warns, "we may reduce imagination to sterile fancy." C. B. Ives, "James's Ghosts in *The Turn of the Screw*" (*NCF*, XVIII, 183-189), points out that the ghosts follow "patterns of inactivity" and therefore suggest hallucinations, whereas the later Preface misleadingly speaks of them as "figures in an action" and therefore supernatural. Thomas M. Cranfill and Robert L. Clark, Jr., "Caste in James's *The Turn of the Screw*" (*TSLL*, V, 189-198), show that ideas of caste, considered by James for an unwritten short story (*Notebooks*, Oct. 18, 1895), have a bearing on the interpretation of statements by the governess and by Mrs. Grose, the housekeeper.

George Monteiro, "'Girlhood on the American Plan'—A Contemporary Defense of *Daisy Miller*" (*BBr*, XIX, 89-93), shows that a review (*AtM*, March, 1879), previously assigned to Howells, was written by John Hay. James Scoggins, "'The Author of Beltraffio': A Reapportionment of Guilt" (*TSLL*, V, 265-270), refutes a previous article by Donald H. Reiman (*TSLL*, III, 1962, 503-509). The narrator, Scoggins argues, is not the first to disrupt the tenuous peace in the household of Mark Ambient. Robert L. Gale, "James's 'The Middle Years,' II" (*Expl*, XXII, Item 22), notes that reprints

of this story piously give the "I" in the New York Edition, though by
error or jocular intention no II appears. In "The Abasement of Mrs.
Warren Hope" (*PMLA*, LXXVIII, 98-102), Gale argues that "The
Abasement of the Northmores" is actually the abasement of the
demented Mrs. Warren Hope, who wishes to publish love letters
written her by the late Lord Northmore, in revenge for the neglect
of her own deceased husband. The dementia of Mrs. Hope is in-
ferred. Mary E. Herx, "The Monomyth in 'The Great Good Place'"
(*CE*, XXIV, 439-443), finds that this story follows patterns of myth
and dream: departure from the real world, initiation into the spiritual, and return to the real world with enriched consciousness.
Stephen Reid, "'The Beast in the Jungle' and 'A Painful Case': Two
Different Sufferings" (*AI*, XX, 221-239), traces parallels between
James's story and Joyce's much shorter one, with inferences on the
psychological relevance of stories to authors. George Arms, "James's
'The Birthplace': Over a Pulpit-Edge" (*TSL*, VIII, 61-69), infers
from the religious imagery James's concern with the general problem of religious belief. Fred C. Thomson, "James's 'The Jolly Corner'" (*Expl*, XXII, Item 28), finds the sea-world imagery consistent
and appropriate.

vi. Dramatic Adaptations

Bertram Greene's "The Summer of Daisy Miller" was produced in
New York in May. Howard Taubman (New York *Times*, May 28)
thought the production "novelistic rather than theatrical." C. Taylor's adaptation of *The Wings of the Dove* was produced in London
in December, with Wendy Hiller as Milly's chaperon and Susannah
York as Millie. A reviewer (*New Statesman*, December 13) re-
marked on the interest of "the unique Jamesian idiom—with its
slangy primness."

7. Faulkner

Richard P. Adams

Aside from a few intuitive essays such as those by Maurice Edgar Coindreau in 1931 and André Malraux in 1933, serious publication on Faulkner may be said to have begun in 1939 with George Marion O'Donnell's "Faulkner's Mythology" (*KR*, I, 1939, 285-299) and Conrad Aiken's "William Faulkner: The Novel as Form" (*AtM*, CLXIV, 1939, 650-654). These articles laid down two of the main lines along which Faulkner scholarship has developed.

O'Donnell approached his subject from a historical and sociological direction and reduced the Yoknapatawpha material to a conflict between the aristocratic Sartorises and the poor-white scalawag Snopeses, in which the latter were victorious because the former had more virtue. This suggestive oversimplification has been elaborated and corrected by such critics as Malcolm Cowley, in his introduction to *The Portable Faulkner* (New York, Viking Press, 1946, pp. 1-24); Robert Penn Warren, in "Cowley's Faulkner" (*NR*, CXV, 1946, 176-180, 234-237); and more recent writers in a number of books and articles.

Aiken set out to explain and partly to justify Faulkner's style and technique. The marathon sentences and "the whole elaborate method of *deliberately withheld meaning*," he said, were used "simply to keep the form—and the idea—fluid and unfinished, still in motion, as it were, and unknown, until the dropping into place of the very last syllable." Many critics have expanded upon this idea, notably Karl E. Zink in "William Faulkner: Form as Experience" (*SAQ*, LIII, 1954, 384-403) and "Flux and the Frozen Moment: The Imagery of Stasis in Faulkner's Prose" (*PMLA*, LXXI, 1956, 285-301); and Walter J. Slatoff, *Quest for Failure* (Ithaca, N.Y., Cornell Univ. Press, 1960).

The quantity of work on Faulkner has increased enormously in the past several years. The 1943 bibliography in *PMLA* had one entry under his name; for 1953 there were twenty; for the current year, 1963, there are eighty.[1] The first book-length study was published in 1951; in the next ten years there were eleven more; in 1963 alone there were six.

i. Bibliography

Irene Lynn Sleeth's *William Faulkner: A Bibliography of Criticism* (Denver, Alan Swallow, 1962) is a reprint in pamphlet form of an article which appeared in *TCL*, VIII, 18-43. It is not only the most nearly up-to-date list, covering the period from 1920 to early 1961, but much the most compendious, with a total of nearly 900 items, including books, essays or chapters in books, articles, and major reviews. Besides American and British publications, it lists 122 French, 18 Italian, 16 Spanish and Latin American, 15 German, 12 Scandinavian, 1 African, 1 Polish, and 6 Japanese. Inevitably, there are some omissions and several errors; but this bibliography is a valuable tool, not only for the beginner but for the expert as well.

Current bibliography on Faulkner may be found in *Twentieth Century Literature, Modern Fiction Studies,* and *American Literature,* as well as in the annual supplement to *PMLA*. A rough count indicates that over two hundred items have been added in 1961, 1962, and 1963, bringing the total to more than a thousand. Even with some allowance for the usual duplication because of scholarly thrift in publishing material in books which has previously appeared in periodicals, the total is impressive. The fact that most of it has piled up in the last ten years is not only impressive but a little frightening.

ii. Texts

No important new texts of Faulkner works were published in 1963. However, a reprint of the first edition of *Sartoris* and a corrected version of *Sanctuary* were brought out by Random House in 1962, in what could be part of a complete, textually reliable edition. James

[1] One of the foreign-language items in the 1963 *PMLA* bibliography could not be located, possibly because of faulty listing: Kay Killingsworth's "L'héritage méridional dans l'œuvre de William Faulkner et d'Albert Camus" (7973). A definitely faulty listing is that of Richard Hughes' "Faulkner and Bennett" (6019), which is said to be in Volume XX, No. 120 of *Encounter,* but which is really in Volume XXI, No. 3. The abbreviation *EJb* for the periodical publishing William Styron's "William Faulkners Beisetzung" (6055), which is not listed in the key, stands for *Eckart Jahrbuch.*

B. Meriwether's "The Text of Faulkner's Books: An Introduction
and Some Notes" (*MFS*, IX, 159-170) clearly shows the need for
such an edition, and indicates which of the existing texts can be
used with confidence and which cannot. Another volume, a newly
corrected and reset version of *As I Lay Dying*, has been added in
1964.

iii. Biography

The long and eagerly awaited authoritative biography of Faulkner
did not appear in 1963, nor did any important contribution toward
it. The biographical items in the 1963 list, Maurice Edgar Coindreau's "Faulkner tel que je l'ai connu" (*Preuves*, No. 144, pp. 9-14),
John Faulkner's *My Brother Bill: An Affectionate Reminiscence*
(New York, Trident Press), and Robert N. Linscott's "Faulkner
without Fanfare" (*Esquire*, LX [July], 36, 38), are composed mainly
of personal anecdotes: raw materials for biography rather than
biography itself. Several competent scholars are working on biographical studies, however, and the deficiency will certainly be
remedied.

iv. Criticism

In spite of the obvious need for other kinds of scholarly investigation, the great bulk of writing on Faulkner in 1963, as in previous
years, has been critical. James B. Meriwether's "Faulkner and the
New Criticism" (*BA*, XXXVII, 265-268) takes note of this fact and
complains that "the scholarly study of Faulkner may hardly be said
to have begun yet." Critics have not been able to use "the conventional approaches of historical scholarship," Meriwether says, because "the Faulkner field is still characterized by a notable lack of
reliable biographical data, of any substantial study of his literary
background, his thought, his reading. We have no general study of
his imagery, symbolism, or structure; we have no adequate or
readily available character index. For half his published work there
is no good text readily available."
   These remarks are mostly true, and they need to be taken seriously; but they were perhaps a bit too stringent, even when they
were first written down, and much has happened since then to modify
the situation. There had been some fairly general studies of imagery,

symbolism, and structure, although there was and still is plenty of room for more. Since Meriwether wrote, five or more books have appeared containing indexes of Faulkner's characters. Three of them were published in 1963: Robert W. Kirk and Marvin Klotz, *Faulkner's People: A Complete Guide and Index to Characters in the Fiction of William Faulkner* (Berkeley, Univ. of Calif. Press), Margaret Patricia Ford and Suzanne Kincaid, *Who's Who in Faulkner* (Baton Rouge, La. State Univ. Press; not listed in *PMLA*), and Cleanth Brooks, *William Faulkner: The Yoknapatawpha Country* (New Haven, Yale Univ. Press). The Kirk and Klotz index is the most useful, containing more than 1,300 names, cross-indexed to individual stories, with page references to specified texts. The Ford and Kincaid has only 820 names, and refers only to the titles of the works in which they occur. The list in Brooks has about 760 names, with page references, but the page references are less complete and specific than those in Kirk and Klotz. At least two books with similar apparatus have appeared so far in 1964, and heaven only knows how many others are on the way. Guides and handbooks, at least to certain aspects of Faulkner's work, can no longer be said to be in short supply. Three of the articles in the 1963 bibliography belong in the same general category: Thomas E. Connolly's "A Skeletal Outline of *Absalom, Absalom!*" (*CE*, XXV, 110-114), Gail B. Little's "Three Novels for Comparative Study in the Twelfth Grade" (*EJ*, LII, 501-505), and W. U. McDonald, Jr.'s "The Time-Scheme of *The Hamlet*" (*MidR*, V, 22-29; misprinted W. V. McDonald, "The Tune-Scheme" in *PMLA*).

Another area in which some work had been done before Meriwether wrote, and more has been done since, is the systematic study of Faulkner's literary background, reading, sources, and parallels. Richard P. Adams' "The Apprenticeship of William Faulkner" (*TSE*, XII [1962], 113-156) is a brief and rather sketchy survey of several categories of reading that Faulkner may have done when young. Emily Kuempel Brady's "The Literary Faulkner: His Indebtedness to Conrad, Lawrence, Hemingway, and Other Modern Novelists" (*DA*, XXIII, 2131-32) covers a narrower range in more detail. Melvin Goldstein's "A Source for Faulkner's 'Nobel Prize Speech of Acceptance': or Two Versions of a Single Manifesto" (*BSTCF*, IV, 78-80), identifying Dylan Thomas' "In My Craft and Sullen Art" as Faulkner's source, is unconvincing. Walter B. Rideout and James B. Meriwether's "On the Collaboration of Faulkner and

Anderson" (*AL*, XXXV, 85-87) corrects the conclusion of an earlier article by H. Edward Richardson, which accused Faulkner of using a story in *Mosquitoes* which had been invented by Anderson; a closer look at the evidence shows that the story was Faulkner's. Robert M. Slabey's "Faulkner's *Mosquitoes* and Joyce's *Ulysses*" (*RLV*, XXVIII [1962], 435-437) is a detailed and persuasive demonstration of the Joyce influence in Faulkner's early career. Slabey in this article and in "The 'Romanticism' of *The Sound and the Fury*" (*MissQ*, XVI, 146-159) goes farther than anyone has previously done in asserting unequivocally that Faulkner used the "mythical method" in the same way that Joyce and Eliot did. A minor detail (which may be more significant than it looks) is Peter Swiggart's identification of Shreve's reference to Byron's wish. Swiggart's "Faulkner's *The Sound and the Fury*" (*Expl*, XXII, Item 31) correctly locates the source in the sixth canto of *Don Juan*, but neglects to mention that Faulkner refers to the same passage more explicitly in *Sartoris*, *A Fable*, and "Divorce in Naples."

Faulkner's imagery and symbolism, and to some extent his structural methods, as well as his themes, are illuminated in many ways by studies of his use of mythological materials and references. Lennart Bjork's "Ancient Myths and the Moral Framework of Faulkner's *Absalom, Absalom!*" (*AL*, XXXV, 196-204) shows numerous parallels. Alexander C. Kern's "Myth and Symbol in Criticism of Faulkner's 'The Bear'" (*Myth and Symbol: Critical Approaches and Evaluations*, ed. Bernice Slote, Lincoln, Univ. of Neb. Press, pp. 152-161) draws a highly interesting critical inference from the apparent fact that Sam Fathers' totem is the deer and Ike McCaslin's is the snake. Neil D. Isaacs' "Götterdämmerung in Yoknapatawpha" (*TSL*, VIII, 47-55) develops mythological references underlying the impression of Sutpen as a kind of "horse-god" for Wash Jones. Slabey further pursues his theory of Faulkner's use of the mythical method in "Faulkner's *Sanctuary*" (*Expl*, XXI, Item 45), associating Popeye with Hermes and Miss Reba's house with Hades; but he ignores the much more obvious parallel between Popeye and Pluto, and between the story of *Sanctuary* and the Persephone myth.

There is still relatively little published criticism bearing on the structure of Faulkner's work, but some progress was made in 1963. Leon Edel's "How to Read *The Sound and the Fury*" (*Varieties of Literary Experience*, ed. Stanley Burnshaw, New York, New York Univ. Press, pp. 241-257) touches on an important point in warning the reader not to try to re-establish a supposedly scrambled chronology of events in the story—a favorite pastime of the handbook people—and then goes on to thematic questions. Philip Graham's "Patterns in Faulkner's *Sanctuary* and *Requiem for a Nun*" (*TSL*, VIII, 39-46) finds that "In both books the emphasis is first on the physical, then on the social, and last on Truth—from nature to society to the abstract." The terms seem a bit confused, but a structural sequence is shown in the scenes at the Old Frenchman place, Memphis, and Jefferson in *Sanctuary* and in "The Courthouse," "The Golden Dome," and "The Jail" in *Requiem*. Robert J. Griffin's "Ethical Point of View in *The Sound and the Fury*" (*Essays in Modern American Literature*, ed. Richard E. Langford, DeLand, Fla., Stetson Univ. Press, pp. 55-64) shows a similar structural progression through the four sections from an amoral to a hyper-moral to a hypocritical to a morally realistic point of view. This analysis bears out earlier observations (notably by Carvel Collins) about the progression from relatively concrete subjective views to relatively abstract objective reports of the events and scenes in the book. John Hagan's "*Déjà vu* and the Effect of Timelessness in Faulkner's *Absalom, Absalom!*" (*BuR*, XI [March], 31-52) notices many events in the story which ironically echo earlier situations and prophesy later outcomes, both in Sutpen's personal life and in the history of his family and, by extension, of the South. A similar observation is made in Glauco Cambon's " 'Assalonne, Assalonne!': Il demone della memoria" (*La lotta con Proteo*, Milan, Bompiani, pp. 215-222). Michael Millgate's " 'A Fair Job': A Study of Faulkner's *Sanctuary*" (*REL*, IV [Oct.] 47-62) points out that Faulkner's revision of *Sanctuary* was almost entirely a matter of structural improvement, and that his use of the phrase "a cheap idea" to describe the galley version of the book must therefore refer to the structure and not, as has been generally assumed by critics, to the theme.

By far the largest number of studies published in 1963, as in earlier years, have to do with theme, content, and meaning in Faulkner's work, and often with what are presumed to be Faulkner's own ideas and feelings. This looks like the easiest approach, but in many ways it is one of the more dangerous, as many an unwary critic has unintentionally demonstrated. It goes directly against what Faulkner most often said about his work, that he was not writing about ideas at all, or about the South, or about the theology of the various

myths he used (including Bible stories), or about "sociology." In
a sense, of course, his fiction is about these things, among many
others. But the sense in which Faulkner deals with ideas is always
literary rather than literal, and the pitfalls in the way of interpretation are many and subtle. To cite the most obvious example, what
a character in a Faulkner book says can never safely be taken as
an expression of Faulkner's personal opinion. Neither can Faulkner's
sympathetic portrayal of a character safely be taken as an indica-
tion of his approval of that character, or of the kind of person that
character is. Nor, to be more specific, can Faulkner's nostalgic
evocation of the old, agrarian, aristocratic ante bellum way of life
be taken, as so many critics have taken it, to mean that he is joining
Thomas Nelson Page in lamenting the destruction of a perfect
Southern Eden or the advent of an evil Modern World. The number
of erroneous interpretations and of flat misreadings coming out of
thematic approaches to Faulkner's work should constitute a stern
warning that publication in that field is not for apprentices, unless
they are highly industrious as well as clever, or for amateurs in any
but the very best sense of the term.

The most voluminous and well-seasoned contributor to the thematic criticism of Faulkner in 1963 was Cleanth Brooks, who published four articles, a chapter in a book, and a whole book. The
articles, "The Community and the Pariah" (*VQR*, XXXIX, 236-253),
"Faulkner's *Sanctuary*: The Discovery of Evil" (*SR*, LXXI, 1-24),
"Faulkner's Savage Arcadia: Frenchman's Bend" (*VQR*, XXXIX,
598-611), and "History, Tragedy, and Imagination in *Absalom,
Absalom!*" (*YR*, LII, 340-351), reappear considerably expanded,
somewhat revised, and corrected in a few minor details in *William
Faulkner: The Yoknapatawpha Country*. The chapter, originally
delivered as one of a series of lectures, is "William Faulkner: Vision
of Good and Evil," in *The Hidden God: Studies in Hemingway,
Faulkner, Yeats, Eliot, and Warren* (New Haven, Yale Univ. Press,
pp. 22-43). The main emphasis in Brooks's criticism, ever since he
began to publish on Faulkner in 1951, has been sociological rather
than technical or aesthetic; and *The Yoknapatawpha Country* carries out that emphasis at length in detailed discussions of the
community and its history, and the relation of various individual
characters to the community. The lecture on Faulkner's "Vision of
Good and Evil" defines his position as that of "a profoundly religious writer" whose "characters come out of a Christian environ-

ment, and represent, whatever their shortcomings and whatever their theological heresies, Christian concerns": a judicious though still perhaps oversimplified statement. Brooks promises another book on Faulkner which he says will deal more with technical matters and with the non-Yoknapatawpha fiction. Although his work on Faulkner has not been quite what one might have expected of a "New Critic," Brooks's expertness as a close reader of texts has been well used in preventing the kind of misreadings that disfigure so much of what passes as scholarship on Faulkner.

Various thematic matters are explored in a number of articles by other authors in 1963. Bobby Ray Dowell's "Faulkner's Comic Spirit" (*DA*, XXIII, 4355) notes the function of Faulkner's comedy in support of his belief that man will prevail. Elmo Howell's "William Faulkner and Tennessee" (*THQ*, XXI, 251-262) presents some useful historical information, but misinterprets Faulkner's attitude toward the Confederacy. E. R. Hutchinson's "A Footnote to the Gum Tree Scene" (*CE*, XXIV, 564-565) contends that in the final scene of "The Bear" Boon Hogganbeck is guarding the squirrels against the encroachments of mechanical civilization—but does not explain why Boon says, "They're mine!" One of the most successful efforts to boil Faulkner down to a single theme is made in Kenneth E. Richardson's "Quest for Faith: A Study of Destructive and Creative Force in the Novels of William Faulkner" (*DA*, XXIII, 3384). Richardson suggests that the destructive force is inflexibility, and that its "creative opposite . . . is embodied in a life that possesses an adaptability to change." Allen Tate's "William Faulkner 1897-1962" (*SR*, LXXI 160-164) is an attempt to establish the "Greco-Trojan" myth of the South as the single main theme of Faulkner's work. The attempt is not successful, but much of what Tates says is valuable.

Existentialist approaches, which have never been very convincing, were still unconvincing in 1963, but four attempts were made: Thomas Francis Loughrey's "Values and Love in the Fiction of William Faulkner" (*DA*, XXIII, 2915), Robert M. Slabey's "*As I Lay Dying* as an Existential Novel" (*BuR*, XI [Dec.], 12-23), and William J. Sowder's two articles, "Faulkner and Existentialism: A Note on the Generalissimo" (*WSCL*, IV [Spring-Summer], 163-171) and "Lucas Beauchamp as Existential Hero" (*CE*, XXV, 115-127).

Discussion of individual characters is especially risky, because of the temptation to treat them as if they were real people, which

Faulkner's characters never are. This temptation is only partly resisted in three 1963 studies focused on characters as such. Richard E. Fisher's "The Wilderness, the Commissary, and the Bedroom: Faulkner's Ike McCaslin as Hero in a Vacuum" (*ES*, XLIV, 19-28) maintains that Ike's failure in marriage prevents his effective action in ethical matters. John K. Simon's "What Are You Laughing at, Darl?" (*CE*, XXV, 104-110) proposes that Darl is the "pivotal" character and in some sense "the surrogate of the author within" *As I Lay Dying*. John L. Longley, Jr., has the most systematic and comprehensive investigation yet made from this point of view in *The Tragic Mask: A Study of Faulkner's Heroes* (Chapel Hill, Univ. of N.C. Press). Longley explicitly says that he thought "there would perhaps be some profit in undertaking . . . an analysis and assessment of the various characters—individual human beings—in the Faulkner canon," particularly because "many Faulkner characters appear in more than one book." In spite of being on such slippery theoretical ground, Longley makes a number of valuable observations.

The only full-length general study to appear in 1963 is Lawrance Thompson's *William Faulkner: An Introduction and Interpretation* (New York, Barnes and Noble, Am. Authors and Critics Series), which attempts "a detached and objective reassessment of his many strengths and weaknesses . . . ." The result, though somewhat idiosyncratic and marred by a number of misreadings and misprintings, presents some very interesting interpretations, such as its discussion of the Joyce-Eliot influence on Faulkner. It is probably more useful to a mature Faulkner scholar than to a beginner, who might not know that (for example) the MacCallums in *Sartoris* are not Negroes.

It may be worth mentioning that thirteen of the eighty items in the 1963 bibliography are in languages other than English: five in Italian, four in French, two in German, and one each in Spanish and Russian, although it should also be mentioned that several of these essays are by American authors. The number of serious studies of Faulkner in Italian has been rapidly increasing during the past few years; American Faulkner scholars may do well to cultivate a reading knowledge of that language, as well as others more commonly taught in this country.

8. Hemingway and Fitzgerald

Frederick J. Hoffman

i. Bibliographies and Texts

In the cases both of Ernest Hemingway and of F. Scott Fitzgerald, scholarship is just beginning the work of checking facts and texts, and of judging the appropriateness of the early criticism. It is natural enough that Fitzgerald, who died December 21, 1940, should have been given more exacting attention so far than Hemingway, whose death occurred on July 2, 1961. Both of them were supremely personalities of their time, and are still celebrated as persons as much at least as they are studied as artists. This fact does make a survey of this kind more difficult than it might otherwise be. On the other hand, the close perspective provided by their near contemporaneity offers its own kind of excitement. The initial stage in each case has been critical, consisting largely of readings of the texts, with some attempts to apply to the texts (or to infer from them) theoretical and even philosophical "lessons." This critical pioneering has yielded a rich variety of speculations; many of them have what strongly appears to be lasting quality.

Meanwhile, bibliographic work has tended to be mostly a matter of collecting checklists of works by and about the authors. To this necessary task the magazine *Modern Fiction Studies* has made substantial contributions: in the number of August, 1955, for Hemingway (Maurice Beebe); and in the issue of Spring, 1961, (Beebe and Jackson Bryer) for Fitzgerald. Subsequently, the best work on the latter is contained in Jackson Bryer's essay, "F. Scott Fitzgerald: A Review of Research and Scholarship" (*TSLL*, V, 147-163). Bryer begins by discussing checklists of Fitzgerald's works, proceeds to an analysis of the present state of his texts, explains the principal university depositories of Fitzgerald MSS, and concludes with a discussion of biography and criticism.

In some ways the availability of texts of Fitzgerald's books has vastly improved. At his death all of them were out of print; today almost all of them have returned, thanks to Scribner's having brought out inexpensive hard-cover and paperback editions. In England the four-volume Bodley Head Scott Fitzgerald has provided the first English uniform edition. Lists of translations into French and Japanese have appeared in recent issues of the *FN* (Spring and Fall, 1961). The latest collection of Fitzgerald stories is *The Pat Hobby Stories* (New York, Scribner's, 1962).

While the numbers of texts are in Fitzgerald's case most satisfying, the establishment of accurate texts, comparisons with holographs, and publication of authentic editions are tasks that are just beginning. We of course are aware of what Fitzgerald (at least in terms of his contracts with Scribner's) accepted as first editions; presumably his readers also accepted these as *their* editions. But there are many disparities between the cloth-bound edition and various holographs and galley-proof variants. In the case of Fitzgerald at least, the task of describing these differences can offer more than a merely mechanical determination of *the*'s and *and*'s. Matthew Bruccoli (editor of *FN*) has produced a study (*The Composition of* Tender Is the Night: *A Study of the Manuscripts*, Pittsburgh, Univ. of Pittsburgh Press) which testifies abundantly to the genuine contribution a search of and in documents can make. Bruccoli used some 3,500 pages of holograph manuscript, typescript, and proof, "representing seventeen drafts and three versions of the novels" (p. xv). The result does much to consolidate facts and speculations about the nine years (1925-1934) that passed without a major work from Fitzgerald. Attempts to establish the text of *The Great Gatsby* and other works are under way, and speculations about them continue to form an important fraction of Fitzgerald scholarship.

The years between *Gatsby* and *Tender* have been widely acknowledged as both a crucial and a fascinating period in Fitzgerald's career. He moved from one radical notion to another, but finally his own life led to the major decisions regarding the book's form and direction. We have had the history of these years given us with an admirable sense of their meaning and their excitement. Bruccoli presents us here with the gratifying proof of our suspicions concerning their direct correspondence with his creative work. The power of Fitzgerald's person is nevertheless acknowledged. Even Bruccoli, who is most anxious to preserve the novel from "personality fanciers," does admit that: "As does all of Fitzgerald's best work, *Tender Is the Night* draws upon intensely—even painfully—

personal material. . . . The novel, originally planned as a study of matricide, became a fictionalized account of Fitzgerald's life during the period in which he was writing it" (p. 17). This fact is not surprising. Bruccoli is after all supporting the convictions of almost every critic before him. The important fact of his work is that he offers chapter and text of the story, and of its relevance for modern American literature.

As for bibliographical and textual aids to Hemingway scholarship, the two early bibliographies (L. H. Cohn, 1931, and Lee Samuels, 1951) must shortly be superseded by a fully definitive bibliography. They are nevertheless useful within their limits; Samuels's is in some sense an updating of Cohn's. In addition to the Beebe checklist, mentioned above, there are three collections of Hemingway criticism: John K. M. McCaffery, *Ernest Hemingway:The Man and His Work* (Cleveland, World, 1950), the oldest and the least satisfactory (there is no scholarly apparatus of any kind); Carlos Baker, ed., *Hemingway and His Critics: An International Anthology* (New York, Hill and Wang, 1961); and R. P. Weeks, ed., *Hemingway* (New York, Prentice-Hall, 1962). Only the second of these provides a useful checklist of Hemingway criticism. Hemingway texts have received much the same treatment as Fitzgerald's: that is, Scribner's has been producing a uniform hard-cover and paperback series of most of them. Examination of the actual holograph and typescript copies has been less active. Indeed, much of this activity is now going on and will have to be completed in connection with Carlos Baker's work on the authorized biography. Meanwhile, most of the actual surviving MSS are in the hands of Mary Welsh Hemingway and will apparently be put at Professor Baker's disposal. Baker has himself speculated upon the difficulties of his task (*NYTBR*, July 26, 1964), his attempt to discover, "in some systematic fashion, what he [Hemingway] did for his epoch and what his epoch did for him."

There have actually been two new Hemingway publications since his death: *The Wild Years*, ed. Gene Z. Hanrahan (New York, Dell, 1962), a collection of his contributions in the 1920's to the Toronto *Daily Star* and the Toronto *Star Weekly*; and *A Moveable Feast*, a memoir of the years 1920-1927 in Europe, released by his widow and published in 1964. A valuable listing of Hemingway's foreign editions is Hans W. Bentz's *Ernest Hemingway in Über-*

setzungen (Frankfurt, Hans W. Bentz Verlag). This book, in three
languages (German, French, and English), lists translations of all
Hemingway works, arranged alphabetically by title. The total picture is most impressive; whether it suggests anything regarding
Hemingway's "immortality" or not, it certainly does testify to European excitement in Hemingway's work over the years.

ii. Memoirs and Biography

At the end of his bibliographical essay on Fitzgerald, Jackson Bryer
expressed the hope that "commentators will begin to detach Fitzgerald the writer from Fitzgerald the legend ..." (p. 163). Despite
the number of times this hope has been voiced, on behalf of both
Fitzgerald and Hemingway, it has not yet been realized, except
occasionally in formalist exercises in reading. The reasons for this
situation are various; one of them, given above, has to do with the
remarkably *public* reputations of both artists, and the inevitable
associations of them with certain peculiarities of their times. Their
careers are almost always used—by critics and by journalists alike—
as "symptomatic" or "symbolic" of certain aspects of the twentieth-
century world. It is hard to dissociate the two from each other,
because both Fitzgerald and Hemingway were in various ways
(some of them affirmative, others pathetic) very close to their contemporary worlds—so much so that each in a sense lends substan-
tially to the "image" generally attached to aspects of twentieth-
century history.

We may assume, therefore, that much of the active work on both
authors should be in the nature of memoirs and biographies. In the
case of Hemingway, there are three books of memoirs, one of them
(*A Moveable Feast*, Scribner's) his own. The other two are by
members of Hemingway's family: sister Marcelline (Marcelline
Hemingway Sanford) published *At the Hemingways: A Family Portrait* (Boston, Little, Brown, 1962); and brother Leicester published his memoir (*My Brother, Ernest Hemingway*, Cleveland,
World) in the same year. Both of these must be called "useful"
rather than in any way definitive or penetrating. Nevertheless, there
is no doubt that Carlos Baker will be grateful to them when he
works on the opening years of the authorized *Life*. They are essentially family accounts, with all of the loyalties, prides, and sentiments
associated with a closely woven, intimate family center; their per-

suasiveness *depends* upon the fact that Ernest was brother, not author or "cultural hero."

There are odds and ends of biography, besides these. Leo Lania gathered together a *Pictorial Biography* (New York, Viking, 1961), which is an interesting album with commentary. In the months following Hemingway's sensational death, a number of paperback biographies, hastily thrown together from available sources, appeared in the market; the only one of these that is worthy of mention is *Ernest Hemingway: The Life and Death of a Man*, by Alfred G. Aronowitz and Peter Hamill (New York, Lancer Books, 1961).

The significance of *A Moveable Feast* is perhaps twofold: it belongs with other memoirs and biographies that have appeared in recent times and is in many ways dependent upon them for its meaning (that is, Hemingway, Morley Callaghan, Gertrude Stein, Sylvia Beach, and Robert McAlmon have all to be counted into the final estimate of Hemingway's life); and it is prefaced by the rather astonishing remark: "If the reader prefers, this book may be regarded as fiction. But there is always the chance that such a book of fiction may throw some light on what has been written as fact" (p. ix). The book presents a remarkable self-portrait of the young Hemingway, in Paris for the most part, learning to write, tightening his belt in the interests of integrity and "the real thing." Individual portraits (of Fitzgerald, Gertrude Stein, Ford Madox Ford, and others) are malicious. But the main atmosphere is romantic-heroic: the young couple and their baby living in Verlaine's former garret, loving much and eating little, above all awaiting his "great chance" which must, after all, come to such heroically decent people. There seems to be no one (except Sylvia Beach and, briefly but not ultimately, Gertrude Stein) who escapes the creative and imaginative censure which Hemingway visits upon his contemporaries. In contrast to almost all of them, he sees himself (at one or another café, nursing one or two drinks and shutting himself off from hunger in the greater interest of supporting his art) as a man of regular habits, great courage, and absolute dedication to the art to which (he is confident) his skill will eventually make a great contribution. There is something terribly true about his insistence; Hemingway depended upon his art, defended and defined it all his life in any number of metaphors (bullfighting, hunting in Africa, etc.), and finally (one much suspects) giving up his life because he had lost it.

An example of Hemingway's special talent for speaking quietly and maliciously of his friends is his treatment of Fitzgerald. One has the feeling here that Fitzgerald was an alcoholic misfit, entirely irresponsible, who needed constant guidance from a friend who was morally steady and sure. Since *A Moveable Feast* was written in 1960 at Fincia Vigia, his villa in Cuba, one must ascribe to it (and to several other portraits) some of the special feelings and distortion of memory which the passing of almost four decades of time must have caused. Morley Callaghan's *That Summer in Paris* (Coward-McCann) speaks much of the relationship and helps to right the balance: as do Andrew Turnbull's *Scott Fitzgerald* (Scribner's, 1962) and William Goldhurst's *F. Scott Fitzgerald and His Contemporaries* (World). The last book, divided into chapters on major contemporary influences, while it should be called criticism, is more aptly described as a "biography of his career."

Turnbull manages to write a biography that communicates the pathos of Fitzgerald's life remarkably well. He had, of course, the advantage over Arthur Mizener in having known Fitzgerald (even though Turnbull was only eleven and Fitzgerald was thirty-six when they first met on the Turnbulls' Maryland estate). Unlike Mizener's *The Far Side of Paradise* (1951), which attempted critical analyses (and often provided distinguished ones), Turnbull is mainly concerned to present the man, and he often succeeds in giving a close portrait of him. But the most important biographical event of recent years was the publication in 1963 of Turnbull's edition of *The Letters of F. Scott Fitzgerald* (New York, Scribner's). These represent about one-half of the total number of letters, chosen, as Turnbull explains, mainly in the interest of illuminating his creative work (p. xviii). The arrangement in terms of Fitzgerald's correspondents has several interesting results, the principal one being a series of perspectives upon Fitzgerald's life; in each case the special nature of his correspondent defines the quality and the intensity of Fitzgerald's opinions and feelings. In general, *The Letters* (distinctive also because, aside from *The Pat Hobby Stories*, they are the only recent original material collected, edited, and published) provide a remarkable portrait of a serious artist, often generous to his friends, suffering much from the agonies brought on both by his and by Zelda's excesses, but mainly a substantial literary person.

The Letters are perhaps the beginning of a reappraisal of Fitzgerald and a successful attempt to dissociate him from the "legendary Fitzgerald" which he himself encouraged.

The Letters have made several contributions to the understanding of Fitzgerald. While they seem to help support the notion that his work can never be separated from his life, they also represent Fitzgerald in his own variant of objectivity. His advice (to his daughter, to his contemporaries), his support of other writers, his value judgments of contemporary literature (nine out of ten of which hit the mark with great precision): these are all remarkable testimonies to a Fitzgerald who was scarcely ever believed in his public life but may actually survive the popular image he seemed so anxious himself to celebrate.

iii. Criticism

Since we are now in an advanced state of the "first phase" of critical appraisals of both Hemingway and Fitzgerald, several things might be expected of the criticism: that some of it will echo the original kinds of critical evaluation, which were a combination of impressionistic readings, lucky guesses, and insights (some of the last very good indeed); that there will have been time for a summing up by competent scholar-critics, using the information available and the cumulative values of some decades of criticism and reviews; and that the "location" of each author within synoptic cultural and intellectual studies will have been an activity encouraged and perhaps justified by the fact that the perspective upon both is now "post-mortem."

Two useful, stimulating, and informative introductions have appeared: Earl Rovit's *Hemingway* and Kenneth Eble's *Fitzgerald* (both in Twayne's TUSAS). They are competent; they gather together all available approaches to their subjects, and indeed add their own. Annotated checklists are provided in each case. They are high on the TUSAS list, and they fulfil the purpose of the series intelligently. The University of Minnesota Pamphlet series also has its studies of *Hemingway* (by Philip Young, 1959) and *Fitzgerald* (by Charles E. Shain, 1961); both are good, but scarcely more than small essays. The same might be said of S. F. Sanderson's *Ernest Hemingway* (New York, Grove Press, 1961), which is short, derivative, and quite obviously intended for the Hemingway "be-

ginner." A German translation by Elmer Tophoven of the French
Editions du Seuil biographical and critical study of Hemingway
by Georges-Albert Astre (Hamburg, Rowohlt, 1961) has as its principal advantage an attention paid to documents and photographs.
Collections of criticism have appeared within recent years on
both writers. For Hemingway there are the *Configuration critique
d'Ernest Hemingway* (Paris, Minard, 1958), many of the selections
originally from *MFS*; Carlos Baker's *Hemingway and His Critics*
(New York, Hill and Wang, 1961); and Robert P. Weeks's *Hemingway: A Collection of Critical Essays* (Englewood Cliffs, N.J., Prentice-Hall, 1962). The most recent collections of Fitzgerald criticism
are Arthur Mizener's *F. Scott Fitzgerald* (Englewood Cliffs, N.J.,
Prentice-Hall) and Frederick J. Hoffman's The Great Gatsby: *A
Study* (New York, Scribner's, 1962). The second of these is concerned with *The Great Gatsby* as a culmination of five years (1920-
1925) of Fitzgerald's working to improve his craft. Most of these
collections, of course, draw upon critical essays from the past, and
they do not therefore constitute recent criticism, except insofar
as they are organized and introduced in special ways. Carlos Baker's
has the special feature of being "international" (eight of the essays
are by other than American critics), and it is in general very intelligently edited and informed by Baker's superior knowledge of
Hemingway criticism. R. P. Weeks's is the least valuable of the
collections. Though he claims to have collected the essays that
"have proved most fruitful," many of them are brief notes or mere
impressions. Except for a few (E. M. Halliday, Philip Young, Carlos Baker, Mark Spilka), either the critics are scarcely authoritative,
or they are not represented by their best work. Among special issues
of magazines devoted to Fitzgerald's work, the Fitzgerald number
of *MFS* (VIII, Spring, 1961) should be cited for both its checklist
and its very able collection of essays (John Kuehl, A. E. Dyson,
Bruccoli, others).

Besides these collections, there have been several book-length
studies. The major work in either case has been Turnbull's editing
of the Fitzgerald *Letters*, already discussed. The two introductions,
by Earl Rovit and Kenneth Eble, are also noteworthy publications.
Three special approaches should be mentioned: William Goldhurst's
F. Scott Fitzgerald and His Contemporaries (Cleveland, World);
Sergio Perosa's *L'Arte di F. Scott Fitzgerald* (Rome, Edizioni di
Storia e Letteratura, 1961); and Joseph de Falco's *The Hero in*

Hemingway's Short Stories (Pittsburgh, Univ. of Pittsburgh Press).
Goldhurst's book is useful mainly because of the approach to Fitzgerald in terms of his contemporary friends and "influences"; occasionally the relationship is profitably revealed, but much of the time
the conclusions from a rather careful presentation of the facts are
not much more than enlightened guesswork. There is some critical
analysis, but it rarely helps to bring the scholarly work to any specific conclusion. The work of Perosa is distinguished as the first
substantial book-length study of its subject in Italian. De Falco's
book is too much concerned with the "mythic," and lets it get in the
way of what should have been a good subject. The following sentence, based upon a reading of Joseph Campbell's *The Hero with
a Thousand Faces*, testifies to his having "spoiled" his treatment by
hiding it behind theoretical material, the relevance of which he has
only superficially explored: "Whenever the hero does proceed
through all the stages [he has cited three earlier], a more coherent
and complete design is effected at the narrative level" (p. 17).

The year's work in Hemingway and Fitzgerald studies is both
ordinary and unusual. Several important publishing events make
it worth examination. Mostly, it marks a transition between some
three and a half decades of pioneering criticism and journalism
and what are bound to be more mature, better informed, and more
advanced reappraisals. This does not mean that the pioneering
work (of Philip Young, Charles Fenton, and Carlos Baker on
Hemingway; of Arthur Mizener, James Miller, and Alfred Kazin on
Fitzgerald) has been done in vain. Many separate essays still
remain classics of the early years (Lionel Trilling, Marius Bewley,
Glenway Wescott, and Edmund Wilson, among others, on Fitzgerald; Wilson, Young, Mark Spilka, Ray West, among others, on
Hemingway). But criticism is beginning now to show more concern over the actual writing (or the writing process) and less of
the specious appeal to temporary intellectual preoccupations. This
tendency impresses me with the feeling that both research and
criticism in modern literature are moving toward a point of maturity
not before observed.

The work has been uneven. Some of it simply adds a useful note
or two to the total accumulation. In the case of Hemingway, good
examples are Barney Childs' "Hemingway and the Legend of Kilimanjaro" (*AN&Q*, II, 3), which discusses H. W. Tilman's discovery
of Leopard's Point on Mount Kilimanjaro; the elaborate syntactical

study by Francis Christenson of "The Undefeated," in "Notes Toward a New Rhetoric" (*CE*, XXV, 7-18); and, especially, Jerzy R.
Krzyżanowski's study of the model for General Golz of *For Whom
the Bell Tolls* (*PolR*, VII, 69-74). Also useful is Soeur Mary Austina
La Forest's "La Vogue de Hemingway en France" (*RUL*, XVIII,
40-61), which does in a smaller way for Hemingway's French reputation what S. D. Woodworth's book (*William Faulkner en France*,
Paris, Minard, 1959) did for its subject.

Other 1963 essays on Hemingway have been more speculative
than scholarly: Jean Malaquais's "Hemingway ou le champion et la
mort" (*Prevues*, No. 147, pp. 32-41) is an interesting re-examination
of a subject often explored; Paul B. Newman's "Hemingway's Grail
Quest" (*UKCR*, XXVIII, 295-303) is a remarkably naïve criticism of
Hemingway within the tradition of Eliot's *The Waste Land*, written
as though no one had ever before suggested the resemblance; Alex
Page's "Pakistan's Hemingway" (*AR*, XXIII, 203-211) is a sprightly
examination of the Pakistani's reasons for liking Hemingway and
their confusion with political relations with the United States; and
Geoffrey Moore's " 'The Sun Also Rises': Notes Toward an Extreme
Fiction" (*REL*, IV, 31-46) is as foolish and ill-informed an editorial-
izing piece as it is arrogant.

The surprising thing is that phenomena like Moore's essay are
so carefully and somberly listed in recent checklists, which one
supposes must be complete and quite impartial. The fact testifies
once again to the basic need for value judgments concerning what
annually appears as "criticism." People like Jackson Bryer have
performed a valuable service to Fitzgerald readers in their offering
discussions of his work as well as checklists. Matthew J. Bruccoli
has applied his bibliographical talents not only to the *Newsletter*
and its checklists, but also to the total issue of criticism and bibliographical examination of texts. Other work during the year is less
valuable: Philip Hobsbaum's "Scott Fitzgerald and His Critics: The
Appreciation of Minor Art" (*BAASB*, No. 6, pp. 31-41) suffers from
insufficient information, and therefore is scarcely able to support a
negative analysis; James F. Light, in "Political Conscience in the
Novels of F. Scott Fitzgerald" (*BSTCF*, IV, 13-25), tries very hard
indeed, but spoils his argument by occasionally seeing evidence
where none exists (this is not to say that his thesis is wrong, only
that it is pushed beyond the need for assertion); John Lucas's "In
Praise of Scott Fitzgerald" (*CritQ*, V, 132-147) is so much an

attempt to atone for such extreme British contempt as that shown by Moore for Hemingway that one is almost hopefully willing to accept it altogether, but it is after all an argument from persuasion and assertion and therefore interesting journalism rather than criticism.[1]

iv. Conclusion

Criticism and scholarship relevant to Hemingway and Fitzgerald are in general a testimony to the kinds of difficulties and triumphs available to work in twentieth-century American literature. There are many extremes. Many explorations of it are so evasive as almost to be called critical fantasies. Yet, despite the persistence of crude applications of wayward theories, the value of real criticism and scholarship is not diminished. Good, sound work has been done; documents are being made available; intelligent people are applying their sensible and sensitive minds to critical evaluation. It should certainly be proved true sometime in the future that the explorations of the twentieth-century literary world that we have observed are at least as valuable as any contemporary criticism has been. More than that, evaluations of the criticism proceed apace: evaluations that are sensibly objective, prudent, and shrewd.

The great deficiencies of twentieth-century criticism are abundantly evident in certain pieces on Hemingway and Fitzgerald: the tendency to read "off the top" of their work, the great temptation to read the man into his work, to the point of denying the intrinsic value of the latter; the romantic projection of the man's life and work into his century (so many historians are victim of this idea that intellectual history seems unjustifiably to be a futile pastime); and the editorial "privilege" of disapproving or condemning a man out of court or countenance. The insights available to the reader are nevertheless important to the ultimate judgment which must be applied to both of these distinguished writers.

[1] Noted too late for extended comment are these two Hemingway items: Philip Young's retrospective essay, "Our Hemingway Man" (*KR*, XXVI, 676-707), and Carlos Baker's anticipatory novel, *The Land of Rumbelow* (New York, Scribner's 1963). Young's essay offers occasionally acid commentary upon the criticism that was published from the date of his first book (New York, Rhinehart, 1952), but is otherwise a very useful running commentary. Baker's novel features a teacher-biographer as hero; the resemblance is not coincidental.

Part II

9. Literature to 1800

Richard Beale Davis

As our bibliographies in *PMLA* and the *LHUS* attest, the term "literature" as applied to books and authors and movements of the period before 1800 is much more inclusive than it usually is for later periods. Men and women who recorded their thoughts on religion, politics, and society, as well as epistolarians and diarists, here far outnumber poets, fiction writers, or formal essayists. Colonial publishing history and libraries, theories of religion and philosophy without close belletristic association, concepts of science and the Negro—subjects such as these supply at least as many individual items as do major and minor authors.

i. Bibliography, Libraries, Periodicals, and Publishing History

Adequate bibliography remains a major need for the period before 1800. Puritan sermons and tracts, political pamphlets, poems and satires in colonial newspapers and magazines, all should be catalogued, not to mention the writings of a Thomas Jefferson or an Edward Taylor. One significant list did get its start in 1963 with Parts A-C and D-G of d'Alté A. Welch, "A Bibliography of American Children's Books Printed Prior to 1821" (*PAAS*, LXXIII, Pt. 1, 121-324; Pt. 2, 465-596).

There are also several more or less informal listings and studies of collections of books and papers. David A. Randall traces the history of significant political pieces which have passed through his hands in " 'Dukedom Large Enough.' III: Thomas Jefferson and the Declaration of Independence" (*PBSA*, LVI, 472-480), a study in public critical attitudes as well as in book history. Whitfield J. Bell, Jr., in "Henry Stevens, His Uncle Samuel, and the Franklin Papers," (*PMHS*, LXXII, 143-211) outlines the hazardous history of one of the two great collections of Benjamin Franklin's personal papers and in so doing shows a good deal about the difficulties in obtaining governmental aid in procuring such materials. Nicholas B. Wainwright in tracing the curious history of "The Penn Collection" (*FMHB*, LXXXVI, 393-419) of the Pennsylvania Historical Society demonstrates that families can be as difficult and undecided as governments in their disposition of such matters. And Edwin Wolf II, an enterprising bibliographer, tells of an exciting find in "Some Books of Early New England Provenance in the 1823 Library of Allegheny College" (*PAAS*, LXXIII, 13-44).

Quasi-medical literature in its relation to the later eighteenth-century novel's preoccupation with virginity and other sexual topics is considered in Otho T. Beall, Jr.'s "*Aristotle's Master Piece* in America: A Landmark in the Folklore of Medicine" (*WMQ*, XX, 206-222). Louis Timothée of the Library Company of Philadelphia is suggested by Walter H. Blumenthal as the "First Librarian of Colonial America" (*AN&Q*, I, 83-84). But Charles T. Laugher in "Some Further Notes on the First Libraries of Colonial America" (*AN&Q*, II, 4-6) offers several earlier candidates. Frank L. Mott in "What Is the Oldest American Newspaper?" (*JQ*, XL, 95-98) examines eight journals with varying claims to primacy.

Two studies of colonial government printing indicate a good deal about the publication of theological works and more about the first recorded ordinances of our political literature. Rollo Silver in "Government Printing in Massachusetts" (*SB*, XVI, 161-200) gives titles, authors, number of copies, distribution, and costs of scores of thanksgiving proclamations, treaties, and election sermons between 1753 and 1781. J. F. S. Smeall offers suggestions about the Revolution in "Revolutionary Process: The Publication of the *Association*, 1774-1775" (*NDQ*, XXX, 89-98).

More personal is Alexander J. Wall, Jr.'s "William Bradford, Colonial Printer—A Tercentenary Review" (*PAAS*, LXXIII, Pt. 2, 361-384), which outlines Bradford's various careers in various places. Ernest Benz, in "Franklin and the Mystic Rocket" (*AGR*, XXIX, 24-26), tells the story of Franklin the printer's use of a rocket drawing in a new edition (1751) of a German pietistic work to symbolize aspiration towards heaven.

In the relatively unexplored field of early periodicals some useful results of spadework are revealed. William H. Castles, Jr., examined one colonial newspaper, "*The Virginia Gazette*, 1736-1766: Its Editors, Editorial Policy, and Literary Content" (*DA*, XXIII, 3350-51). The brief summary indicates that this study probably

deserves publication in its entirety, to stand beside Hennig Cohen's
The South Carolina Gazette 1732-1775 (1953). "*The Columbian
Magazine* and Its Contributions to American Literary Nationalism"
(*DA*, XXIII, 4676-77), by William Joseph Free, considers the five
distinct periods between 1786 and 1792 in this Philadelphia journal's history and the uniquely American theses which were developed in it. In "The Eighteenth Century Philadelphia Almanac
and Its English Counterpart" (*DA*, XXIII 2903-04), Joseph Philip
Goldberg analyzes the literary content of these annuals and finds
that, contrary to general opinion, they sought to inculcate a high
level of morality and "to lead their readers to human happiness"
rather than to material success.

ii. Texts

The year 1963 saw many contributions to the slow but steady
stream of newly edited or first printed texts of colonial authors.
No great multi-volume edition was inaugurated, but a number of
those now in progress were added to, and one "complete edition"
with a new extra volume and critical commentary was brought out.
   The last-mentioned was the *Complete Writings of Roger Williams* (7 vols.; New York, Russell and Russell), the first six volumes
of which are an exact reprint of the Narragansett edition (only two
hundred were originally printed) and the seventh a first collected
text of five rare pamphlets and a critical essay on Williams by Perry
Miller. Another New Englander was edited by Leon Howard in
'*The Mind*' *of Jonathan Edwards: A Reconstructed Text* (Berkeley
and Los Angeles, Univ. of Calif. Press) in an analytical study which
combines the critical search for ideas with bibliographical method.
   The printed papers of four of the founding fathers have been
augmented. Under the editorship of L. H. Butterfield, *et al.*, the
Adams Family Correspondence (Cambridge, Harvard Univ. Press),
the first two volumes of letters 1761-1768, have continued the series
of records of this remarkable family. Less appealing as literature
but equally as valuable as record of mind and activity is Volume
VII of *The Papers of Benjamin Franklin . . . 1756 . . . 1758* (New
Haven, Yale Univ. Press), ed. Leonard W. Labaree, *et al.* Volume
VII of *The Papers of Alexander Hamilton . . . 1790 . . . 1791* (New
York, Columbia Univ. Press), edited by Harold C. Syrett and Jacob
E. Cooke, depicts that statesman in his early days as Secretary of

the Treasury. Perhaps more intrinsically interesting is Volume III of *The Papers of James Madison... 1781* (Chicago, Univ. of Chicago Press), with William T. Hutchinson and W. M. E. Rachal as editors, which demonstrates Madison's movement, or development, within his states' rights position, toward nationalism.

Dwight B. Heath, an anthropologist, has edited *A Journal of the Pilgrims at Plymouth: Mourt's Relation* (New York, Corinth Books), the entire text of the 1622 edition of the earliest published account of the coming of the Pilgrims. Equally useful will be Howard C. Rice, Jr.'s edition of the Marquis de Chastellux's *Travels in North America in the Years 1780, 1781 and 1782* (Chapel Hill, Univ. of North Carolina Press), a considerably revised version of the translation of George Grieve.

There are new editions and first editions of the journals and letters of figures minor from a literary point of view: Lothar L. Tresp, ed. and trans., "August, 1748, in Georgia, from the Diary of John Martin Bolzius" (*GaHQ*, XLVII, 204-216, 320-332) and George F. Jones, ed. and trans., "John Martin Bolzius Reports on Georgia in 1739" (*GaHQ*, XLVII, 216-219); Richard B. Davis, ed., *William Fitzhugh and His Chesapeake World, 1676-1701* (Chapel Hill, Univ. of North Carolina Press), a collection of letters and other documents, and "Chesapeake Pattern and Pole-Star: William Fitzhugh in His Plantation World, 1676-1701" (*PAPS*, CV, 525-529); and Edward M. Riley, ed., *The Journal of John Harrower, an Indentured Servant in the Colony of Virginia, 1773-1776* (New York, Holt, Rinehart, and Winston), the account of a schoolmaster and versifier.

Records of the New England mind are already more familiar than those just mentioned. Four or five new editions are worth noting. M. G. Hall has re-edited, with a thoughtful analytical introduction, "The Autobiography of Increase Mather" (*PAAS*, LXXI, 271-360). He shows the first part as conventional Puritan autobiography for the benefit of one's children and the second part as a justification of Increase himself as politician and statesman. "The Diary of Ebenezer Parkman" (*PAAS*, LXXI, Pt. 1, 93-227; Pt. 2, 361-448; LXXII, Pt. 1, 31-233; Pt. 2, 329-481; LXXIII, Pt. 1, 45-120; Pt. 2, 385-464), ed. Francis G. Walett, begun in 1961 and still appearing, is the journal (from 1724) of a country parson of Westborough, Massachusetts. "The Journals of the Rev. Stephen Williams, 1775-1777" (*DA*, XXIV, 285), edited by Alexander G. Medlicott, Jr., are "largely the record of a man who spent his life glorifying God" but also recorded his observations of the secular world. The scientific and international side of the Puritan mind is represented in the sophisticated and knowledge-hungry letters (1659-1660), G. H. Turnbull, ed., "Some Correspondence of John Winthrop, Jr., and Samuel Hartlib" (*PMHS*, LXXII, 36-67).

Belletristic texts of the period are scarce, but there are some minor and single works and a few collected editions. In *JA* appeared the text of a newly identified story, "Eine neu entdecke Kurzgeschichte C. B. Browns" (VIII, 280-296), by William M. Manly. In the same journal Alfred Weber edited "Hugh Henry Brackenridges Epistel an Sir Walter Scott" (VIII, 267-279), the first complete modern printing of a poem from the unique copy in the Historical Society of Pennsylvania. Hennig Cohen has discovered and edited "A Cotton Mather Verse Inscription" (*AN&Q*, I, 53-54) of 1723 to his daughter, a document in "further evidence of the unfortunate esthetic consequences of the didactic role of poetry in Puritan society."

Useful should be the three concise editions from large collections or scattered works. Donald E. Stanford has abridged, with a new introduction, *The Poems of Edward Taylor* (New Haven, Yale Univ. Press), his own standard work of 1960. Arthur Palmer Hudson has gathered *Songs of the Carolina Charter Colonists, 1663-1763* (Raleigh, Carolina Charter Tercentenary Commission) from English and American printed sources. Philip M. Marsh has compiled and edited *A Freneau Sampler* (New York, Scarecrow), an excellent representative assemblage from editorials, verse, criticism, and essays generally.

iii. Biographical

The year produced no full-length lives-in-criticism such as did 1962 in Edmund S. Morgan's *The Gentle Puritan: A Life of Ezra Stiles, 1727-1795* (New Haven, Yale Univ. Press) and Larzer Ziff's *The Career of John Cotton: Puritanism and the American Experience* (Princeton, Princeton Univ. Press). There was one book on a scientific writer, and shorter pieces which add to our knowledge of the careers of a dozen others.

Though Edmund S. Morgan in "Ezra Stiles and Timothy Dwight" (*PMHS*, LXXII, 101-117) avows that his purpose is "historiographical" rather than biographical, this evaluation of Yale student recol-

lections and letters, as guides to his twin subjects' achievement and
reputation at a particular moment, is certainly of the stuff which
makes sound interpretative biography. Janette Bohi portrays another
New Englander in new detail in his village Massachusetts environment in "Nathaniel Ward, a Sage of Old Ipswich" (*EIHC*, XCIX,
3-32).

Bits of data and analyses which perhaps should be useful to a
future biographer appeared concerning the career of Cotton Mather.
Through a study of the still unpublished autobiography "Paterna,"
David Levin in "The Hazing of Cotton Mather: The Creation of a
Biographical Personality" (*NEQ*, XXXVI, 147-171) reconsiders the
picture of the infant prodigy as presented by earlier biographers.
In two brief pieces William R. Manierre corrects the dating of
Mather's letters to the German Pietist August Hermann Francke
("A 'Mather' of Dates," *SB*, XVI, 217-220), and points out ("Notes
from Cotton Mather's 'Missing' Diary of 1712," *AN&Q*, II, 51-52)
how the diary for 1712 provides useful dating references and illuminates his earliest relations with the Royal Society. Then there was
a reprint of Barrett Wendell's *Cotton Mather: The Puritan Priest*
(New York, Harcourt, Brace, and World), with a new introduction
by Alan Heimert.

Also appearing in 1963 was the French edition of A. O. Aldridge's
Benjamin Franklin et ses contemporains français (Paris, Didier),
published in this country in 1957, which will be of interest chiefly
to Americanists abroad, and one brief essay which adds an attractive
day in the philosopher's life for future biography. The latter is
Robert R. Hare's "Electro Vitrifico in Annapolis: Mr. Franklin Visits
the Tuesday Club" (*MdHM*, LVIII, 62-66), a description from the
minutes of a Maryland literary club. Alexander Hamilton receives
new attention from his recent biographer when Broadus Mitchell
poses a number of second-thought queries in "If Hamilton Were
Here Today: Some Unanswered Questions" (*SAQ*, LXII, 288-296).

Perhaps less significant but equally personal are some glances at
the lives of other men. Helen Stone Peterson describes the part
Jefferson's two daughters had in his White House years in "The
President's Daughters" (*VC*, XIII, Autumn, 18-22). Paul F. Butler,
Jr., sees that "Washington's Religious Opinions" (*SWR*, XLVIII,
48-61) suggested as much in his actions and conversation as in his
writings. A world-traveler's whereabouts on the date of an event
he described vividly is considered judiciously in J. Kenneth Mum-

ford's "Did John Ledyard Witness Captain Cook's Death?" (*PNQ*, LIV, 75-78). A significant year in the political career of one of the Hartford Wits is painted in fresh colors through new letters in Milton Cantor's "Joel Barlow's Mission to Algiers" (*Historian*, XXV, 172-194).

Finally we have two biographical studies of colonial scientific writers who set a tradition in which the Bartrams and Burroughses were to follow. Gordon W. Jones in "Dr. John Mitchell of Virginia" (*VC*, XII, Spring, 32-39) outlines the career of the botanist, cartographer, farmer, and physician whose papers and books described much of the flora and rural way of life in his own colony and in North America generally. An equally important Old Dominion fellow-colonist of Mitchell's is depicted at greater length in Edmund and Dorothy S. Berkeley's *John Clayton, Pioneer of American Botany* (Chapel Hill, Univ. of North Carolina Press), the first life of the co-author of *Flora Virginica*.

iv. Criticism and Literary History

The prose criticized in 1963 was largely theological, and even the three poets subjected to analysis were clergymen indulging the Sacred Muse. But the politico-philosophical mind received some attention: three writers examined the place of the classics in early literature, three more looked at the work on the Indian, and others studied the image of the Negro, rhetoric and oratory, and the old but always intriguing question of Puritanism in belletristic literature.

Among the colonial poets Edward Taylor continued to receive considerable attention. Ken Akiyama in "Edward Taylor's Poetry: An Introduction" (*Stud. in Humanities*, Doshisha Univ., No. 64, pp. 27-44) gives in Japanese with English abstract an approach which American students may find of interest. After three pages of annotated bibliography, Mr. Akiyama quotes in full Meditation 91 (Second Series) with a glossary (in English) which is a word-for-word explication of the poem. It is based on the assumption that at least one volume of theological commentary and many Biblical allusions lie behind each line of verse. Two other writers look at this Puritan's imagery. Robert H. Woodward, in "Automata in Hawthorne's 'Artist of the Beautiful' and Taylor's 'Meditation 56'" (*ESQ*, No. 31, pp. 63-66) notes several sources for the images of mechanical marvels present in both writers. Elizabeth Wiley in "Sources of

Imagery in the Poetry of Edward Taylor" (*DA*, XXIII, 2122-23)
reaches the not-startling conclusion that the Bible and the devotional
prose of his time influenced him most strongly and tied his work to
the mainstream of poetry in his time.

Employing somewhat different techniques, Jack Stillinger examines the work of another New England poet in "Dwight's *Tri-
umph of Infidelity:* Text and Interpretation" (*SB*, XV, 1962, 259-
266). The poet laureate of Presbyterianism in colonial America is
the title given a Virginia poet in Craig Gilborn's "Samuel Davies'
Sacred Muse" (*JPH*, XLI, 63-79). Davies' career as sermon and
hymn writer and as devotional poet is traced. For its intrinsic
quality and as an early example of the thread of Puritanism and
Calvinism which yet continues in the writing of Southerners such
as Faulkner and R. P. Warren, this verse deserves the attention it
has received.

Two critics of our first fiction insist on its strongly American
qualities. Jack B. Moore in "A Traditional Motif in Early American
Fiction: 'The Too Youthful Solitary'" (*MF*, XII, 1962, 205-208)
suggests that although Boccaccio and "the boy who has never seen
a woman motif" are present in this periodical piece, they have here
already been domesticated in America. This tale, probably by
Freneau, foreshadows Cooper, Hawthorne, and Melville. In "The
Importance of Point of View in Brockden Brown's *Wieland*" (*AL*,
XXXV, 311-321), William M. Manly sees Clara the narrator as much
more rational and controlled than a typical sentimental heroine
would be. But she also has the tendency to explore her own tor-
mented psyche and the borderlands of fact and fancy as so many
American heroes and heroines have done since her creation.

The theologico-philosophical prose of five New Englanders has
been analyzed, Jonathan Edwards receiving most attention. Leon
Howard's new text and critique of "The Mind" have been noted
above. Paul R. Baumgartner, in "Jonathan Edwards: The Theory
Behind His Use of Figurative Language" (*PMLA*, LXXVIII, 321-
325), finds, contrary to earlier critics, Edwards' use of figurative
language as natural and happy, for this language externalized the
ideas of God. In "From Locke to Edwards" (*JHI*, XXIV, 355-372),
Edward H. Davidson shows how Edwards translated Locke's idea
of "power" into a theory of "tendency." Going on through "Sinners
in the Hands of an Angry God" and *Freedom of the Will*, Davidson

analyzes the direction of Edwards' thought in its relation to orthodox Puritanism and to later literature.

Sidney E. Ahlstrom in "Thomas Hooker—Puritanism and Democratic Citizenship" (*CH*, XXXII, 415-431) examines the founder of Connecticut in "A Preliminary Inquiry into Some Relationships of Religion and American Civic Responsibility." Ahlstrom suggests that legalism, the Achilles' heel of Puritanism, led Hooker and his followers from one movement into another which concluded with secularization and American democracy.

Besides the bibliographical and biographical matter on Cotton Mather noted above, which included a critical discussion of the still unpublished "Paterna," there were separate essays on his writings. Peter H. Smith in "Politics and Sainthood: Biography by Cotton Mather" (*WMQ*, XX, 186-206) shows how the New England pastor in *Johannes in Eremo* and the *Magnalia* continued a Puritan tradition of biography as spiritual guide and yet used his sketches to demonstrate his region's identity of interest with King William's England. Eugene E. White demonstrates that "Cotton Mather's *Manuductio ad Ministerium*" (*QJS*, XLIX, 308-319) is much more than a detailed spiritual, moral, and intellectual guide for the ministerial candidate. In "The Vision of Goodman Brown: A Source and Interpretation" (*AL*, XXXV, 218-225), E. Arthur Robinson sees the *Magnalia* as a pervasive secondary "source" for Hawthorne's tale, *The Wonders of the Invisible World* being its primary source.

Three more general studies of Puritanism and literature should be noted. John F. Warner, Jr., "The Human Side of Puritan Literature" (*EJ*, LII, 587-590, 609) suggests ways of revitalizing the teaching of this literature along lines suggested by his title. Larzer Ziff is concerned with both England and America in "Literary Consequences of Puritanism" (*ELH*, XXX, 293-305). He observes that "revolutionary cultural movements" like Puritanism change the way men perceive and describe reality more than they furnish a different set of customs to serve as subject matter.

Edmund S. Morgan in *Visible Saints: The History of a Puritan Idea* (New York, New York Univ. Press) is concerned with the theory and practice of church membership in New England, its development of tests of experience of grace, the subsequent compromise, and reassertion by Jonathan Edwards of the necessity of test and experience. *Visible Saints* is a swiftly moving narrative and analysis which clarifies for the less-than-specialist many aspects of this segment of the history of the Puritan mind.

The political and social mind of the later eighteenth century is the subject of several essays. Perhaps implying that he is depicting a typical Tory point of view, Philip Evanson in "Jonathan Boucher: The Mind of an American Loyalist" (*MdHM*, LVIII, 123-136) examines his subject's *Reminiscences* and letters and decides that Boucher perceived readily man's weakness but not his potential for greatness—thus the Tory's disquietude. Bernhard Knollenberg attempts to rehabilitate John Dickinson's reputation and to show him as an honest, perhaps great statesman in "John Dickinson vs. John Adams: 1774-1776" (*PAPS*, CVII, 138-144).

Stanley F. Chyet in "Lewisohn and Crèvecoeur" (*CJF*, XXII, 130-136) studies the criticism contained in an edition of the *Letters of an American Farmer* which Lewisohn brought out in the 1920's. Lewisohn's attraction apparently was to Crèvecoeur's "encounter with himself." Albert E. Stone analyzes the author's major work in "Crèvecoeur's *Letters* and the Beginnings of an American Literature" (*EUQ*, XVIII, 1962, 197-213). Certain qualities of this work, Stone finds, lead straight to Melville and Poe; others to Whittier, Thoreau, and Frost.

The mind of Thomas Jefferson holds a perennial fascination for critics of many kinds. In "The Mind of Thomas Jefferson" (*Ethics*, LXXIII, 79-99), Stuart G. Brown assesses his subject as an intellectual in the light of his philosophical backgrounds. In "Nature's God and the Founding Fathers" (*AH*, XIV, Oct., 4-7, 100-106) E. M. Halliday indicates Jefferson's beliefs in natural morality rather than original sin and in inalienable instincts as well as rights. Fred C. Luebke in "The Origins of Thomas Jefferson's Anti-Clericalism" (*CH*, XXXII, 344-356) sees the third president's hostility to the clergy originating not in his religious beliefs but in clerical attacks upon him. Anthony Hillbruner looks at the orator in "Word and Deed: Jefferson's Addresses to the Indians" (*SM*, XXX, 328-334), a study of rhetorical elements in relation to motivation which serve to define Jefferson here as "the idealist as realist." Merrill D. Peterson in "Henry Adams on Jefferson the President" (*VQR*, XXXIX, 187-201) shows that the great historian refused to look at the whole of the great statesman but saw him only as a political force. Peterson points out other shortcomings of Adams' treatment and concludes that to be understood Jefferson "deserves to be interpreted in the humanizing light of pragmatism."

James C. Ching studies another orator-statesman, a new Englander, and the rhetorical elements of his appeal to a particular audience in "Fisher Ames' 'Tomahawk Address' " (*SM*, XXX, 31-40). Observations on two autobiographies suggest the recent interest in the form. M. G. Hall sees two distinct purposes behind Increase Mather's autobiography (see above). R. F. Sayre in "The Worldly Franklin and the Provincial Critics" (*TSLL*, IV, 512-524) views the four parts of Poor Richard's memoirs as installments, each reflecting the time at which it was composed, and insists that each be studied separately. Previous critics have been provincial in trying to read Yankee or American virtues into an account which represents, with irony and humor and naïveté, universal or world verities. John W. Ward in "Who Was Benjamin Franklin?" (*ASch*, XXXII, 541-553) observes that the search for an answer to this question must begin with the memoirs. Ward sees the *Autobiography* in two parts, the first written for his family and the second for the world with a consciousness of offering himself as "a representative type, the American."

The Indian supplies symbols, character, or simple narrative. J. Paul Hunter in "Friday as a Convert: Defoe and the Accounts of Indian Missionaries" (*RES*, XIV, 243-248) argues that seventeenth-century accounts of Indian missions indicate that converts responded just as Friday does. That the tragic figure of Pontiac appeared in belletristic literature as early as 1765 and was utilized in several plays before the end of the century is demonstrated in George H. Orians, "Pontiac in Literature: Part I. 1764-1915" (*NOQ*, XXXV, 144-163). And Philip Young reminds the Japanese of the immortality as American symbol of an Indian maiden in "The Mother of Us All: Pocahontas Reconsidered" (*Nichibei Forum*, VIII, 1962, 100-122, a reprint from the 1962 *KR*).

The national character of the earliest American comedy is emphasized in John Lauber's "*The Contrast*: A Study in the Concept of Innocence" (*ELN*, I, 33-37). This play marks an important stage in the development from a colonial to a distinctively American literature, for it is based on the concept of New World innocence, and presents the now-familiar theme of the moral contrast between the elegant European and the homespun American. Even our first real dictionary implicitly and explicitly underlines this moral con-

trast, thinks P. J. Staudenraus in "Mr. Webster's Dictionary: A
Personal Document of the Age of Benevolence" (*Mid-America*,
XLV, 193-201).

Two essays and a book remind us that the Latin classics were
as alive to the colonial American as Milton or Shakespeare. In
"Colonial American Renderings of Horace in *The Massachusetts
Magazine*" (*CB*, XXXIX, 81-83), Leo M. Kaiser studies one example
of the popularity of the Latin poet in New England. In "John
Beveridge: Latin Poet of Two Worlds" (*CJ*, LVIII, 215-223), the
same critic shows a Philadelphian and his circle as translators and
imitators of several Roman poets, with Horace chief among them.
Richard M. Gummere in *The American Colonial Mind and the Classical Tradition* (Cambridge, Harvard Univ. Press) believes the
American colonists used the classics in no systematic manner but
rather combed ancient literature for pertinent ideas. The author
assembles evidence of references to the classical world from hundreds of places, but he does not attempt to assess indebtedness in
ideas. It is a survey, not a series of probings in depth (cf. H. M.
Jones' review in *AL*, XXXVI, 222-223).

Two more general studies should be noted. A. M. Schlesinger in
"The Aristocracy of Colonial America" (*PMHS*, LXXIV, 1962, 3-21)
makes several suggestions useful to understanding the part of plan-
ter, theocrat, and merchant-prince in a fluid society. Milton Cantor,
working at the other end of the social ladder, looks at "The Image
of the Negro in Colonial America" (*NEQ*, XXXVI, 452-477). He
does not claim that the colonists cared deeply about the matter. But
in the writings of men like Morgan Godwyn, Samuel Sewall, Jefferson, Benjamin Rush, and Samuel Hopkins he sees in the seventeenth
and eighteenth centuries the germs of the two later attitudes toward
slavery and the Negro. As a political animal, white men saw him
like themselves. But as an economic force, some considered the
Negro as slave essential to their survival. Thus was the future
forecast.

10. Nineteenth-Century Fiction[1]

Louis J. Budd

i. Stowe, Tourgée, and Others

When a year's scholarship is sorted out, surprising patterns and emphases appear. Other factors besides aesthetic quality are clearly influencing what the scholars take up and what their editors accept. More particularly, though most of them like to think of working by sidereal rather than local time, their output often reflects the interests of their non-literary contemporaries. Often but not always or perfectly, of course. Zeal to reclaim a very minor figure can defy all patterns, as in a recent flurry of items about John Neal; or a consensus that Bret Harte, for example, was once overrated leads to just as lopsided neglect. Still the main lines in recent scholarship come either from an active dialogue with preceding work or else from debates centered outside the academy.

Proof of this second factor lies in the surge of writing about Harriet Beecher Stowe and Albion W. Tourgée. Though almost every student of Mrs. Stowe discovers that her fiction has vibrancy and resonance, much of the latest commentary borrows force from the Negro problem. Benjamin F. Hudson's "Another View of 'Uncle Tom'" (*Phylon*, XXIV, 79-87) takes off from the irony that the name of her famous slave—who epitomized dignity and courage as well as self-respecting love for mankind—has become a favorite insult of the integrationists. Hudson's main business of deciding whether her Tom had a Christian or a Stoic philosophy unsurprisingly settles on the first. (As for the servile Tom created by the myriad dramatizations of the novel, John H. McDowell, "Original Scenery and Documents for Productions of *Uncle Tom's Cabin*" [*RHT*, XV, 71-79], records the staging and script details of a touring version organized as late as 1903.) More provocative is the analysis by Severn Duvall in "*Uncle Tom's Cabin*: The Sinister Side of the Patriarchy" (*NEQ*,

[1] This essay excludes four major figures: Hawthorne, Melville, Twain, and James.

XXXVI, 3-22). Bolstered by Southern reviews it argues brilliantly that the novel challenged the Cotton Kingdom's vision of itself as a happy family with Old Testament overtones. This analysis also shows that Mrs. Stowe's sensitivity to miscegenation, because of the unhappy families it made for, both gave fervor to her characters and flayed a quivering nerve in white Southern women. Indeed, her sensitivity to family relationships is proclaimed as the key to her entire body of fiction by Janet A. Emig in "The Flower in the Cleft: The Writings of Harriet Beecher Stowe" (*BHPSO*, XXI, 223-238), which links the emotional habits of her characters with attitudes toward her own upbringing. In pre-Freudian naïveté she evidently poured her childhood and youth into every heroine or, more revealingly, every hero. This theory, by no means new, also underlies John R. Adams' *Harriet Beecher Stowe* (New York, Twayne). However, taking account of her most casual essays, Adams stresses her writing rather than her neuroses, judging it with respect but also firm taste. Backed by wide secondary research, he convinces us that she served a full apprenticeship before her success and that she moved beyond Uncle Tom into local-color fiction of underrated value.

Nobody dares to find much intrinsic value in Tourgée. But, as Monte M. Olenick points out in "Albion W. Tourgée: Radical Republican Spokesman of the Civil War Crusade" (*Phylon*, XXIII [1962], 332-345), he is virtually unique for novels that took the Negro's side after Emancipation. The carpetbagging career that underlay his novels is seen in Otto H. Olsen's summary of his dissertation ("Albion W. Tourgée: Carpetbagger," *NCHR*, XL, 434-454). Another dissertation by Theodore L. Gross has led to two articles and a book that incorporates them. His critical biography, for the Twayne series, fills a gap in our literary history though hobbled as criticism by Tourgée's bottomless faults. On political questions it vacillates between Tourgée's viewpoint and overstraining to give his enemies fair play; yet it sheds light on attitudes toward the Negro between 1870 and 1900, especially as expressed through fiction.

Many of those short stories and novels were still set in the Old South. In fact, for almost a hundred years both fictionists and historians have found it more intriguing than Reconstruction days. Richard Beale Davis, "The 'Virginia Novel' Before *Swallow Barn*"

(*VMHB*, LXXI, 278-293), pushes further into it with very informed and meticulous proof that well before 1830 Virginians were already creating a literary vision of their region, partly impelled by a feeling that its heroic age was over. William Gilmore Simms also continues to attract research, as in the account of his trips to Alabama by Wm. Stanley Hoole, "Alabama and W. Gilmore Simms" (*AlaR*, XVI, 83-107, 185-199). But, spurred on by Edmund Wilson's *Patriotic Gore* (1962), interest is now shifting toward the postbellum period. *The Faraway Country: Writers of the Modern South* (Seattle, Univ. of Washington Press), by Louis D. Rubin, Jr., symptomatically begins with George Washington Cable (in a chapter titled "The Road to Yoknapatawpha") and tries to reclaim his *John March, Southerner* as a near-major novel. Another sign of the times is an anthology labeled *After Appomattox: The Image of the South in Its Fiction, 1865-1900* (New York, Corinth Books), whose editor, Gene Baro, contends like Rubin that Cable's generation made a necessary bridge to the Southern masters.

Current affairs have also encouraged work on our "native" humorists. David Ross Locke's modern-day relevance heavily shapes an anthology, *The Struggles of Petroleum V. Nasby* (Boston, Beacon Press), introduced by Joseph Jones and graced by some of Thomas Nast's drawings. Likewise, more of George Washington Harris' political sketches are being unearthed by *The Lovingood Papers* (Knoxville, Univ. of Tennessee Press). To be sure, this annual founded in 1962 welcomes anything on its subject; its first two issues add importantly to the Lovingood canon, which appeals mainly to a special breed (that included William Faulkner). Still, even the latest article on Johnson J. Hooper, "Simon Suggs: A Burlesque Campaign Biography" (*AQ*, XV, 459-463) by Robert Hopkins, centers on his alertness to political rhetoric. While Artemus Ward was alert mostly in blander ways, he has the enduring claim of having schooled Mark Twain, who admired Lovingood too. James C. Austin, "Artemus Ward, Mark Twain, and the Limburger Cheese" (*MASJ*, IV, ii, 70-73), suggests a specific borrowing; John Q. Reed works out an itinerary in "Artemus Ward's First Lecture Tour" (*AL*, XXXIV, 571-573) and, more vitally, the text of the lecture which so impressed Twain in 1863 ("Artemus Ward's 'The Children in the Wood' Lecture on the Tour of 1861-1862," *MASJ*, IV, ii, 58-69).

ii. Irving, Cooper, and Others

In other words the native humorists get added play because they merge into the development of American fiction. Ironically, the very high mission that the nineteenth century proclaimed for its poetry helps to make us prefer mostly its prose. Washington Irving therefore keeps holding respect as a founding father of our short story. This respect is furthered by Lewis Leary's graceful yet expert and ripe addition to the University of Minnesota Pamphlets on American Writers. More currently, Irving's work is profiting from the era of explication, now somewhat hungry for new materials. Robert A. Bone, "Irving's Headless Hessian: Prosperity and the Inner Life" (*AQ*, XV, 167-175), ingeniously argues that "The Legend of Sleepy Hollow" protested in detail against the fatal lures that acquisitiveness exerts on the imagination. Barbara D. Simison, "Some Autobiographical Notes of Washington Irving" (*YULG*, XXXVIII, 3-13), prints random but valuable jottings, sure to touch off more commentary.

As for James Fenimore Cooper, another founding father, a reissue of *The Red Rover* (ed. Warren S. Walker, Lincoln, Univ. of Nebraska Press) adds to Thomas Philbrick's book (1961) maintaining that he was an important novelist of the sea who partly cleared the way for *Moby-Dick*. In another sub-genre, "A Neglected Satire on James Fenimore Cooper's *Home As Found*" (*AL*, XXXV, 13-21) by W. B. Gates details a rebuttal to one of his novels of American manners. More challenging is his current appeal to a band of sensitive literary critics. Supporting their view that he achieved much subtler form than usually granted, Donald A. Ringe's "Chiaroscuro as an Artistic Device in Cooper's Fiction" (*PMLA*, LXXVIII, 349-357) decides that he handled light and shade functionally and tellingly. Yet he must survive primarily as a mythmaker on our central experiences, as can be seen in the germane chapter of A. N. Kaul, *The American Vision: Actual and Ideal Society in Nineteenth-Century Fiction* (New Haven, Yale Univ. Press). A native of India, Kaul brings fresh insight to Cooper's tension between the hoped-for community and democracy as it was; Kaul also contrasts valuably the import of the Leatherstocking tales and the Littlepage trilogy.

Every new brief for Cooper's contemporaries only ends by revealing that their best falls far short of his. This is true of a rich sampling of John Neal's fiction and essays, edited by Hans-Joachim

Lang and flanked by comment and a bibliography by Irving T. Richards (*JA*, VII [1962], 204-319). A claim that Robert Montgomery Bird reached the Leatherstocking level once—Joan Joffe Hall, "*Nick of the Woods*: An Interpretation of the American Wilderness" (*AL*, XXXV, 173-182)—builds up to conceding that his strongest novel faltered between the only alternatives it held out. Assuming Bird's lesser stature, Curtis Dahl's judicious and packed book (*Robert Montgomery Bird*, New York, Twayne) stresses his importance to the times, his versatility, and his talent for romantic tragedy. The Twayne United States Authors Series is bringing forth critical biographies that even the bravest university press might not gamble on. Though too wavering in quality, it is turning into our most detailed literary history.

Another volume in the series, Rayburn S. Moore's *Constance Fenimore Woolson* (New York, Twayne), lessens the relative neglect of our female writers. Rounded, thorough, and untendentious, it suggests that we are missing worthwhile fiction by cleaving more and more to a few giant figures. This is surely true with Sarah Orne Jewett, as shown again in Robin Magowan's "Pastoral and the Art of Landscape in *The Country of the Pointed Firs*" (*NEQ*, XXXVI, 229-240), which expertly links her best work with pastoral concepts and the impressionist painters rather than the local colorists. Yet she gets less space again than Ambrose Bierce, who is studied in two more doctoral dissertations, recommended to German readers (Gisela Pira, "Ambrose Bierce," *NS*, 425-430), and praised as a theorist (Howard W. Bahr, "Ambrose Bierce and Realism," *SoQ*, I, 309-331). Another exotic, who does not have the credit of influencing Stephen Crane, as did Bierce, will apparently rebound with the fresh concern about Asia, as indicated in Erwin Jahn, "Lafcadio Hearn's Image of Japan" (*OW*, VIII, i, 33-40).

Temporarily cast into neglect by the theory that the romance is the vital artery of American fiction, the minor realists are again being discussed for their merits as well as their help toward our supposed maturity. In a bold synthesis, George W. Johnson, "Harold Frederic's Young Goodman Ware: The Ambiguities of a Realistic Romance" (*MFS*, VIII, 361-374), insists that *The Damnation of Theron Ware* solidly renders surfaces while grappling with moral choice and cosmic perspectives; but, revealingly, he concludes that it does not reach the goals set for it. Perhaps without intending so, William Randel's return to Edward Eggleston (for the Twayne series) stimulates more curiosity in Eggleston's historical writing than his fiction. However, with respect for the lately maligned "rise" of realism and with infectious confidence in his durability, Randel proves that Eggleston was neither a shaggy maverick nor a lucky amateur. Clarence A. Glasrud's scholarly biography (Northfield, Minn., Norwegian-American Hist. Assn.) makes no strong explicit or implicit claims for its subject, Hjalmar Hjorth Boyesen, but it documents his activities as a magazine champion of realism and as a liaison with Continental writers.

Neglected from the start, John William De Forest can hardly fail to have his personal rise soon, if only because of Joseph Jay Rubin's handsome Monument Edition. It has now reached its third volume with *Kate Beaumont* (State College, Pa., Bald Eagle Press), a witty and finely paced as well as honestly observed novel of the antebellum South. Hamlin Garland, on the other hand, has seemingly had more than his share of glory; John E. Higgins' deft survey, "A Man from the Middle Border: Hamlin Garland's Diaries" (*WMH*, XLVI, 294-302), will not touch off a chain reaction. But Frank Norris' broad canvases have attracted more and more of the critics who like to fashion their own panoramas. Now James K. Folsom, "Social Darwinism or Social Protest? The 'Philosophy' of *The Octopus*" (*MFS*, VIII, 393-400), rejoins that they overlook the obvious reading—its attack on the railroad for brutally insisting on much better than a fair profit. More broadly Donald Pizer, "Synthetic Criticism and Frank Norris; Or, Mr. Marx, Mr. Taylor, and *The Octopus*" (*AL*, XXXIV, 532-541), warns against distorting it to fit preconceived patterns and advises that an "eclectic" approach will go deepest here. Pizer has also been rethinking basic terms. His incisive note, "Frank Norris' Definition of Naturalism" (*MFS*, VIII, 408-410), narrows the tangle created by Norris' calling Zola a "romantic" novelist; for Norris "naturalism" could point toward technique rather than deterministic ideas.

iii. Howells and Crane

The William Dean Howells revival of the 1950's has settled in for an indefinite run. Edwin H. Cady, his premier biographer, adds more impetus by probing keenly our most exciting literary friendship in "Howells and Twain: The World in Midwestern Eyes" (*BSTCF*, III, 3-8). But the busiest Howellsians of late have been Clara and

Rudolf Kirk. Their critical biography (Twayne, 1962), focused on the primary texts rather than psychodynamics, works in a wealth of facts while exerting judgment and taste. On her own, Clara Kirk has done a political study in depth, *W. D. Howells, Traveler from Altruria* (New Brunswick, Rutgers Univ. Press, 1962), and two essays. The first, " 'The Brighter Side' of Fiction—According to Howells and James" (*CE*, XXIV, 463-464), reveals that Henry James objected to the "wanton melancholy" of the Russian masters and called for an "ideal of joy" similar to the famous, derided preference for the "smiling aspects" of American life. The second, "Toward a Theory of Art: A Dialogue Between W. D. Howells and C. E. Norton" (*NEQ*, XXXVI, 291-319), contrasts Howells and a late Brahmin in their social and, more interestingly, aesthetic principles and makes clear why the democratic-hearted realist had to break away finally from the Boston elite. Her analysis remains important even after a tough-minded scrutiny by Kermit Vanderbilt, "Howells and Norton: Some Frustrations of the Biographer" (*NEQ*, XXXVII [1964], 84-89).

In part Howells scholarship hums so busily because the avenues are so many. The fourth volume of Jacob Blanck's *Bibliography of American Literature* (New Haven, Yale Univ. Press) having reached him as well as John Hay and Hearn, needs over sixty pages to list the facts of his publications. On his prominent sociopolitical side Stanley Cooperman, "Utopian Realism: The Futurist Novels of Bellamy and Howells" (*CE*, XXIV, 464-467), compares *A Traveler from Altruria* with *Looking Backward*, as social program and as art; his brisk chiding of both books is clouded by signs that he would praise no utopian vision. Without bias, Howard A. Wilson edits "William Dean Howells's Unpublished Letters about the Haymarket Affair" that went to William M. Salter (*ISHSJ*, LVI, 5-19). Syntheses of his opinion on other live questions are given by James W. Mathews, "Howells and the Shakers" (*Person*, XLIV, 212-219), and Alma J. Payne, "William Dean Howells and the Independent Woman" (*MidR*, V, 44-52). "Howells' *A Foregone Conclusion:* Theme and Structure" (*CLAJ*, VI, 216-220) by Richard Giannone takes up the contrasted views of Venice and, by extension, Old World society in one of the apprentice novels. More ambitious but not based on enough texts, Annette K. Baxter's "Caste and Class: Howells' Boston and Wharton's New York" (*MQ*, IV, 353-361) contrasts two treatments of high society, finding its "compactness and repose" dominant in the first as against "breadth and mobility" in the second.

As with Cooper, the aesthetic qualities that distinguish Howells from the social historian have been stressed recently. William McMurray, "The Concept of Complicity in Howells' Fiction" (*NEQ*, XXXV [1962], 489-495), daringly uses one of his social principles—not yet hunted back to its source—to trace his technique of characterization. Similarly, John E. Hart, "The Commonplace as Heroic in *The Rise of Silas Lapham*" (*MFS*, VIII, 375-383), expands a cardinal tenet of Howells' realism into a reworking of mythic romance, contending that Lapham engages us so deeply because a symbolic death and heroic rebirth are made to spring out of ordinary details and events. Sister Mary Petrus Sullivan's "The Function of Setting in Howells' *The Landlord at Lion's Head*" (*AL*, XXXV, 38-52), relying on his own critical vocabulary, shows that one of his later novels subtly and successfully integrates its hero's character with his New England property. Appearing unfortunately in a rare journal, the best new piece of criticism is Harry R. Garvin's "Howells, Venice, and the American Novel" (*AION-SG*, V [1962], 249-261). Garvin affirms his strengths as a realist but makes him out centrally a novelist of manners, committed to reasonableness rather than metaphysics or tragic passion and lacking the highest pitch of sensitivity rather than courage.

Always generous, Howells would be more surprised than envious at the booming fame of Stephen Crane, whose partisans are now so ebullient that dissent seems rude. Undaunted, Malcolm Bradbury and Arnold Goldman, "Stephen Crane: Classic at the Crossroads" (*BAASB*, No. 6, pp. 42-49), cry that he ducked the larger issues, using ambiguity as a shield and raw experience as a substitute for evaluation. These charges would have wounded him but will not lessen the tide recorded carefully in Robert N. Hudspeth, ed., "A Bibliography of Stephen Crane Scholarship: 1893-1962" (*Thoth*, IV, 30-58), which already has its first annual supplement (V [1964], 85-87). Thomas A. Gullason's gathering of *The Complete Short Stories and Sketches* (Garden City, N. Y., Doubleday) adds new items and details, makes a stepping stone toward the definitive edition needed, and invites the explicators to go beyond a few battered masterpieces. Showing incidentally how thin the line between fiction and taut-lipped feature stories was for him, Olov W. Fryckstedt's *Stephen Crane: Uncollected Writings* (Studia

Anglistica Upsaliensia No. 1, Stockholm, Almqvist & Wilksell) reprints scarce journalistic items. Another invaluable, broader-gauged tool is Edwin H. Cady's critical biography (New York, Twayne, 1962), which adds much fresh research and sturdily persuasive interpretation. But the definitive life necessarily lies ahead, after more articles like William Randel's "Stephen Crane's Jacksonville" (*SAQ*, LXII, 268-274) and James B. Stronks' "Stephen Crane's English Years: The Legend Corrected" (*PBSA*, LVII, 340-349). The first casts doubt on Thomas Beer's assertion that Florida bored Crane in 1896-1897; the second deflates the cheering belief that he commanded big prices after becoming famous. Such close, original work makes the intelligent essay in H. Wayne Morgan's *Writers in Transition: Seven Americans* (New York, Hill and Wang) seem outmoded because too general and too much guided by the "ironic hero."

The soundest new approach, Max Westbrook's "Stephen Crane and the Personal Universal" (*MFS*, VIII, 351-360), reconciles his naturalistic impulses and his search for value; holding that he accepted abstractions, though only after confirmed by life, it concludes that he saw human values as defined *in* but not merely *by* actuality. A related approach, George W. Johnson's "Stephen Crane's Metaphor of Decorum" (*PMLA*, LXXVIII, 250-256), sees him as increasingly frustrated in his drive to find pattern while still reacting to experience directly; from this dilemma the artist emerges once more as the only possible hero, who can both live with barbaric honesty and yet create order which has a tradition. Though Johnson helpfully shows that Crane shied away from solipsism, he also shied away from glorifying himself as artist, choosing to talk on the workmanlike scale of Robert P. Weeks' "The Power of the Tacit in Crane and Hemingway" (*MFS*, VIII, 415-418). Still closer in scale, Maurice Bassan, "Misery and Society: Some New Perspectives on Stephen Crane's Fiction" (*SN*, XXXV, 104-120), fills in the topical context of "An Experiment in Misery." Likewise, while tying in "The Monster" with the imagery of his earlier stories, Sy Kahn's "Stephen Crane and the Giant Voice in the Night: An Explication of *The Monster*" (*Essays in Modern American Literature*, ed. Richard E. Langford, De Land, Fla., Stetson Univ. Press) points up its satire of the gossips who hounded him in Port Jervis and elsewhere.

Scrutiny of his famous novel has become especially meticulous.

Harold R. Hungerford, " 'That Was at Chancellorsville': The Factual Framework of *The Red Badge of Courage*" (*AL*, XXXIV, 520-531), proves irrefutably that Crane drew on an actual battle for setting and other details. From a more difficult angle, James W. Tuttleton, "The Imagery of *The Red Badge of Courage*" (*MFS*, VIII, 410-415), offers an inviting end to the debate over the Christian imagery, maintaining that it is used not as key symbolism but as an ironic contrast with imagery recognizing a pagan, satanic god of war. The struggle to classify his masterpiece is carried on by Marvin Klotz's insistence, "Romance or Realism?: Plot, Theme and Character in *The Red Badge of Courage*" (*CLAJ*, VI [1962], 98-106), that it belongs to realism, that most critics ignore Henry Fleming's commonplace, typical quality; on the other hand, arguing from figurative passages, William Joseph Free's "Smoke Imagery in *The Red Badge of Courage*" (*CLAJ*, VII, 148-152) stakes it out for naturalism because it denies that courage can be a "moral quality." In loose agreement with both, William B. Dillingham, "Insensibility in *The Red Badge of Courage*" (*CE*, XXV, 194-198), decides that too much individuality has been ascribed to Fleming, who bears out the naturalists by betraying that only the "insensible" can be brave; however, Dillingham goes too far toward having Crane deny the beauties of courage.

His poetry, its value taken for granted since Daniel G. Hoffman's fine study, is elevated further by Harland S. Nelson, "Stephen Crane's Achievement as a Poet" (*TSLL*, IV, 564-582). Partly differing with Hoffman, he submits that the best poems, the parables about "human nature," stem from a Methodist sense of the corrupt and overweening sinner and that irony rather than symbolism is their forte. Max Westbrook's "Stephen Crane's Poetry: Perspective and Arrogance" (*BuR*, XI, iv, 24-34), which integrates his two major genres, pieces out a pair of opposing masks, with Crane naturally approving that of kindness, willingness to learn from actuality, and humility to be content with what slender lessons can be wrung from it. He did try the third major genre, as Robert W. Stallman, "Stephen Crane as Dramatist," reminds us before the first printing of a two-act play written about 1899 (*BNYPL*, LXVII, 495-511). Set in Cuba, it is a posturing melodrama, a companion piece to our Rough-Rider novelists.

Though sorely fallible and distracted by hackwork before his early death, Crane is standing up very well under the critical microscope. When his best work is compared with that of Irving and Cooper, our literature can be said to have come a long way. So can, more recently, the scholarship devoted to it; a core of hard-won, sophisticated consensus about Cooper or Howells or Crane is close. Nor has the publication explosion showered us with trivia. Some of the younger scholars and critics are bagging big answers as they approach the nineteenth century with a respect that their generation mostly saved five or ten years ago for the contemporary masters. A heartening number of these critics are eager to learn from historical scholarship. Conversely, the literary historians are now seldom satisfied to dredge up a fact without judging its size or its use for criticism. Much remains to be done, Americans always say. But the year's scholarship in nineteenth-century fiction is a good vintage by any standard.

11. Nineteenth-Century Poetry

J. Albert Robbins

i. Edgar Allan Poe

a. **Bibliography.** Two brief articles add to the printing history of "The Raven." A new early printing of "The Raven" has been found by G. Thomas Tanselle ("An Unknown Early Appearance of 'The Raven,'" *SB*, XVI, 220-223) in the February 8, 1845, issue of the New York *Weekly News*. Tanselle includes a convenient list of the several early printings of the poem. He also adds information about the first appearance of the poem in a book, known for some time to have been in the second edition of George Vandenhoff's *A Plain System of Elocution*. Discovery of a mid-April review of this 1845 volume makes more certain the place of this printing in the publication history of the poem, ten weeks after its first appearance, seven and a half months before Poe collected it in *The Raven and Other Poems* ("Poe and Vandenhoff Once More," *AN&Q*, I, 101-102).

b. **Texts.** Earl N. Harbert ("A New Poe Letter," *AL*, XXXV, 80-81) gives the text of a letter written from Richmond, September 18, 1849, affirming Poe's intention of calling upon the poetess, Mrs. St. Leon Loud, an engagement he did not live to fulfil. The letter is not in Ostrom's checklist. John C. Miller provides an accurate text of a Poe letter hitherto printed in garbled form, a letter written to Thomas Mackenzie, April 22, 1843, seeking information about sale terms for the *Southern Literary Messenger* ("A Poe Letter Re-Presented," *AL*, XXXV, 359-361). This letter also is not in Ostrom. From a manuscript fragment in Sarah Helen Whitman's hand, J. A. Robbins adds a small passage to the conjectural text of a letter of November 14, 1848—Ostrom 285 ("An Addition to Poe's 'Steamboat Letter,'" *N&Q*, X, 20-21).

c. **Biography.** The familiar Edward Wagenknecht and a younger scholar, Sidney P. Moss, have written useful studies of Poe's temperament and career. As to the former, perhaps the chief virtue of Professor Wagenknecht's *Edgar Allan Poe: The Man Behind the Legend* (New York, Oxford Univ. Press) is the sensible and reasonable view of a complex topic—Poe's mind, personality, temperament, and character. Eschewing the "poor Poe" school of sentimental sympathizers and the "nasty Poe" school of psychoanalysts, Wagenknecht takes a sympathetic, yet very honest, look at Poe. The novice can gain a good insight into Poe in this volume, and in the liberal documentation come upon much of the useful research; and the more knowledgeable, though they will find much that is familiar, will consider this a handy refresher course and will surely applaud the author's facing facts. Without unduly reiterating the contradictoriness in Poe, Wagenknecht rightly records unpleasant truths: Poe could be both ridiculous and stupid in his remarks on Longfellow's *The Waif*; though so astute about Hawthorne's fiction, there are such lapses of taste as his preferring "Little Annie's Ramble" to "Young Goodman Brown"; and this "omniscient" critic could and did commit literary sins for which he castigated others. The topical rather than chronological organization will appeal to many, for, after a quick look at biography, we are conducted on a tour of relevant topics: Poe's temperament, self-opinion, truthfulness, erudition, knowledge of literatures past and present, literary theory and practice, method of composition, critical judgments, relations with women, and religious convictions. The book is able and useful.

Given the topic of Moss's *Poe's Literary Battles: The Critic in the Context of His Literary Milieu* (Durham, N.C., Duke Univ. Press), one will at once wish to know how this study differs from Perry Miller's *The Raven and the Whale* (1956). Miller dealt with a whole literary era and treated both Poe and Melville; Moss, confining himself to Poe, sets out exhaustively to examine the primary evidence of the chief engagements in which Poe earned his literary Purple Hearts: his assault upon the New York coterie in *Southern Literary Messenger* days; his carrying the offensive to the enemy on their own territory, particularly his encounters with Willis Gaylord Clark; his flank attacks upon Longfellow; his Boston Lyceum "hoax," nothing to recall with pride; his nightmarish involvement with Mesdames Osgood and Ellet; and his clash with Thomas Dunn English. Moss has dug into the scattered archival records and he quotes liberally, so liberally that the book becomes a resource for scholars rather than a synthesis of the issues—which is what Miller accomplished so well in his broader, undocumented study. Moss is so transfixed by the masses of material, and so reluctant to speculate on the nature of Poe's complex temperament, that this Poe seems a shadowy protagonist caught in a preternaturally hostile world. One wishes that the author would note, other than in summation, that Poe asked for many of the blows that he received, however noble his original aims.

Collaterally but not directly pertinent is the biography of Rosalie Poe. John C. Miller has summarized the unhappy life of "Poe's Sister Rosalie" (*TSL*, VIII, 107-117).

There are two other volumes on Poe, but one, a fictionized biography, complete with imaginary dialogue (Irwin Porges, *Edgar Allan Poe*, Philadelphia, Chilton) contributes nothing; and the sensation peddling of G. M. Tracy's *Les Amours extraordinaires d'Edgar Poe* (Paris, La Palatine) is sheer journalism.

d. **Criticism.** The broadest critical assessment of Poe is Floyd Stovall's "The Conscious Art of Edgar Allan Poe" (*CE*, XXIV, 417-421). Stovall classifies the critics and students of Poe into six categories, ranging from those who genuinely like Poe to those who, admittedly or not, dislike him; from those who, lacking the man himself, place the works on the analyst's couch, to those who, like Stovall, feel that we should consider the poems and tales as "the product of conscious effort by a healthy and alert intelligence." In brief, no-nonsense analyses of selected poems and tales Stovall indicates central meaning and variety of method to show how one may give Poe a sensible and forthright reading and so escape the obfuscation and irrelevance of much fashionable but *outré* criticism.

Edward Stone ("Poe in and out of His Time," *ESQ*, No. 31, pp. 14-17) proposes that Poe had to wait a century to be heard clearly and truly. Poe is less of his century than of ours, which has as its hero "normal man, gazing out at the world and finding in what he sees food only for cynicism and despair."

"Ulalume" is considered by Eric W. Carlson and Thomas E. Connolly. The former, in "Symbol and Sense in Poe's 'Ulalume'" (*AL*, XXXV, 22-37), after a long look at previous scholarship, argues convincingly that the protagonist-narrator is reliving a subconscious experience; that the form is basically dramatic; and that the symbolism and impressionistic use of word sounds operate perfectly (not fatally, as Brooks and Warren contend) to convey a psychological meaning ("the protagonist is driven to despair in an effort to recapture his ideal integrity"). Connolly (*Expl*, XXII, Item 4) believes that the poem is more successful than James E. Miller, Jr., indicated in his *PQ* article (XXXIV, 1955, 197-205). There is throughout a careful control of images and sound patterns and in the climactic last stanza Ulalume is risen from the tomb and the narrator "now entombed in a loveless life with the haunting memory of Ulalume to stand guard between him and the invitation to a new love and to life."

As for "The Raven," J. Lasley Dameron ("Another 'Raven' for Edgar Allan Poe," *N&Q*, X, 21-22) calls attention to a poem of the same name in the May, 1838, *Bentley's Miscellany*, but I fail to see the "tonal resemblance" to Poe's poem that Dameron does. A very early criticism of the poem, written about 1850 by the English Shakespearean scholar and editor, is recorded by Francis F. Burch ("Clement Mansfield Ingleby on Poe's 'The Raven': An Unpublished British Criticism," *AL*, XXXV, 81-83), of interest now as being an early and disinterested verbal analysis of the poem.

Believing the subject poem one of Poe's best, Eric W. Stockton ("Celestial Inferno: Poe's 'The City in the Sea,'" *TSL*, VIII, 99-106) synthesizes previous criticism, examines structure, sound patterns, sources, revisions, and allegorical elements, and looks upon the poem as a fusion of Heaven and Hell, reminiscent of Poe's familiar life-in-death paradox.

James W. Gargano has written a very sound essay on "The Question of Poe's Narrators" (*CE*, XXV, 177-181). In a look at five of the better serious tales, he distinguishes the function of the narrator from the position of Poe as author. Many a critic has wrongly assumed that the narrator speaks for and reveals the author— W. H. Auden, for example, in belittling "The Cask of Amontillado." Montresor in no way is Poe's mouthpiece; instead, the story "is one of the supreme examples in fiction of a deluded rationalist who cannot glimpse the moral implications of his folly." Poe's sick narrators by no means reveal an auctorial sickness: indeed, the tight control of the author attests his sanity, clarity of mind, and aesthetic percipience. This article is eminently sane and, it seems to me, right in all its judgments.

The year's best criticism of a single piece of Poe's fiction is L. Moffitt Cecil's "The Two Narratives of Arthur Gordon Pym" (*TSLL*, V, 232-241). His hypothesis does much to explain what in *Pym* has troubled scholars for a long time—disunity and unevenness in a work by a writer uniquely devoted to unity and singleness of effect. In part, the anomaly can be explained biographically, for the novel was written at a time when Poe's fortunes were low and when he was attempting to follow the advice of Paulding and of Harper's to produce a long work. Whatever the cause, the internal evidence, Cecil believes, shows that Poe began with one narrative—that of a Nantucket youth romantically drawn to the sea with "visions of shipwreck . . . famine . . . captivity" taking place "upon some grey and desolate rock"—and in the last third of the book shifted to an altogether different story of polar exploration, a narrative which is "both independent and artistically complete" and reminiscent of "MS. Found in a Bottle." Quite aware of the resultant disunity, Poe tried to explain it away in the elaborate pretense of dual authorship in the introductory and terminal notes.

"Usher" continues to invite critical impulsiveness. In one essay ("The Vampire Motif in 'The Fall of the House of Usher,'" CE, XXIV, 450-453) Lyle H. Kendall, Jr., sees evidence aplenty that vampirism is the hereditary Usher curse, culminating in Madeline's vampire assault on Roderick at the end. John S. Hill would quite disagree ("The Dual Hallucination in 'The Fall of the House of Usher,'" SWR, XLVIII, 396-402). If Madeline was not dead upon interment, she soon was by virtue of the airtight coffin and copper-lined vault—and no one, much less the weak, wraithlike Madeline, could possibly have escaped that stronghold. Thus what Roderick and his friend saw was a specter of their demented minds. Finally, in his brief "A Tour of the House of Usher" (ESQ, No. 31, pp. 18-20), James Hafley gives no thorough guided tour but a series of thought-provoking, hit-and-run suggestions about meaning and method. More is suggested than demonstrated.

More convincing are an essay on "Ligeia" and another on "The Assignation." Muriel West (Expl, XXII, Item 15) considers the first an allegory in which Ligeia represents "the poetic, harmonious, natural truths that characterize the intuitive wisdom of the ancients" and represents also Poe's poetic muse; conversely Rowena stands for the "Gothic grotesquerie in which he found himself involved" unwillingly. And, she suggests, perhaps the reincarnation of Ligeia dramatizes the transformation of the disliked Gothic tales into "a prose poem—a work of the loftiest imagination." Viewing the other tale, Richard P. Benton answers his question in the affirmative ("Is

Poe's 'The Assignation' a Hoax?" *NCF*, XVIII, 193-197), arguing convincingly that Poe set out to hoax Byron-worshipers by a parody of the Byron–Countess Guiccioli affair and by mocking Byron's friend and confidant, Thomas Moore, through the narrator of his tale. The identified situational and verbal echoes attest the comic purpose of the story.

The German scholar Franz H. Link, in "Edgar Allan Poes 'Ligeia' und das Paradoxon der modernen Dichtung" (*DVLG*, XXXVII, 363-376), merely uses "Ligeia" as a referent for a general summary, largely derivative, of Poe's aesthetic principles—such matters as Poe's private imaginary world; his interest in the ontological status of that world; and the essentiality of beauty, perceptible only to the artist. His world of imagination is separate from and hostile to the real, everyday world, yet paradoxically this timeless imaginary world of the artist can be perceived only in a real world of time. There is little here that goes beyond previous criticism on Poe.

For all his display of vinous erudition, Poe really had an amateur's knowledge of wines and liquors, William Bittner argues in "Poe and the 'Invisible Demon'" (*GaR*, XVII, 134-138). When he says that Luchresi "cannot distinguish Sherry from Amontillado," Poe records his ignorance of the fact that Amontillado is a variety of sherry. The preference of the hero of "Bon-Bon" for Sauterne, rather than Medoc, is absurd, for one is white and the other red—for a connoisseur rather like preferring candy to steak. Obviously Poe was not knowledgeable about wines from experience, nor did he go to the literature on the subject to acquire the expertise he pretended.

In a series of interesting remarks upon "Poe's *Eureka* and Emerson's *Nature*" (*ESQ*, No. 31, pp. 4-7), Patrick F. Quinn notes many parallels (similar assumptions, observations, grandiose affirmations, reliance upon intuition; relation of man to deity, earth to cosmos; search for an ultimate unity) but also distinct differences (an attempt at logical demonstration and completeness not found in Emerson; a fascination with destruction and death in Poe, but an emphasis upon vitality and life in Emerson).

Many of Poe's ideas on reviewing could have come, J. Lasley Dameron says ("Poe and *Blackwood's* on the Art of Reviewing," *ESQ*, No. 31, pp. 29-30), from an essay by William Stevenson in the November, 1824, issue of the magazine.

ii. Longfellow, Lowell, Holmes

It is hard to say why a scholar and critic so esteemed as the late
Newton Arvin would choose Longfellow to follow his excellent
trilogy on Hawthorne, Whitman, and Melville. He has also elected
to write a "complete" critical biography (*Longfellow: His Life and
Work*, Boston, Little, Brown) with the consequence that one must
join Mr. Arvin in looking at a good deal of insignificant poetry. Of
necessity he is forced into qualification and apology, into the use
of pale words ("engaging," "charm," "tenderness," "graceful," "fra-
grance") or of damning ones ("jejune," "ingenuous," "perfunctory,"
"inept"). To defend a misunderstood Longfellow, and yet to be
critically honest, he must balance deficiencies (as on page 121:
"frankly subjective," "commonplaces of romantic aesthetics," "taste
often sadly astray") with saving graces ("At his best, however, he
wrote sensitively, warmly, and imaginatively").

Perhaps one should read the Epilogue first, for here the rationale
emerges. Critics have gone too far, he believes, and have narrowed
the roster of beatified authors too greatly; yet even here the apologetic tone is inescapable: "Unless we are to throw into the discard
all writers who do not satisfy our post-metaphysical and post-
symbolic needs, we shall wish to preserve many of these poets in
our memory, and keep them available for states of feeling that
respond to their styles."

There are perceptive judgments on individual poems and the
scholar will always need to consult Arvin's *Longfellow*. Most will
not agree that *Hiawatha* and *Tales of a Wayside Inn* are quite as
good as Arvin believes, but will find many a shorter work lucidly
discussed.

In his review article ("The Poetry of Longfellow," *HudR*, XVI,
297-304), Marius Bewley assesses the book and the poet without
judicial mercy. For him Longfellow "never discovered a unique
quality," as did Bryant, and never found moral vitality, as did Whittier. His poetic dulness is unmatched until we reach Edwin Arlington Robinson. With telling statistics, he reminds us that Arvin
requires two more pages for *Hiawatha* than for *The Scarlet Letter*
and twice the space for *Evangeline* as for *Billy Budd*. It is, for
Bewley, necessarily "a downhearted book."

The long-vexed question of Longfellow's use of sources and the
charges of plagiarism are treated definitively in Ernest J. Moyne's

Hiawatha *and* Kalevala: *A Study of the Relationship between Long-fellow's "Indian Edda" and the Finnish Epic* (Helsinki, FCC, No. 192). Moyne presents the evidence with clarity and thoroughness, and renders his decision without qualification: the accusers generally were uninformed and critically trigger-happy; Longfellow was as indebted to authentic Indian sources as to *Kalevala*; and, inasmuch as there was no servile imitation, the charges of plagiarism are "utter nonsense."

To document Longfellow's early renown with more than mere sales figures, Loring E. Hart ("The Beginnings of Longfellow's Fame," *NEQ*, XXXVI, 63-76) samples the review-criticism from the beginning (a laudatory 1825 review by Bryant of poems identified only with the then-unknown initials H. W. L.) through the first volume of collected verse, *Voices of the Night* (1836). The early opinion was largely approving and often enthusiastic, though a quartet of sceptics (Poe, John Neal, J. T. Buckingham, and Park Benjamin) provided sour notes.

Others have argued the influence of David Hartley's psychology of the association of ideas upon Bryant, as transmitted by Archibald Alison's *Essays on the Nature and Principles of Taste* (1790). Now Marston LaFrance ("Longfellow and Archibald Alison," *CLQ*, Ser. VI, pp. 205-208) attempts by inferential evidence, and not with clear success, to show how Longfellow may have been so influenced and how this *"probably* helped Longfellow realize that man, not external nature," was most worthy of attention in poetry.

The philosophical influence of *Wilhelm Meister* on *Hyperion* is generally known, but Martin L. Kornbluth ("Longfellow's *Hyperion* and Goethe's *Wilhelm Meisters Lehrjahre*," *ESQ*, No. 31, pp. 55-59) explores the artistic similarities—structure, narrative incident, characterization, relationships between characters, irrelevancies, and over-all theme and intent. The similarities are so extensive that "*Hyperion* may be considered Longfellow's version of *Wilhelm Meister*, lacking only (or perhaps masking only) the so-called immoralities of its German prototype."

Twenty-seven unpublished poems by Lowell, written between 1841 and 1891, have been collected by Martin B. Duberman (*AL*, XXXV, 322-351), virtually all of them occasional poems or personal poems written in letters and albums. They range from little rhymes on cheese and on gargling with claret to a long and rather ambitious poem, "The New Persephone." "James Russell Lowell's Study of the

Classics before Entering Harvard" (George P. Clark, *JA*, VIII, 205-209), though difficult to assess because of the fragmentary evidence, was solid and thorough in both Greek and Latin and comparable to the best preparatory training of that time.

"Lowell's 'The Washers of the Shroud' and the Celtic Legend of the Washer of the Ford" (John Q. Anderson, *AL*, XXXV, 361-363) summarizes this despairing Civil War poem and comments on how Lowell enhanced his poem by a Breton legend in which a prophetic war goddess warns the hero of approaching defeat. By this joining of mythology and contemporary issues Lowell expresses his fear that the Union, though young, may be about to die. An unpublished essay by Lowell, "virtually the last of his literary excursions into contemporary politics" and a bitter attack on Andrew Johnson is presented with brief comments by LeRoy P. Graf and Ralph W. Haskins ("'This Clangor of Belated Mourning': James Russell Lowell on Andrew Johnson's Father," *SAQ*, LXII, 423-434).

Oliver Wendell Holmes' varying and often perceptive views on the creative process (he rejected the theory of automatism but realized that past reading and experience can function subconsciously to produce new art) are detailed in "The Underground Workshop of Oliver Wendell Holmes," by Karl P. Wentersdorf (*AL*, XXXV, 1-12).

iii. Emily Dickinson

A convenient sampling of critical judgments is supplied by Richard B. Sewall's *Emily Dickinson: A Collection of Critical Essays* (Englewood Cliffs, N.J., Prentice-Hall), which begins with Conrad Aiken, 1924, and ends with David Higgins on her prose (this from an unpublished dissertation of 1961). The six "pre-Johnson" essays are pioneer pieces which show creative criticism in the process of identifying and specifying greatness. Then, with the indispensable variorum text of Johnson in 1955 (signaled here by a passage from Johnson's critical biography of that year) come three commemorative reviews by Blackmur, Ransom, and Austin Warren. Finally, Phase III, the critical consolidation, is represented by essays from James Reeves, Richard Wilbur, Louise Bogan, Charles R. Anderson, Archibald MacLeish, and Higgins. Altogether there are general assessments, explorations of central themes, studies of prosody and language, explications, and appreciations. What is clear is that much is yet to be done before we feel that we fully know this remarkable poet, but here is the foreground of understanding, much of it brilliant. One can hardly quarrel with Sewall's choices in a volume of this size beyond questioning the absence of Richard Chase and Theodora Ward.

Beyond this volume, the scholarship is quite miscellaneous. In the more general short studies, there are treatments of the white-robe image, structural patterns, and the use of dashes. In "Emily Dickinson's White Robes" (*Criticism*, V, 135-147), J. S. Wheatcroft explains the orthodox, New Testament origin of the image and probes into her varied use of it to express her heritage and sensibility, and particularly to convey her ideas and feelings on love and death. Citing many of these allusions, Wheatcroft attempts to show how basic the image and metaphor is, expressing for Dickinson both religious tradition and personal feeling. Drawing upon an examination of poetic structure in her doctoral dissertation, Suzanne M. Wilson ("Structural Patterns in the Poetry of Emily Dickinson," *AL*, XXXV, 53-59) finds that one major pattern predominates, with several variations—the three-part sermon organization (statement, elaboration, conclusion). The increasing sophistication of the pattern, here illustrated by examples, "very strongly suggests conscious artistry." The broad conclusions proposed are difficult to demonstrate amply in so short an article as this. Many a scholar and critic has dealt tentatively with Dickinson's strange punctuation, including Charles R. Anderson, who, in his 1960 book, said that "It is impossible to say positively whether [the varied dashes] are accidental or deliberate, and if the latter, what they mean" (p. 307). Edith Perry Stamm proposes an answer in "Emily Dickinson: Poetry and Punctuation" (*SatR*, XLVI, March 30, pp. 26-27, 74). Several textbooks of rhetoric and elocution of the poet's time used a system of symbols to indicate rising or falling inflection of the voice in oral reading, and one of these (Noah Porter's *Rhetorical Reader*, 1837) was used at Amherst Academy when Dickinson was a student there. Such marks, then, were "meant to direct the reading of her verse." In a letter to the editor (April 27, p. 25) Theodora Ward disagreed, observing that such notations increased markedly in both poems and letters in the years of greatest personal stress and emotional tension, and stating that the frequent use of dashes in letters clearly could not have been intended to indicate oral stress. In a rebuttal (May 25, p. 23) Miss Stamm countered weakly and inconclusively.

A German scholar, Teut Andreas Riese of Heidelberg, has, as a European, fresh and meaningful things to say about Dickinson in "Emily Dickinson und der Sprachgeist amerikanischer Lyrik" (NS, XII, 145-159). Like Whitman, Melville, and more recently Wallace Stevens, Dickinson, he believes, has a view of language completely different from the European. The unique tradition of this country encourages a differing view of reality and hence of language. The American artist has a need, and even a delight, in defining and creating a new reality for himself, in transcending orthodox reality—even, on occasion, in demonstrating the unreality of the real. The American *Sprachgeist*—the spirit of the language—involves a renouncing of traditional norms of poetic language. Thus, with Dickinson, there is a boldness, abrupt changes from one sphere of meaning to another, juxtaposition of irreconcilables, a seeming nonchalance with vital issues, an intent and ever alert disciplining of consciousness and will, an employment of language often as hieroglyph which deliberately, and perhaps necessarily, escapes exactness. For all her uniqueness, Dickinson resembles other great American writers in this quite national and un-European concept of the function and uses of language.

Jack Lee Capps has written a dissertation on "Emily Dickinson's Reading, 1836-1886: A Study of the Sources of her Poetry" (DA, XXIV, 1611-12) based on references in letters, poems, Mount Holyoke textbooks, Houghton Library materials. In an appendix there is an annotated index to her reading.

The several explicatory articles and notes are generally unimpressive, but we might take note of William Rossky (Expl, XXII, Item 3) who differs with Anderson's reading of "A Clock Stopped" in Emily Dickinson's Poetry (1960). The poem, he believes, is not static and does not indicate conventional views of immortality, but shows steady emotional development and closes on a note of the awful mystery of the complete impenetrability of death. Beyond this the year's scholarship runs to theorizing or speculation, often on single lines or words. A. Scott Garrow ("A Note on Manzanilla," AL, XXXV, 366) takes a close look at the place name in the last line of "I taste a liquor never brewed" and decides that Johnson is wrong in thinking she meant Manzanillo, the Cuban city known for exporting rum. Dickinson indeed meant Manzanilla, a city in Spain known for a sherry of that name. Ergo, change your thinking from rum to sherry.

iv. Higginson, Whittier, Aldrich, Miller

From Higginson's point of view it is rather sad that this prolific, popular, and long-lived author has little significance to us beyond his friendship with Emily Dickinson, but the fact is recognized in the title of a new biography by Anna Mary Wells, *Dear Preceptor: The Life and Times of Thomas Wentworth Higginson* (Boston, Houghton Mifflin). To Dickinson he was alternately Preceptor and Master. Miss Wells goes beyond this title reference to say unequivocally at the beginning of one chapter, "The preservation of Emily Dickinson's poems for posterity was incomparably the most important literary work of Higginson's life."

In regard to this part of the biography, Miss Wells is sure that Dickinson's biographers have undervalued and misjudged Higginson's role. Miss Dickinson, recall, did approach Higginson and for her this move must have been long and carefully pondered. His response to her appeal and his recognition of her genius was immediate and, if ill-equipped actually to guide her art, he certainly provided what Dickinson sought, gentlemanly and paternal understanding and professional reassurance. Where others, in ignorance and temerity, laid their heavy editorial paws on her fragile poetry, Higginson apparently did not. Contrary to what many believe, he did try to persuade her to publish. It was to him, in her letters, that she opened her heart and hopes. Her faith and need for his assurance continued to her death. By some strange but proper justice on the part of the family, Higginson had a part in her funeral service. His posthumous testimony about her is vital and his quiet offices as junior editorial partner to Mrs. Todd (and Mrs. Todd was running the operation) surely made the early volumes of poetry better than they otherwise would have been. Miss Dickinson needed Mr. Higginson and she had no cause to regret her choice of preceptor.

This is no place to describe the other areas of this author's life and career, but they are not without interest or significance, though that significance must inevitably be a reflection of the important age in which he lived. As Henry James observed, he had "the interesting quality of having reflected almost everything that was in the New England air, of vibrating with it all round." As Miss Wells notes, we treasure nineteenth-century writers who differed with

their age—and clearly Higginson was of it. Both kinds help us to
know that age with completeness.

Five letters by Whittier and two by Rose Terry Cooke (Jean
Downey, "Whittier and Cooke: Unpublished Letters," *QH*, LII,
33-36), written between 1858 and 1892, the year when both died,
document a tender literary friendship and a mutual respect for
each other's work.

Aldrich wrote an effective and suspenseful detective story at a
time when the genre was still evolving; but into it he interjected
twelve chapters on capital-labor problems, apparently because he
favored the small-town capitalist over labor organizers and unions
(Donald Tanasoca, "*Stillwater Tragedy*: A Socio-Detective Novel,"
AN&Q, I, 148-150).

Norman Talbot traces "Joaquin Miller's Reception in English
Periodicals" (*REL*, IV, iv, 63-79). There was general and swift
critical applause after Miller printed a few of his *Pacific Poems*;
and his new English admirers, led by W. M. Rossetti, took him from
grubby lodgings and led him through fashionable drawing and
dining rooms, a celebrity. Talbot samples the criticism between 1871
and 1886, universally admiring in the first flush of discovery, then
increasingly disenchanted as the novelty of picturesqueness and
poetic roughness dissipated.

v. General

It is unfortunate that the one general study of nineteenth-century
poetry to appear during the year should dwell upon the most
poetically arid segment of the century and do it so unproductively.
In *The Poet and the Gilded Age: Social Themes in Late 19th Century American Verse* (Philadelphia, Univ. of Pennsylvania Press),
Robert H. Walker has examined 5,883 volumes of largely dreary,
shabby, and worthless verse; explored it topically; and capped it all
with a statistical summation ("an experiment in quantification"),
which, he hopes, will lead to new co-operation between literary
scholar and social scientist. If you are curious about what versifiers
had to say about city life, Mr. Walker can tell you that 19.0 per cent
are tributes to urban achievement, 13.6 per cent contrasts of rural
virtues and urban vices, 22.8 per cent reactions to the unpleasant
side of city life, etc. up to a full 100.0 per cent. Should you wish
to know how the "poets" reacted to economic conditions (material

progress, inventions, exploitation of the poor, housing, child labor, etc.), Mr. Walker has the answers and the observation that "diet, perhaps oddly, received little attention unless it reached the starvation level." The waste of scholarly ability and energy on such subliterary materials is depressing.

Ben Harris McClary poses a question he cannot answer, if answerable it is. In "Melville, Twain, and the Legendary 'Tennessee Poet'" (*TFSB*, XXIX, 63-64) he notes Melville's reference to "the poor poet of Tennessee" in the sixth paragraph of *Moby-Dick* and the longer reference to such a poet, along with mention of the name Edward J. Billings, in the latter half of *Extract from Captain Stormfield's Visit to Heaven*. Whether there is any basis in fact for this shadowy poet McClary is unable to say.

12. Fiction: 1900-1930

C. Hugh Holman

Most of the writers of fiction in America between 1900 and the early thirties are either realists or naturalists. Since neither of these kinds of fiction is critically fashionable today and these writers are not yet far enough removed in time to call forth extensive historical study, the quantity and quality of work done on them—when Henry James, Fitzgerald, Faulkner, and Hemingway are treated separately—is distressingly low, even when such late and popular borderline cases as Thomas Wolfe and John Steinbeck are included.

Perhaps the most important single work published in 1963 for students of the fiction of the period is George J. Becker's *Documents of Modern Literary Realism* (Princeton, Princeton Univ. Press), a collection of critical judgments, theories, and manifestoes from Europe, England, and America, with an illuminating introduction by Becker on "Realism as a Literary Movement," which is marred to some extent by Becker's failure to distinguish between realism and naturalism. Only Dreiser from the American novelists of this period is represented, although some important critical essays on naturalism by Americans are reprinted, notably those by Philip Rahv and Malcolm Cowley. The volume is rich with documents on the intellectual and cultural implications of realism.

i. General Studies

Several general studies deal in part with the fiction of this period. D. E. S. Maxwell's *American Fiction: The Intellectual Background* (New York, Columbia Univ. Press), although it gives most of its attention to the nineteenth century, in Chapter VI, "Edith Wharton and the Realists," deals with Mrs. Wharton as a successful portrayer of the mercantile and banking society of old New York, and gives only brief treatment to other realists, principally Sinclair Lewis and Fitzgerald. John Bradbury's *Renaissance in the South: A Critical History of the Literature, 1920-1960* (Chapel Hill, Univ. of North

Carolina Press) is a useful record of extensive writing activities, and it describes the work of a wide variety of writers, such as Julia Peterkin and the early Southern social protest novelists, as well as better-known figures like Thomas Wolfe. Few books have made intelligent remarks about a greater number of writers in as brief a space. That its critical acumen does not equal its inclusiveness was inevitable.

The work which treats the fiction of this period most completely is H. Wayne Morgan's *Writers in Transition: Seven Americans* (New York, Hill and Wang), which examines, "as spokesmen of cultural transition and as representatives of many of the changes that have accompanied the twentieth century in America," Stephen Crane, Edith Wharton, Ellen Glasgow, Willa Cather, Sherwood Anderson, Hart Crane, and Thomas Wolfe. With disarming modesty, Mr. Morgan calls his essays "old-fashioned . . . appreciations." However, these essays, which summarize their subjects' literary careers as "artistic attempts to meet the challenges of a changing world order," are good introductory treatments. Mr. Morgan is best when he is dealing with Edith Wharton as a novelist of manners and with Ellen Glasgow's efforts to define the qualities of endurance. What he has to say of Willa Cather's artistic quest and of Sherwood Anderson's search for unity is interesting though of lesser value. Only in his essay on Wolfe does he appear to be retracing well-known ground.

Although Chester E. Eisinger's *Fiction of the Forties* (Chicago, Univ. of Chicago Press) deals with writers doing their best work in a later time, it has some interesting things to say about John Dos Passos, whom it treats in some detail as a radical naturalist, and about James T. Farrell, Sinclair Lewis, Willa Cather, and John P. Marquand. Mr. Eisinger's intention seems to be the examination of novelists as a portion of the history of ideas; hence his work, although historically useful, is largely uncritical in its approach. Anthony C. Hilfer, in a 1963 University of North Carolina dissertation, "The Revolt from the Village in American Literature," studied the social criticism in the work of Willa Cather, Sinclair Lewis, Thomas Wolfe, T. S. Stribling, and Zona Gale.

Frederick J. Hoffman, in "Dogmatic Innocence: Self-Assertion in Modern American Literature" (*TQ*, VI, Summer, 152-161), argued that twentieth-century American writing has suffered from the "blight of naturalism," that writers in the 1920's were free to

improvise artistically, a freedom which in the thirties gave way to
social pressures. These pressures were examined by L. Barnes in
Marxist terms in "The Proletarian Novel" (*Mainstream*, XVI, July,
51-57) which greeted a "reviving interest" in politically radical fiction with a brief sketch moving from Jack London to Howard Fast
and Richard Wright.

ii. New Editions

One of the most significant projects of the year was the republication
of fiction written in the early decades of the century and long out
of print. In a new series, Chicago in Fiction, under the general
editorship of Saul Bellow, three volumes were published by the
University of Chicago Press. George Ade's short novels, *Artie* (1896)
and *Pink Marsh* (1897), appeared in a volume with an informative
introduction by James T. Farrell. Frank Harris's early proletariat
novel about the Haymarket anarchists, *The Bomb* (1909), has a
biographical introduction by John Dos Passos. Ben Hecht's novel
Erik Dorn (1921) has an introduction by Nelson Algren that over-
praises both Hecht and his novel. Two other reprints of the "Chicago
school" of writers appeared outside the Chicago in Fiction series.
George Ade's *Chicago Stories*, a selection of fifty-six of Ade's "Stories
of the Streets and the Town" sketches in the Chicago *Record*, 1893-
1900, with an introduction by Franklin J. Meine, originally published in 1941 in a limited edition, was sumptuously reprinted
(Chicago, Henry Regnery & Co.). Robert Herrick's *The Memoirs
of an American Citizen* (1905), his best work, was reprinted in The
John Harvard Library with an excellent and highly informative
introduction by David Aaron (Cambridge, Mass., Harvard Univ.
Press). Another Midwestern writer was reintroduced to the reading
public in *The Ring Lardner Reader* (New York, Charles Scribner's
Sons), with a warmly appreciative introduction by Maxwell Geismar. The publication of the motion picture script of *Storm in the
West*, by Sinclair Lewis and Dore Schary (New York, Stein and
Day), a satiric allegory of World War II as a Western movie (never
produced), adds to the corpus of Lewis' published work without
adding any luster to it.

Riding John Steinbeck's new popularity as a Nobel prize winner,
his *Short Novels*, edited with an informative and thoughtful intro-

duction by Joseph Henry Jackson, was issued in a new edition (New York, Viking Press)—it had originally appeared in 1953.

The Collected Stories of Ellen Glasgow, ed. Richard K. Meeker (Baton Rouge, Louisiana State Univ. Press), assembles all Miss Glasgow's short fiction—twelve from *The Shadowy Third and Other Stories* (1923), four uncollected stories from magazines, and one from manuscript. The introduction sketches Miss Glasgow's career as a short story writer—it was neither extensive nor distinguished, contrary to Mr. Meeker's beliefs—and the notes on individual stories are meticulous. The volume makes available to scholars a minor but largely unavailable aspect of an important novelist's work.

iii. Studies of Authors

No book-length study of the novelists of this period appeared in 1963 which approached in importance Richard S. Kennedy's *The Window of Memory: The Literary Career of Thomas Wolfe* (Chapel Hill, Univ. of North Carolina Press, 1962) or Mark Schorer's *Sinclair Lewis: An American Life* (New York, McGraw-Hill, 1961). Ten short volumes dealing with individual authors were published, but seven of them were in series of short introductions: four from the very uneven Twayne United States Authors Series, one from Barnes and Noble's relatively small American Authors and Critics Series, and two were in the University of Minnesota Pamphlets on American Writers series of brief but distinctive critical introductions. A relatively small number of articles on the fiction writers of the first three decades were published during the year, and the bulk of them were biographical or personal reminiscences. The writers that elicited the most critical attention were the naturalists in whose works critics demonstrated a greater interest in imagery, mythic patterns, and artistry than they showed in the works of other writers of the period.

In addition to the attention which D. E. S. Maxwell and H. Wayne Morgan gave Edith Wharton (see above), Patricia R. Plante studied the critical reception of her short fiction in "Edith Wharton as a Short Story Writer" (*MQ*, IV, 363-379), a portion of her very useful 1962 Boston University dissertation on "The Critical Reception of Edith Wharton's Fiction in America and England with an Annotated Enumerative Bibliography of Wharton Criticism from 1900 to 1961." Diana Trilling refurbished a 1947 *Harper's Bazaar*

article, "*The House of Mirth* Revisited" (*ASch*, XXXII, 113-128).
James Tuttleton, in a doctoral dissertation at the University of
North Carolina, examined "Edith Wharton as a Novelist of Manners."

Ellen Glasgow, in addition to the publication of her *Collected
Stories* and her examination in Morgan's *Writers in Transition*, supplied in one of her novels an illustration of method for textual
bibliography by Oliver L. Steele ("Evidence of Plate Damage as
Applied to the First Editions of Ellen Glasgow's *The Wheel of Life*
[1906]," *SB*, XVI, 223-231). Robert Hudspeth, in "Point of View
in Ellen Glasgow's *The Sheltered Life*" (*Thoth*, IV, 83-87), found
in the contrasting points of view (maturity *vs.* youthful passion) a
statement of the novel's theme. Douglas Day published, in "Ellen
Glasgow's Letters to the Saxtons" (*AL*, XXXV, 230-236), primary
material not included in Blair Rouse's *Letters of Ellen Glasgow*.

Stanley Cooperman, in "Willa Cather and the Bright Face of
Death" (*L&P*, XIII, 81-87), interpreted *One of Ours* as "a case
history of phallic substitution: the unmarried hero for whom death
is the only possible aphrodisiac"—a reading which Miss Cather
would have liked only a little less than that of John J. Murphy
(*"Shadows on the Rock*: Cather's Medieval Refuge," *Ren.*, XV, 76-
88), who saw her retreating from the present in order to "forget
the breakdown in her own country of the genteel tradition." Robert
E. Scholes, in "Hope and Memory in *My Antonia*" (*Shenandoah*,
XIV, Autumn, 1962, 24-29), saw that novel as "an elegy over the
dying myth of the heroic innocent, over the days that are no more."
Robert Gale, in two notes ("Cather's *Death Comes for the Arch-
bishop*," *Expl*, XXI, Item 75; and "Manuel Lujon, Another Name by
Willa Cather," *Names*, XI, 210-211) supplied new data on one of
her novels. However, H. Wayne Morgan's essay in *Writers in Transition* (see above) was the best single piece of work on a seriously
neglected writer.

Winston Churchill, by Warren I. Titus (New York, Twayne)
is a useful study of the historical and Muckraker novelist, and probably gives the student of twentieth-century literature as much biographical and bibliographical information as he needs. Mr. Titus
wisely recognizes that Churchill is important because he was popular rather than because he was good; yet he devotes much of his
short work to the summary and criticism of novels that no one any
longer reads.

Theodore Dreiser was the recipient of the most serious critical attention given any of this group of writers. William A. Freedman took "A Look at Dreiser as Artist: The Motif of Circularity in *Sister Carrie*" (*MFS*, VIII, 384-392) and found "a circular quest for happiness." Sheldon N. Grebstein, in "Dreiser's Victorian Vamp" (*MASJ*, IV, Spring, 3-12), saw *Sister Carrie* as a portrait of a Victorian "vamp" who commits sexual sins without penalty. Richard Lehan, in "Dreiser's *An American Tragedy*: A Critical Study" (*CE*, XXV, 189-193), examines Dreiser as an artist rather than as social critic, studying the novel in terms of setting, characters, scenes, symbols, irony, and style, and concluding convincingly that Dreiser has been unjustly downgraded because of his mechanistic philosophy. Ellen Moers, in "The Finesse of Dreiser" (*ASch*, XXXIII, 109-114), examined Dreiser's use of the language of the inarticulate, particularly in *Sister Carrie*, and found it "careful to the point of finesse." William L. Phillips studied "The Imagery of Dreiser's Novels" (*PMLA*, LXXVIII, 572-585) and gave a detailed and well-documented "close reading" of five novels. His article, however, tends to underestimate Dreiser's scientific imagery and to "overread" sensational "stock" images from popular sentimental fiction of Dreiser's day. William E. Wilson, in "The Titan and the Gentleman" (*AR*, XXIII, 25-34) contrasted Dreiser and Booth Tarkington.

Gertrude Stein is the subject of *What is Remembered* by Alice B. Toklas (New York, Holt, Rinehart, and Winston), a remarkably readable and informative book, which probably should be entitled *The Autobiography of Gertrude Stein*. The richness of its glimpses of writers and artists is enhanced by an excellent index. In a fine article by George T. Wright ("Gertrude Stein and Her Ethic of Self-Containment," *TSL*, VIII, 17-23), her career is divided into the period up to 1909, naturalistic; 1909-1932, highly abstract; and post-1932, coherent and personal. Only when she talks of herself is her "talent for sentence making" allowed to play over a recognizable world, Mr. Wright concludes.

Sherwood Anderson, in addition to his treatment by H. Wayne Morgan, was the subject of an issue of *RLM* (No. 78-80, pp. 1-158), made up of translations of earlier articles with the only new essay being Roger Asselineau's study of style in *Winesburg, Ohio* ("Langue et style de Sherwood Anderson dans *Winesburg, Ohio*"). G. Thomas Tanselle's "Realist or Dreamer: Letters of Sherwood Anderson and Floyd Dell" (*MLR*, LVIII, 532-537) presents two new Anderson letters. Epifanio San Juan argues cogently for Anderson's importance in "Vision and Reality: A Reconsideration of Sherwood Anderson's *Winesburg, Ohio*" (*AL*, XXXV, 137-155)—an important piece of Anderson criticism.

Ashley Brown, in "An Interview with Conrad Aiken" (*Shenandoah*, XV, Autumn, 19-40), presents Aiken's comments on his work, chiefly on his poetry and criticism but also illuminatingly on his fiction. James W. Tuttleton, in "Aiken's 'Mr. Arcularis': Psychic Regression and the Death Instinct" (*AI*, XX, 295-314), sees the story as a struggle between Eros and Thanatos, using the categories of the psychologist to explain "the exploration of the frontier of consciousness-unconsciousness" in the story.

Walton R. Patrick's *Ring Lardner* (New York, Twayne) is adequate biographically and excellent as a study of style, structure, and narrative technique in Lardner's short stories, although it tends to underestimate him as a humorist and satirist, so that Geismar's essay in *The Ring Lardner Reader* (see above) is a needed counterpoise. Both Patrick and Geismar are convincing reminders that in Ring Lardner we have a neglected important writer.

Sinclair Lewis was the subject of two books. Mark Schorer's *Sinclair Lewis*, in the University of Minnesota Pamphlets on American Writers series, is a brief, graceful summary of his gargantuan *Sinclair Lewis* (1961). Schorer has more sympathy for Lewis as a tragic figure than as a novelist and he tends to "damn with faint praise." *Dorothy and Red*, by Vincent Sheean (Boston, Houghton Mifflin) is a narrative interspersed with letters and diaries, telling the story of the marriage of Lewis and Dorothy Thompson. A fascinating record of a tragic relationship, it contributes little to literary history and nothing to literary criticism. A shortened version, "The Tangled Romance of Sinclair Lewis and Dorothy Thompson," was published in *Harper's* (CCXXVII, Oct., 121-172). Charles E. Rosenberg, in "Martin Arrowsmith: The Scientist as Hero" (*AQ*, XV, 447-458), sees Arrowsmith as a martyr hero in a materialistic world, and views the novel as both an indictment of the handicaps put in the scientist's path and a rejection, too, of the attitudes of the scientific community.

John Dos Passos was the subject of four articles, none of them completely convincing. John P. Diggins compared "Dos Passos and Veblen's Villains" (*AR*, XXIII, 485-500). Dan Wakefield viewed Dos Passos's apparent political and social shift from extreme left to extreme right and asked, "Dos, Which Side Are You On?" (*Esquire*,

LIX, April, 112-114). E. D. Lowry, in "*Manhattan Transfer*: Dos Passos's Wasteland" (*University Review*, XXX, Autumn, 46-52), presented a not totally convincing argument that Dos Passos was indebted to T. S. Eliot, particularly with regard to fire and water symbolism, and concluded that *Manhattan Transfer* was not naturalistic and was better than we had thought. Ben Stolzfus examined one aspect of Dos Passos's popularity abroad in "John Dos Passos and the French" (*CL*, XV, 146-163) and found him well-known and highly praised.

Frederick P. W. McDowell's *Elizabeth Madox Roberts* (New York, Twayne) is primarily an examination of her literary artistry. Mr. McDowell believes that her patterns of imagery and her multivariant symbols should work to yield her a more significant place in the modern novel than she presently occupies. Mr. McDowell's "revival" may be getting underway with Robert Penn Warren's "Elizabeth Madox Roberts: Life Is from Within" (*SatR*, XLVI, March 9, 20-21, 38).

John J. Gross, in *John P. Marquand* (New York, Twayne), gives an inadequate biographical and critical study of an important, popular, and underrated novelist of manners. It is marred further by Mr. Gross's failure to examine the extensive work of Marquand as a popular professional writer and his concentration on Marquand's social comedy after 1936. It is also marred by some careless errors and omissions.

Lionel D. Wyld, in "Canallers in *Waste Land*: Considerations of *Rome Haul*" (*MQ*, IV, 335-341), concludes that Walter D. Edmonds almost founded the "Erie Canal" novel and at the same time defined the *Waste Land* attitudes of its time.

Heinz Kosok, in "Thornton Wilder: A Bibliography of Criticism" (*TCL*, IX, 93-100), does not list Wilder's works but supplies a useful bibliography of comment on them. Julián Marías, in "*Los idus de marzo*: La recreatíon del mundo clásico en Thornton Wilder" (*Insula*, XVIII, No. 197, p. 10), examines *The Ides of March*.

Thomas Wolfe continued to be the subject of a substantial number of articles, although the year saw no Wolfe publications of the importance of Richard S. Kennedy's *The Window of Memory*, which appeared in December, 1962, nor was any new collection of Wolfe's materials published. In H. Wayne Morgan's *Writers in Transition*, Wolfe's career was examined in sympathetic terms but without adding anything truly fresh. The majority of articles were personal reminiscences. Charles Angoff, in "Thomas Wolfe and the Opulent Manner" (SWR, XLVIII, vi-vii, 81-84), recounts his experiences as an editor of the American Mercury with Wolfe, describes his slashing editorial work on Wolfe's short novel Boom Town, and acknowledges that, viewed from after the fact, he "over edited" this work. V. L. O. Chittick, in "Tom Wolfe's Fartherest West" (SWR, XLVIII, 93-110), recounts through personal reminiscence Wolfe's final Western trip, his illness, and his death. The historian Clement Eaton, in "Student Days with Thomas Wolfe" (GaR, XVII, 146-155), describes his acquaintance with Wolfe when the two were students at Chapel Hill and Harvard. Mr. Eaton credits the University of North Carolina with having instilled in Wolfe the quality of dissent and encouraged inquiry and a liberal view of life. B. R. McElderry, Jr., in "Thomas Wolfe: Dramatist" (MD, VI, 1-11), examined Wolfe's abortive career as a playwright and found in these efforts many of the seeds of his later novelistic work. Francis E. Skipp, in "The Editing of Look Homeward, Angel" (PBSA, LVII, 1-13), described the typescript carbon copy of Look Homeward, Angel, which is in the William B. Wisdom Collection at Harvard, and compared this version with the printed work. He found that about 95,000 words had been deleted from the more than 330,000 of the original manuscript, but that the cuts were made in large blocks to eliminate the material which seemed to be outside the central narrative or to delineate characters to an extent greater than they merit through the role they play in the work. This essay is an outgrowth of Skipp's important dissertation, "Thomas Wolfe and His Scribner's Editors," Duke, 1963. Robert C. Slack, in "Thomas Wolfe: The Second Cycle" in Lectures on Modern Novelists (Carnegie Series in English, No. 7, Pittsburgh, Dept. of Eng., Carnegie Inst. of Tech., pp. 41-53), found Wolfe's career to fall into two cycles, the first of which he called the "romantic quest" and second "the search for America." Mr. Slack's gracefully expressed essay contributes little that is fresh to our understanding of Wolfe's work. Edward Stone, in "A Rose for Thomas Wolfe" (OUR, V, 17-24), wrote with feeling about the impression that Wolfe made upon him; the title of his graceful essay describes its nature accurately. Louis D. Rubin, Jr., in a brilliantly written study in his book The Faraway Country (Seattle, Univ. of Washington, pp. 72-104), found Look Homeward, Angel to be an excellent novel, but concluded that bad editing of the later books had distorted our standard views of Wolfe. In a sense, Mr. Rubin here repudiates some of the stands that he took in *Thomas Wolfe: The Weather of His Youth* (Baton Rouge, Louisiana State Univ. Press, 1955). However, in a study of the contemporary autobiographical novel ("The Past Recaptured," *KR*, XXV, 393-415), dealing with Wolfe and Proust, Mr. Rubin treated thoughtfully and well Wolfe's use of personal experience. Margaret Church, in *Time and Reality: Studies in Contemporary Fiction* (Chapel Hill, Univ. of North Carolina Press), in "Thomas Wolfe: Dark Time," presented a revision of her important 1949 *PMLA* article (LXIV, 629-638), which was reprinted in Richard Walser, *The Enigma of Thomas Wolfe* (1953).

James T. Farrell, whose career was launched at the beginning of the 1930's, was examined by Thomas F. Curley in "Catholic Novels and American Culture" (*Com*, XXXVI, 34-42) and praised for trying "to cope with his experience as ... a Catholic," and thus becoming a major influence on contemporary Catholic writers. Edgar M. Branch presented a succinct and graceful record and criticism of Farrell in his pamphlet, *James T. Farrell* (Minneapolis, Univ. of Minnesota Press), which also has a good selective bibliography.

John Steinbeck, whose career also was launched as the thirties began, received a large amount of attention, principally because of his receiving the Nobel Prize. A catologue of his work, *John Steinbeck: An Exhibition of American and Foreign Editions* was published by the University of Texas Humanities Research Center (Austin). His *Short Novels* were reprinted (see *Editions* above). The recognition of mythic and religious motifs is becoming a commonplace of Steinbeck criticism, and it continued during 1963. Joseph Fontenrose in an American Authors and Critics volume, *John Steinbeck: An Introduction and Interpretation* (New York, Barnes and Noble), studies Arthurian, Biblical, and classical myth as a conscious basis and framework for his novels. This short book is full of interesting erudite comment (its author is a professor of classics), but it tends (admittedly with encouragement from Steinbeck's work itself) to "over-read" myth and symbol. Daniel R. Brown, in "A Monolith of Logic against Waves of Nonsense" (*Ren*, XVI, 48-51), tested Steinbeck's creed against orthodoxy and found him denying that any one religion can satisfy human needs. Robert J. Griffin and William E. Freeman, in "Machines and Animals: Pervasive Motifs in *The Grapes of Wrath*" (*JEGP*, LXII, 569-580),

asserted that these motifs "contribute considerably to the structure
and thematic content of the novel." J. P. Hunter's essay "Steinbeck's
Wine of Affirmation in 'The Grapes of Wrath,'" in *Essays in Modern
American Literature* (ed. Richard E. Langford, De Land, Fla., Stetson Univ. Press, pp. 76-89), is a defense of the novel as a work of
art, particularly in its closing scene. Mr. Hunter emphasizes the use
of Biblical material. Harry Morris, in *"The Pearl*: Realism and Allegory" (*ES*, LII, 487-495, 505), uses the short novel as a text to
demonstrate how to read allegorical fiction and declares Steinbeck
to be "a professed parabolist." Francis X. Connolly's essay (translated by Marcelle Sibon in *TR*, No. 180, pp. 93-99), "Lettre de New-
York: John Steinbeck, prix Nobel," shared two concerns—interpreting
a new Nobel Prize winner to a European audience, and emphasizing Steinbeck's philosophy—in this case as "non-teleological,"
scientific, interested in what *is*.

The interpretations of Steinbeck for European readers included
Franceso Bruno's essay (*Ausonia*, XVII, vi, 41-43), Alfred Feldges'
interpretation of "The Raid" (*NS*, pp. 234-239), John T. Grindley's
essay on Steinbeck as a naturalist (*RNC*, XXV, clv, 1962, 110-119),
Nils Lie's essay (*Vinduet*, XVII, 14-16), Gianfranco Randelli's
(*Fenarete*, XV, ii-iii, 17-21), and Gloria Stolk's (*RNC*, XXIV, cliv,
1962, 91-96).

But the best single piece of work on this suddenly popular writer
was *A Companion to* The Grapes of Wrath (New York, Viking
Press), a casebook edited by Warren French. Here are assembled
primary documents, including Steinbeck's *Their Blood is Strong* (a
1938 pamphlet), reviews, and critical estimates, with an informed
running commentary by the editor. This work is almost a model
"casebook" and one important to an understanding of the novel as
social document and, to a lesser extent, as art.

If 1963 can be considered a typical year, the authors of fiction
covered in this brief survey represent a group of writers of great
cultural and social importance and of not inconsiderable artistic
value who deserve more and better treatment than they are receiving. One does not need to subscribe to Taine's doctrine of "race,
epoch, and era" in order to see that an understanding and at least
a qualified appreciation of these writers is needed if their greater
contemporaries are to be understood.

13. Fiction: 1930 to the Present

Louis D. Rubin, Jr.

Not very many years ago the accepted hypothesis in graduate schools of literature was that any author not thoroughly dead, preferably for several decades, was no fit subject for important scholarly activity. How, the reasoning went, could one understand and evaluate a writer's work until all his books were written and all his writing done?

Happily this is no longer the case; we have come to realize that the scholar can bring to bear on a contemporary writer's work a perspective and understanding that must of necessity be denied to later generations, so that the loss in objectivity and long-range critical judgment is compensated for by a gain in topicality and immediacy. Furthermore, the breaking down of the artificial division between literature and what contemporary novelists and poets are writing can serve to invigorate the study of the past as well as to strengthen and make sounder the criticism of contemporary literature.

For the student who would survey and evaluate a year's scholarship in the contemporary field, however, the new dispensation raises problems. To wit: no less than twenty essays were published during the year 1963 on the fiction of J. D. Salinger (and indeed, probably more than that, for numberless and Traceless are the little magazines containing criticism of contemporary authors.) During that same year, four essays worth commenting on were devoted to the fiction of Saul Bellow, and three to that of William Styron. Now this hardly represents any sort of statistical reflection on the relative importance of these three novelists. In evaluating such scholarship, one will obviously have to use different measures of the worth of individual essays. Furthermore, one's own personal reaction to the work of one's contemporaries is likely to color one's judgments much more than if one were dealing in a field in which all the main problems are fairly well known and agreed upon. If one feels as I do, for example, that J. D. Salinger is an excellent writer whose work is currently being worked over to an extent out of all proportion to its importance, one is hard put to it to read through the umpteenth explication of what the figure of Seymour Glass means in the total mythic structure of the Salinger canon without becoming a trifle impatient. Yet in a field where there are as yet few guideposts and little agreement on essentials, each man's approach is almost as valid as the next fellow's, and deserves a full hearing. One can only console oneself with the reflection that not only will such measurements of contemporary interest in a writer be of some concern to future scholars, but that in evaluating the evaluations, one is no doubt also providing material for some scholar a hundred years from now who will perhaps find it a matter of some astonishment that in the year 1963 a number of intelligent literary scholars occupied themselves with discussing the works of some long since forgotten novelist, while the now classic novels of some other novelist were not even noticed. With that startling reflection, I proceed to the task at hand.

i. General Studies

The only general evaluation of post-1930 fiction of importance to appear in 1963 was Chester E. Eisinger's *Fiction of the Forties* (Chicago, Univ. of Chicago Press). Mr. Eisinger performed the unenviable task of surveying all the important fiction written from the opening of World War II up to the Korean Police Action. Such considerations as the decline of naturalism and social protest literature, the impact of the Russo-German Pact on the liberal mind, the vogue of the war novel and its special problems, the massive fact of the existence of the big bomb, the onset of the Cold War, the rise of McCarthyism and so forth all have their place in such a study. Mr. Eisinger sees the forties as a time of relatively little literary experimentation, of a growing pessimism, and a movement from public and social literature to that involving the individual's confrontation of his own existential identity. Implicit in Mr. Eisinger's approach is the division of fiction according to the author's social, political, and sociological attitudes, with the result that, for example, a chapter entitled "The Conservative Imagination" deals with James Gould Cozzens, assorted Roman Catholic novelists, William Faulkner, Caroline Gordon, Andrew Nelson Lytle, Peter Taylor, and Robert Penn Warren. On the other hand, another entitled "The

New Fiction" devotes itself to Truman Capote, Carson McCullers, Eudora Welty, Paul Bowles, J. P. Marquand (in passing), and Jean Stafford. I find the comparisons implied here of very limited usefulness, and would have preferred a very different system of grouping these writers, though I suppose that any such conceptual scheme is bound to fit some writers better than others. But I do not think that views of society and politics make the best approach to evaluating and understanding writers of fiction; and I say this despite the fact that Mr. Eisinger has good things to say about a number of good writers.

When William Faulkner and Ernest Hemingway died within a year of each other, some persons began looking around and asking themselves and each other who was now the leading American novelist. Two editors of the *New York Times Book Review*, Miss Nona Balakian and Mr. Charles Simmons, decided to edit a book of essays in which the merits and demerits of the logical candidates for the top spot were set forth by qualified critics. The result was an uneven volume, *The Creative Present* (New York, Doubleday), in which several good essays—Diana Trilling's "The Radical Moralism of Norman Mailer," Mark Schorer's "McCullers and Capote: Basic Patterns," and Alan Pryce-Jones' "The Fabulist's Worlds: Vladimir Nabokov" were mixed in with a number of highly ordinary evaluations.

Good source material for literary scholars and critics was provided by two collections, Herbert Gold's *First Person Singular: Essays for the Sixties* (New York, Dial Press), and George Plimpton's *Writers at Work: The Paris Review Interviews, Second Series* (New York, Viking Press), in which a second group of contemporary writers were asked questions, some of them revealing, about their work and their state of mind. Neither of these volumes, I think, is as valuable as either Granville Hicks' collection of several years ago, *The Living Novel*, or the first set of *Paris Review* interviews, which naturally skimmed off the cream.

John M. Bradbury performed a useful function in his *Renaissance in the South: A Critical History of the Literature, 1920-1960* (Chapel Hill, Univ. of North Carolina Press) which provided brief descriptions and estimates of an incredible number of Southern writers. The future historian who wants, for example, to find out something about Ovid Williams Pierce, Wesley Ford Davis, Isa Glenn, Dorothy Scarborough, and George Madden Martin, to name a few at

random, will find them all here, with a description of their books and
an estimate of their abilities. Considerably less inclusive is Louis
D. Rubin, Jr.'s *The Faraway Country: Writers of the Modern South*
(Seattle, Univ. of Washington Press), which concentrates on six
novelists and four poets from the standpoint of their relationship
to the changing South of the twentieth century.

ii. J. D. Salinger

Why is it, one wonders, that the work of J. D. Salinger has attracted
the critical attention of so many scholars? There are not only numerous essays on Salinger, but a full-length study and a new collection of essays in the 1963 crop. I suspect that at least two factors
are involved, in addition to the genuine merit of Salinger's work,
which is considerable. One is that most scholars are teachers, and
most college students like Salinger very much, with the result that
The Catcher in the Rye has found its way into most college cur-
ricula, whereupon the teacher who must deal with it finds himself
impelled to publish his findings. Another factor is that within the
last several years Salinger has published two new books, *Frannie
and Zooey* and *Raise High the Roof Beam, Carpenters*, and since
his work constitutes a kind of *roman fleuve*, with the same characters appearing here and there, and with a common philosophical
mystique unifying the whole thing, the result is a body of fiction
peculiarly adapted to the working out and the proclaiming thereof
of ideological systems.

Warren French's *J. D. Salinger*, in the continuing Twayne
United States Authors Series (New York, Twayne), traces Salinger's
development from the early short stories, using "Uncle Wiggily in
Connecticut" to show how Salinger's vision involves the confrontation of two worlds, a "nice" and "phony" one. After reviewing criticism of *The Catcher in the Rye*, he interprets the novel not as an
attempt on Holden Caulfield's part to escape from a monotonous,
humdrum world, but as a search for tranquillity, in which he passes
through various crises and begins to discover his uniqueness. The
later work, French decides, involves the account of a search for
individual salvation, which is marred by the author's growing use
of exposition at the expense of narrative. "Seymour: An Introduction," he says, is "self-indulgent *kitsch*," and the quest for salvation
is thus far still unfulfilled.

Salinger's fiction is the subject of a symposium in *WSCL*, IV, No. 1, in which various positions are staked out. Ihab Hassan in "Almost the Voice of Silence: The Later Novelettes of J. D. Salinger" finds that Salinger's work exemplifies a new conception of form becoming rife in contemporary literature, in which all the resources of language, including accidental distortion, are used to convey an unmediated, unrestricted vision of reality. Silence, he says, has become not merely a theme or motif in Salinger, but a principle of form and language. Warren French discusses the inability of sociological realism to deal with Salinger's fiction in "The Phony World and the Nice World." Tom Davis, in "J. D. Salinger: 'The Sound of One Hand Clapping,'" finds that Salinger's involvement in Zen Buddhism has led him to a masked form of rejection and withdrawal. Sam S. Baskett ("The Splendid/Squalid World of J. D. Salinger") sees the Glass family stories as a refusal on Salinger's part to commit himself to a naturalistic world in which the American dream has become a nightmare, and an effort to reclaim delight and wonder. John O. Lyons ("The Romantic Style of Salinger's 'Seymour: An Introduction'") honors Salinger's deliberate flaunting of academic standards for fiction, and his Romantic affirmation of the work of Man. For John Russell, in an excellent essay entitled "Salinger, from Daumier to Smith," the early story "De Daumier-Smith's Blue Period" is pivotal in Salinger's work, the last of the 'formally excellent' early stories, and one which looks forward to present a dramatized "transcendent" appearance. He discerns three types of Salinger heroes, the mystic and the striving artist, and finally the God-knowing pure artist; De Daumier-Smith goes through two such stages, and Buddy Glass achieves the third in the later work. Arthur Schwartz ("For Seymour—With Love and Judgment") sees Salinger as striving to keep emotion, insight, and expression reasonably commensurate with each other; notes that he tries to distract his readers by calling up his reserves of language when he fears that the reader may reject the heart of the entire Glass saga; but feels the author's fears are ill-founded, because the style is "right." Finally, Joseph Blotner ("Salinger Now: An Appraisal") wonders how long the thin body of Salinger's work can continue to support so much extensive analysis, sees Salinger as preoccupied with the need to discover the way whereby love can balance squalor to such an extent that his work has now turned in on itself, and hopes for a moratorium on Salinger criticism while

Salinger works his problem out for himself. A bibliography of
Salinger's work is provided by Donald M. Fiene.

The Catcher in the Rye is not neglected in other critical pieces
on Salinger. John D. Margolis ("Salinger's *The Catcher in the Rye*,"
Expl, XXI, Item 23) asserts that at the carrousel, Holden Caulfield
denies his earlier wish to catch little children when they threaten
to fall over the cliff of adolescence, thus moving closer toward
maturity. Robert M. Slabey ("*The Catcher in the Rye*: Christian
Theme and Symbol," *CLAJ*, VI, 170-183) works out a scheme
whereby the several days of Holden Caulfield's hegira become the
time of Advent, between Fall and Redemption, until finally at the
sanitarium he has traversed the desert toward a land of renewal
and rebirth. Charles Cagle ("*The Catcher in the Rye* Revisited,"
MQ, IV, 343-351) reviews the criticism and finds Salinger's novel
"really the distilled and heady vibration of our own time, the same
unquiet beating of restless feet which Fitzgerald heard thirty
years ago...." Fred H. Marcus ("*The Catcher in the Rye*: A Live
Circuit," *EJ*, LII, 1-8) advises high-school teachers to emulate their
college colleagues in teaching Salinger's novel.

The Glass family of the two later books comes in for study by
a number of scholars. Alfred Chester ("Salinger: How to Love without Love," *Com*, XXXV, 467-474) declares that Salinger's progres-
sive alienation from the sensual world has resulted in a loathing
of things physical and a passion for abstract words. The truth is, he
says, that Salinger doesn't love the Glasses; he hates them, because
in their refusal to live off themselves, they have walled up what is
the author's only possible path to salvation, his art. Donald P.
Costello ("Salinger and His Critics," *Cweal*, LXXIX, 132-135) takes
a different view; Salinger has in the Glasses replaced Holden Caulfield's rejection of life with an acceptance of the world through love,
and has invented a manner which *does* this—personal, intimate,
uneconomical, spontaneous, leisurely, delightful. Mary McCarthy
tees off on the Glasses, in "J. D. Salinger's Closed Circuit" (*Harper's*,
CCXXV, Oct., 1962, 46-48) as constituting a "terrifying narcissus
pool," and wonders whether Seymour Glass's suicide in "A Perfect
Day for Bananafish" came because "he had been lying, his author
had been lying, and it was all terrible, and he was a fake."

Meanwhile there were general estimates. Donald Barr's "Ah,
Buddy: Salinger," in Balakian and Simmons, *The Creative Present*,
pp. 27-62, gives Salinger the full Freudian treatment. Ann L. Hayes

("J. D. Salinger: A Reputation and a Promise," in Arthur T. Broes
et al., *Lectures on Modern Novelists*, Carnegie Series in English,
No. 7, Pittsburgh, Dept. of English, Carnegie Institute of Technology, pp. 15-24) sees Salinger's continued theme as the need to
find oneself and one's world through love, declares that the Glass
family is Salinger's major image of the power to love, and predicts
that if Salinger can answer the question he asks, how to live in the
world with others and yet be oneself, the result will be a major work
of art. Arthur F. Kinney ("J. D. Salinger and the Search for Love,"
TSLL, V, 111-126) views the quest for love through *The Catcher
in the Rye* and the later work, finds that when Salinger kept a social
dimension to his quest he was relevant and perceptive, but when he
began extolling love in mysticism, his work becomes self-conscious
and contrived.

In addition to all this, Marvin Laser and Norman Fruman have
edited a book, *Studies in J. D. Salinger: Reviews, Essays, and Cri-
tiques of* The Catcher in the Rye *and Other Fiction* (New York,
Odyssey), which contains a generous supply of reprinted criticism.

iii. Katherine Anne Porter

Perhaps because publication of *Ship of Fools* in 1962 added a
new and very striking dimension to the fiction of Katherine Anne
Porter, there was much interest in her work in 1963. Daniel Curley
used the new novel as the occasion for a general estimate ("Katherine Anne Porter: The Larger Plan," *KR*, XXV, 671-695) in which
he finds that so long as Miss Porter treated the human being as
simply a human being, she produced stories such as those involving
her character Miranda, magnificent in the exploration of the alienation of the human being from the world and the past. But when
she began striving for a broader context, abandoning her own personal legend to seek a new fable in the great world, her work is
fragmented and unconvincing, resulting finally in *Ship of Fools*,
which he finds a bad book in which love is missing all the way.
For Smith Kirkpatrick, however, *Ship of Fools* is "a lament for us
all" ("Ship of Fools," *SR*, LXXI, 94-98); the novel shows humans
journeying through life wearing the mask of the fool. It comes to
no conclusions, answers no questions, for the answer is life itself,
moving into eternity. John P. McIntyre ("*Ship of Fools* and Its
Publicity," *Thought*, XXXVIII, 211-220) likens *Ship of Fools* to

Melville and Hawthorne, as "forcefully demonstrating how the
heresy of abstraction compels intolerance," but finds that her work,
unlike that of the earlier novelists, is intensely social. Her characters are not aware of evil, and their prejudice, weakness, and sin
portend catastrophe. The novel, he says, is written in an ironic
mode: it "persuades everyone that human living requires decision
and involvement; it assures that all personal failure is equally society's loss." A similar verdict is that of Patricia R. Plante ("Katherine Anne Porter: Misanthrope Acquitted," XUS, II, 87-91), who
describes the new novel as showing men proceeding to a hell of
their own making, and declares that Miss Porter is asking for nothing
less than a re-beginning for us all.

Ray B. West, Jr.'s volume, *Katherine Anne Porter*, in the Twayne
Series (New York, Twayne) surveys all her work. Miss Porter has
found her principal theses in the tensions provided between fixed
social and moral positions and the necessities of movement and
alteration, he says. He stresses her "historic memory," which causes
her rendering and utilization of myth to be both her method and
her subject matter, reviews her career, analyzes the short stories,
discusses *Ship of Fools*, and sets forth her critical position. Brother
William Leslie Nance, S. M., in a Notre Dame dissertation ("The
Principle of Rejection: A Study of the Thematic Unity in the Fiction
of Katherine Anne Porter," DA, XXIV, 1172-73), sees the central
impulse in her fiction as the principle of rejection, and traces this
through her work, as it manifests itself in writing procedures, style,
structure, choice of material, and meaning.

Other items on Miss Porter include a study of her use of animal
imagery as a metaphor of the human struggle against animal forces,
by Sister M. Jocelyn, O.S.B. ("Animal Imagery in Katherine Anne
Porter's Fiction," in Bernice Slote, ed., *Myth and Symbol: Critical
Approaches and Applications*, Lincoln, Univ. of Nebraska Press,
pp. 101-115), and an interview with Miss Porter, chatty and sometimes informative, by James Ruoff ("Katherine Anne Porter Comes
to Kansas," MQ, IV, 205-234).

iv. James Baldwin

Interest in James Baldwin is high just now, partly, one supposes,
because of the prominent role he has played in recent civil rights
activity. Maurice Charney reviews "James Baldwin's Quarrel with

Richard Wright" (*AQ*, XV, 65-75) as indicative of Baldwin's refusal to separate the Negro's past from the history of the human race, or to consider the Negro's fate apart from man's fate. He remarks on Baldwin's awareness of the conflict within him of his real life as a human being and his social, mythic, and fantasy life as a Negro, and concludes that Baldwin's recent novel, *Another Country*, has a turbulence and a passionate eloquence that Wright could never achieve. Colin MacInnes discusses Baldwin's entire career ("Dark Angel: The Writings of James Baldwin," *Encounter*, XXI, ii, 22-33). *Go Tell It on the Mountain* is a "densely-packed, ominous, sensual, doom-ridden story lit by rare beauty"; *Up in Giovanni's Room*, though a brave try, is a melodrama; *Another Country* is the most ambitious and least successful of the novels. Baldwin's latest book of essays, *The Fire Next Time*, makes "a last desperate appeal—anguished if not yet utterly bereft of hope," to the white man. Baldwin, he concludes, is "a premonitory prophet, a fallible sage, a soothsayer, a bardic voice falling on deaf and delighted ears."

Therman B. O'Daniel ("James Baldwin: An Interpretive Study," *CLAJ*, VII, 37-47) finds Baldwin, like Wright, a writer of protest, using both the Negro and the homosexual to make an implied plea for acceptance of difference by society. He likens *Another Country* to Greek and Elizabethan tragedy, showing human beings consumed by passions of hate and thirst for revenge. John V. Hagopian ("James Baldwin: The Black and the Red-White-and-Blue," *CLAJ*, VII, 133-140) notes that Baldwin says he wants to be not a Negro but a writer, yet expends his energies on the genre of the protest essay instead of the protest novel, which is a way of being a Negro instead of a writer. He shows in an analysis of a Baldwin story, "This Morning, This Evening, So Soon," what enormous literary talents Baldwin possesses if he would use them.

Finally, in reviews of *The Fire Next Time*, Stephen Spender ("James Baldwin: Voice of a Revolutionary," *PR*, XXX, 256-260) declares that Baldwin proposes an impossible solution to race hatred by demanding that we all love one another, while in his own work he solves the race problem not by love but by imagination; and James Finn ("James Baldwin's Vision," *Cweal*, LXXVIII, 447-449) notes that racism has hurt Baldwin into poetry, but has also hurt him into a lot of dangerous nonsense in leading him to attack the very Western civilization and Christianity which must provide the sources for the strength needed to win the battle for equality.

There is an essay by Harvey Breit in *The Creative Present* ("James Baldwin and Two Footnotes," pp. 5-23) in which Baldwin's career as a novelist is discussed as if Baldwin were not a novelist but a journalist.

v. Robert Penn Warren

The autumn, 1963, number of *SAQ* (LXII) contains an interesting symposium on the work of Robert Penn Warren as novelist, poet, social historian, and literary critic, consisting of papers read at the joint session of the South Atlantic Modern Language Association and the Southeastern American Studies Association in Miami, November, 1962. Madison Jones ("The Novels of Robert Penn Warren," pp. 488-498) notes that Warren's principal theme has been modern man's failure to achieve wholeness or full identity, and he traces this through all of Warren's novels. Warren shows his protagonists dealing with public issues, which in turn reflect on the inner conflicts, Jones declares; this gives Warren great range and relevance for his novels, but also is Warren's most damaging weakness, because it provides too important a role for philosophy at the expense of fiction. The best of Warren's novels, Jones concludes, clearly survive their shortcomings.

M. L. Rosenthal finds Warren ("Robert Penn Warren's Poetry," pp. 499-507) best as a narrative poet rather than as a lyricist, praises the new clarity in his later work, notes that Warren too often "stands between us and the poem," "commenting, performing, advocating," but is poet enough to make it all worthwhile. John Hicks ("Exploration of Value: Warren's Criticism," pp. 508-515) analyzes Warren's critical approach, and finds that the existentialist problem of alienation and communion dominates his thinking. Warren finally believes that criticism can only lead the reader to the work, which must be experienced immediately and intuitively. William C. Havard ("The Burden of the Literary Mind: Some Meditations on Robert Penn Warren as Historian," pp. 516-531) views Warren's novels in the light of his historical writings, and concludes that the dual interest on Warren's part provides a rare phenomenon of a "novelist who accepts historical experience as fundamental to philosophical understanding" as that understanding is unfolded through the creative imagination.

In other essays on Warren, John R. Strugnell ("Robert Penn

Warren and the Uses of the Past," *REL*, IV, iv, 93-102) discusses
the novelist's theme of the arrival at self-understanding through the
contemplation of the past, and finds that sometimes Warren fails
to link his special concerns with a successful story. A. L. Clements
("Theme and Reality in *At Heaven's Gate* and *All The King's Men*,"
Criticism, V, 27-44) analyzes these two novels in terms of the individual's success or failure in achieving self-knowledge, responsibility,
and awareness of his place in time. Louis D. Rubin, Jr., ("Burden's
Landing," *The Faraway Country*, pp. 105-130) sees Warren's de-
piction of Jack Burden and the community of his origins in *All The
King's Men* as affording an image of the clash of past and present
in the individual's engagement in modern society.

vi. Eudora Welty

Miss Welty's work is the subject of four essays and a doctoral dissertation. The latter, by Sarah Allman Rouse ("Place and People
in Eudora Welty's Fiction: A Portrait of the Deep South," *DA*,
XXIII, 3901), analyzes Miss Welty's Southern settings to show her
skill at assembling a portrait of the Deep South as a microcosm of
society. Her characters, Miss Rouse concludes, are firmly established
as Southern, yet are representative of humanity at large. Equally
revelatory is the conclusion that Alun R. Jones reaches in his essay
on Miss Welty in *The Creative Present* (pp. 175-192): she has
"developed a vision of life that is matched by her consummate skill.
Writing with love, she restores our illusions about the world of
love."

Robert B. Holland studies Miss Welty's *The Ponder Heart* to
show how the structure of the dialogue is a vocalization of the
design of the culture in which they move. Words, he declares, are
an essential nourishment to people who have learned to remain
noble in spite of humiliation, proud in spite of debasements in-
flicted upon them and monstrosities which they themselves have
created ("Dialogue as a Reflection of Place in *The Ponder Heart*,"
AL, XXXV, 352-358). Neill D. Isaacs analyzes the short story "A
Worn Path" as traditional "road" literature, involving the Christian
nature-myth as well as the primitive myth of the Phoenix and
regeneration, with its magic element. The design of the story he
finds a symbol of life itself, and of death so that life may continue
("Life for Phoenix," *SR*, LXXI, 75-81). Louis D. Rubin, Jr.'s essay

"The Golden Apples of the Sun" (*The Faraway Country*, pp. 131-154) deals with the societies of *Delta Wedding* and *The Golden Apples* in terms of the contrast between private personalities and the role of the community. A checklist of book reviews written by Miss Welty is provided by McKelva Cole in *BB*, XXIII, 240.

vii. Flannery O'Connor

The all too early death of Flannery O'Connor last summer was a loss to American letters. Some measure of that loss can be determined from the high estimate of her work by five critics whose essays appeared during 1963. For Maurice Bassan ("Flannery O'Connor's Way: Shock, with Moral Intent," *Ren*, XV, 195-199, 211), Miss O'Connor's attitude toward the blasted moral sensibilities of her time is one of complete disapproval; the story "A Temple of the Holy Ghost" depicts the flowering of the religious sensibility in a world of brutality, outrage, and denial of salvation. Jonathan Baumbach, in a sensible essay ("The Creed of God's Grace: The Fiction of Flannery O'Connor," *GaR*, XVII, 334-346), discusses the novel *Wise Blood* perceptively and concludes that "we don't like to look at our moral sores; Flannery O'Connor rubs our noses in them." (If I may say so, Mr. Baumbach contributed no less than three of the essays examined for this study, each of them a model of its kind.)

Brainard Cheney responds to John Hawkes' 1962 *SR* (LXX, 395-407) essay on Miss O'Connor with a rebuttal entitled "Miss O'Connor Creates Unusual Humor Out of Ordinary Sin" (*SR*, LXXI, 644-652) in which he denies that Miss O'Connor views the human condition as existentially absurd. He declares her work is not similar to that of Nathaniel West, as Hawkes had asserted; unlike either West or Hawkes himself, the Georgia writer, Mr. Cheney says, believes in the Devil, and in her work the naturalistic surface becomes metaphysical, and the appropriate action becomes incongruous, grimly humorous. Richard H. Rupp ("Flannery O'Connor," *Cweal*, LXXIX, 304-307) says that Miss O'Connor exemplifies the Catholic artist at grips with reality, her stories pushing through humor, grotesqueries, and caricature to a vision of men before God, forcing the reader to examine her world *sub specie aeternitatis*. Rainulf Stelzmann finds that Miss O'Connor's theme is that modern man does not lose his faith innocently, but deliberately rejects God and prides himself on his atheistic or agnostic superiority. Her heroes want to be free and independent of God. Her attempt to represent Christian theology by "unorthodox" means causes misunderstanding on the part of some readers, he says, but does not impair the beauty and artistic immediacy of her work ("Shock and Orthodoxy: An Interpretation of Flannery O'Connor's Novels and Short Stories," *XUS*, II, 4-21).

viii. John Barth and John Hawkes

The work of two highly imaginative writers whose books have received all too little critical attention is discussed in a symposium in the valuable Minnesota little magazine *Critique* (VI, ii). Alan Trachtenberg ("Barth and Hawkes: Two Fabulists," pp. 4-18) asserts that both of them have abandoned the traditional novel of society in favor of more personal forms. Both are demanding, erudite, fluent writers, and European ideas have helped both to develop their personal visions. Hawkes' work, he says, is characterized by a sense of dream, of psychic order imposed on and accenting the physical and moral disorder of the world. Barth, at first glance seemingly a comic realist, is actually deeply concerned with the problem of existence and identity; his heroes suffer from too much consciousness and imagination, which poison the will.

Richard Schickel finds that Barth's first novel, *The Floating Opera*, is full of ironic skill, an absurd comedy characterized by set pieces full of truth and exuberant delight, with exceptional manipulation of language and the ability to give fictional life to symbolic characters and situations ("The Floating Opera," pp. 53-67). Herbert F. Smith ("Barth's Endless Road," pp. 68-76) decides that Barth's *The End of the Road* is satiric criticism of the limited goals of existentialism, succeeding as fiction because of the non-realistic effect of a series of allegorical tableaux representing ethical positions rather than characters in opposition. Earl Rovit ("The Novel as Parody: John Barth," pp. 77-85) pronounces Barth's most recent novel, *The Sot-Weed Factor*, an example of a *cul de sac* because it exemplifies one of the positions that contemporary fiction has resorted to since *Finnegans Wake*. The eighteenth-century parody that is the form of the novel smothers more crucial matters under an excessive paraphernalia of antiquarianism, he says, so that the parody imprisons the reader instead of liberating him. If Barth is to employ parody as a willing instrument of his vision, Mr. Rovit declares, he must learn to let his butterfly have a life that transcends his capturing design. (The "butterfly," I might note, is about the size of *War and Peace*, which makes it a pretty big insect.)

Albert J. Guerard analyzes John Hawkes' style as it evolves through his work, from a murky, groping, brilliant, eccentric expression, toward growing irony and control in which the elevated prose of the "implied author" and the more relaxed colloquialism of the personalized narrator are played against each other ("The Prose Style of John Hawkes," pp. 19-29). D. P. Reutlinger (*"The Cannibal*: The Reality of Victim," pp. 30-37) finds that Hawkes' first novel is "a depersonalized vision of cyclic disaster" in which the theme parallels the method of writing, an "anti-realism" whereby the artist replaces "lived" reality with "observed" reality. Charles Matthews ("The Destructive Vision of John Hawkes," pp. 38-52) declares that Hawkes' nightmare landscapes, the sense of arrested flight, pleasureless sexuality, and the disjunction of time are identical with our own nightmares, and that Hawkes has mastered the art of re-creating dream experience and its terrible reality.

Accompanying the essays are bibliographical essays on Barth and Hawkes by Jackson R. Bryer (pp. 86-89, 89-94).

ix. Saul Bellow

Saul Bellow is the subject of two excellent essays by Malcolm Bradbury. The first, "Saul Bellow and the Naturalist Tradition" (*REL*, IV, iv, 80-92), declares him the most substantial young novelist to appear since the second world war, belonging "with that remarkable efflorescence of Jewish writing that has widened the stream of American literature—a writing distinctively soul-searching and Russianized, concerned with nothing else than the condition of man." Bellow's theme is the engagement of one man with all others, together with the claims that his own personal existence and search for place and meaning impose on him. Bellow has moved toward a more open form and greater rhetorical extravagance, Bradbury says; he is a metaphysical novelist whose picture of the human condition is both profoundly absurd and intensely noble. In another essay, "Saul Bellow's *The Victim*" (*CritQ*, V, 119-128), Bradbury relates that novel to the American genre of novels about heroes who, working from spare, existentialist premises, attempt to realize their whole character and duties and the significance of their humanity. The analysis of the novel is both close and subtle.

Geoffrey Rans ("The Novels of Saul Bellow," *REL*, IV, iv, 18-30) discusses Bellow's novels one by one in terms of their growing sophistication and richness, and finds *Henderson the Rain King* straight out of American literature, with Henderson's quest the typically American and Emersonian one of redeeming the present and discovering the future. Bellow, Rans finds, is the natural inheritor of Melville and Whitman.

Robert Gorham Davis ("The American Individualist Traditions: Bellow and Styron," *The Creative Present*, pp. 111-141) also analyzes the novels in sequence, finding much to praise, but worries that the hero of *Henderson the Rain King* shows signs at the end of backsliding into his old misanthropy and thus becoming less optimistic than a good American should be.

x. Other Novelists

Willam Burroughs is the subject of an intensive analysis by Ihab Hassan ("The Subtracting Machine: The Work of William Burroughs," *Crit*, VI, i, 4-23), who describes Burroughs as a didactic writer who affirms his moral passion in the language of denial and derision. His central metaphor is the dreadful technology of science fiction; Burroughs' work, Hassan concludes, gives new meaning, however limited, to outrage, assaulting language to express a "piteous respect for creation."

Reviewing the *Selected Writings of Truman Capote*, David Littlejohn ("Capote Collected," *Cweal*, LXXVIII, 187-188) finds the collection "presumptuously premature," and argues that Capote's work after *Other Voices, Other Rooms* has, except for certain short stories, moved in the direction of sentimentality. Mark Schorer ("McCullers and Capote: Basic Patterns," *The Creative Present*, pp. 83-107) takes a very different view; he sees Capote's work as steadily evolving from the nightmare hallucinatory technique of the earlier work toward a denser social structure and more solid substance.

Raymond Chandler is the subject of an excellent book-length study by Philip Durham (*Down These Mean Streets a Man Must Go: Raymond Chandler's Knight*, Chapel Hill, Univ. of North Carolina Press). Mr. Durham shows how Chandler made extended use of the American vernacular to create a symbolic American man living in the melting pot city of Los Angeles and acting in traditional American style. Chandler's hero, he declares, brings together in a single personification the images of the frontier hero, the war hero, the political hero, the athletic hero, and the chivalric hero.

Discussing "John Cheever and Comedy" (*Crit*, VI, i, 66-77), Frederick Bracher sees Cheever as more than a "facile bright-side writer"; a man of sensibility rather than a social critic or analyst, Cheever has a pervading sense of the fragility of life that makes possible his moment of illumination.

James Gould Cozzens is the subject of an essay by Richard P. Adams and a book by Harry John Mooney, Jr. Mr. Adams, whose appraisal appears in a useful collection edited by Richard E. Langford ("James Gould Cozzens: A Cultural Dilemma," *Essays in Modern American Literature*, De Land, Fla., Stetson Univ. Press, pp. 103-111), questions the general view of Cozzens as conservative, rationalistic, realistic, and classical; his most pervasive theme is change, Mr. Adams says; in his fiction everything is relative, everything changes, and each action must be planned to meet the circumstances in which its effects will be felt. Thematically Cozzens is a pretty thorough and consistent romantic, Mr. Adams concludes. Mr. Mooney (*James Gould Cozzens: Novelist of Intellect*, Pittsburgh, Univ. of Pittsburgh Press) takes a different view; no other novelist of our time has dared to make such an extreme commitment to reason as Cozzens has done, he says. Reviewing the criticism, he then discusses the Cozzens novels, finding the last three dominated by the theme of the individual who, moving after the fact to reduce the effect of folly, finds himself inextricably involved and even committed to it. He quotes approvingly Brendan Gill's modest judgment in the *New Yorker* concerning *By Love Possessed*: "Such is the power of Mr. Cozzen's masterpiece that life may never be the same for us."

Edward Dahlberg is the subject of a study by Jonathan Williams, "Edward Dahlberg's Book of Lazarus" (*TQ*, VI, 35-49). Examining most of Dahlberg's work from *Bottom Dogs* to the present, he finds that Dahlberg's "rock wall" of prose in *The Sorrows of Priapus* "looms above the boneyard of contemporary slovens like the vatic batholith it is." The issue also contains a brief Dahlberg checklist, a Dahlberg essay on the expatriates, and a poem.

A dissertation by Cornelius John Ter Maat discusses the work of Peter DeVries, Frederick Manfred, and David Cornel de Jong in terms of their Dutch Calvinist Midwest backgrounds, finding that they make singularly little use of the past, and that they share the common trait of opposing the rigid, authoritarian mentality, the traditional, highly intellectualized theology, the formal religion and puritanical attitudes which are characteristic of the communities in which they grew up ("Three Novelists and a Community: A Study of American Novelists with Dutch Calvinist Origins," *DA*, XXIV, 751).

Ralph Ellison's novel *The Invisible Man* is discussed by Floyd Ross Horowitz ("The Enigma of Ellison's Intellectual Man," *CLAJ*, VII, 126-132), who fears that Ellison's protagonist may only have arrived at a humanity without the higher rationalization of principle, and hopes that he will choose to live by principle in the face of adversity as mature men do; and by Jonathan Baumbach ("Nightmare of a Native Son: Ralph Ellison's *Invisible Man*," *Crit*, VI, i, 48-65), who finds the novel's inconsistency of method often jarring but often amazingly effective, and concludes that Ellison excels in satire and surrealism, is less adept at realism, and all in all has written a major novel.

Vardis Fisher is the subject of a special number of the *American Book Collector* (XIV, i) containing testimonies, critical analyses, memoirs, and a bibliography; and of a dissertation by Joseph Martin Flora ("Vardis Fisher's Story of Vridar Hunter: A Study in Theory and Revision," *DA*, XXIII, 3372), in which Fisher's tetralogy of the 1930's is viewed in the light of recent revisions to show that the earlier emphasis on the hero's task of balancing conflicting racial and ego drives has been superseded by an emphasis on man's history and myths.

Caroline Gordon's recent novel *The Malefactors*, according to Brainerd Cheney ("Caroline Gordon's Ontological Quest," *Ren*, XVI, 3-12), is the final fictional flower of a quest for a "recognition of man's ontological motivation—toward God, however impaled in flesh he may be," that extends from her earliest work through her Southern past toward a Christian vision. Another Southern woman novelist, Shirley Ann Grau, is seen by Alwyn Berland ("The Fiction of Shirley Ann Grau," *Crit*, VI, i, 78-84) as possessed of first-rate technical skills, but with an essentially mimetic vision that denies her work the firm center of conviction as to why her characters behave as they do.

Jack Kerouac is chastised by Eliot D. Allen for failing to portray
the normal, healthy American woman in his novels ("That Was No
Lady—That Was Jack Kerouac's Girl," *Essays in Modern American
Literature*, pp. 97-102). By Granville H. Jones he is seen as a
serious novelist, with a purpose, a definite rationale, a "constant
and conscious awareness of America and being an American." Mr.
Jones discusses the pros and cons of spontaneous writing, finds
philosophical inconsistency Kerouac's chief fault, and decides that
for Kerouac hope lies within the individual who can believe in love
and act on his belief (*Lectures on Modern Novelists*, pp. 25-39).
Davis L. Stevenson ("James Jones and Jack Kerouac: Novelists of
Disjunction," *The Creative Present*, pp. 195-212) links Kerouac
with James Jones as writing outside the social order, and decides
that both of them provide certain insights into American life thereby,
but their characters basically do not know what they are after, or
why.

Norman Mailer is the subject of a sensitive essay by Diana
Trilling ("The Radical Moralism of Norman Mailer," *The Creative
Present*, pp. 145-171), who argues that Mailer's work is not to be
discussed apart from his belief in the impending downfall of freedom before the onslaught of reaction. She proceeds through a
cogent analysis of Mailer's novels to conclude that Mailer's "moral
imagination is the imagination not of art but of theology," and sees
him finally as issuing "a call to a time when religion was still a
masculine discipline—a call, that is, to an Hebraic world." R. D.
Lakin ("D. W.'s: The Displaced Writer in America," *MQ*, IV, 295-
303) views Mailer as an example of the difficulty the contemporary
American writer faces in having to exist in a postwar world in
which he must choose either to be a tradesman or the victim of a
haunting uneasiness caused by a sense of artistic irrelevancy in an
affluent society.

Bernard Malamud, Jonathan Baumbach declares in a well-
constructed essay ("The Economy of Love: The Novels of Bernard
Malamud," *KR*, XXV, 438-457), has extended the tradition of the
American romance-novel; for Malamud love is the redemptive grace,
the highest good, defeat of love is the tragedy, and in what Mr.
Baumbach considers his best novel, *The Assistant*, the disparate
concerns of mythic ritual and transcendent realism are united in a
novel about an ambivalent saint. Malamud is also discussed by
Granville Hicks, along with Herbert Gold and John Updike ("Gen-

eration of the Fifties: Malamud, Gold and Updike," *The Creative Present*, pp. 217-237). Like Gold, Mr. Hicks asserts, Malamud "dares to believe that men can be better than they are." Updike is apparently not so sure about it.

The symbolism of the novels of Carson McCullers, according to Wayne D. Dodd ("The Development of Theme through Symbol in the Novels of Carson McCullers," *GaR*, XVII, 206-213), emphasizes the discreteness of individuals from each other and from God himself: for proof, see the conclusion to the *Ballad of the Sad Café*. Mark Schorer, in a perceptive analysis of Miss McCullers' development of the theme of love and loneliness ("McCullers and Capote: Basic Patterns," *The Creative Present*, 83-107), discusses three novels and a novella in terms of the interaction of technique and atmosphere, and concludes that Miss McCullers' abandonment of this theme in *Clock without Hands* results in disjunction and confusion.

Partisans of Henry Miller cannot complain of his being neglected by scholars in 1963. A book-length study by Kingsley Widmer (*Henry Miller*, New York, Twayne) sees him as "a minor but intriguing writer whose best works are the rhetorical gestures of a rebel buffoon" and analyzes his work in terms of a growing obsession with the life that led to his becoming an artist. Miller is good at the bittersweet portrayal of his all-too-ordinary family life, Mr. Widmer says, and when his pyrotechnic style and buffoonish gesturing come together, he produces distinctive work. George Wickes has edited, for the Crosscurrents series of the Southern Illinois University Press in Carbondale, a series of memoirs, tributes, favorable critical estimates, testimony from the obscenity trial of *Tropic of Cancer*, and a postscript by Miller himself (*Henry Miller and the Critics*).

Vladimir Nabokov's fiction is the subject of three essays. Carol T. Williams ("'Web of Sense': *Pale Fire* in the Nabokov Canon," *Crit*, VI, iii, 3, 29-45) cites Nabokov's interest in chess problems as the key to the method of that novel; she gives it a close reading and proposes for Nabokov's fiction an Hegelian structure of "thesis" (his twenty years in Russia), "antithesis" (twenty-one years of voluntary exile in Europe), and the "beginning of a synthetic development" (his American years). Charles Mitchell ("'Mythic' Seriousness in *Lolita*," *TSLL*, V, 329-343) interprets *Lolita* as dealing with three myths, the Quest, Beauty and the Beast, and the Garden, and like

Miss Williams proposes an Hegelian structure, this time from Child, or Image, to Nymphet, or Image and Flesh combined, to Woman, or Flesh. Alan Pryce Jones ("The Fabulist's Worlds: Vladimir Nabokov," *The Creative Present*, pp. 65-78) notes that Nabokov is essentially a moralist, views his art as that of the fabulist rather than the novelist, discusses each novel in terms of Nabokov's career, and sees *Lolita* as likely to remain a landmark in the history of the novel.

Harriet Zinnes uses the occasion of the reissue of Anaïs Nin's fiction by Alan Swallow to review and evaluate her work. Miss Nin is one of the few writers to understand modern woman's striving, she declares; psychoanalytical description is made glowing by Miss Nin through the use of language, and she exults in life and being a woman (*BA*, XXXVII, 283-286).

For Jesse Bier, John O'Hara's *Appointment in Samarra* provides a steady picture of a fiercely competitive personal and business life, in which O'Hara is bent on examining the collaboration between predetermining forces and a virtual principle of weak American character that conspires against adulthood ("O'Hara's *Appointment in Samarra*: His First and Only Real Novel," *CE*, XXV, 135-141).

James Purdy's novels and his short stories are analyzed by Warren French ("The Quaking World of James Purdy," *Essays in Modern American Literature*, pp. 112-122) as explorations of the attempt to effect communication in a world of unbearable loneliness, in which Purdy turns his wit on a degenerate society that seeks only physical sensation in a quest for eternal youth. What Purdy advocates, Mr. French says, is a society in which man accepts gracefully his maturing and aging, and gives to youth the affectionate guidance that might enable it to fulfil itself.

William Styron's work is discussed by three critics. Jerry H. Bryant ("The Hopeful Stoicism of William Styron," *SAQ*, LXII, 539-550) declares that Styron's theme is, What must man endure? *Lie Down in Darkness* offers too pat and easy a solution; *The Long March* is a definite artistic advance; *Set This House On Fire*, though written with a deeper stoicism, provides too uncomfortably vague a solution, without development through action. Robert Gorham Davis ("The American Individualist Tradition: Bellow and Styron," *The Creative Present*, pp. 111-141) likes the first novel best, though it is, he says, marked by a falsely portentous rhetoric and concerns some very uninteresting people; while *Set This House On Fire* is

unreal, melodramatic, larger than life, and is saved only by its
American qualities. Louis D. Rubin, Jr., ("William Styron: Notes
on a Southern Writer in Our Time," *The Faraway Country*, pp. 185-
230) discusses Styron's two novels as they illustrate the changing
assumptions and attitudes from one generation of Southern writers
to the next.

John Updike is viewed by Father Guerin La Course, O.F.M., as
having failed thus far to pass beyond the frontiers of the pleasant
and unpleasant, the agreeable and disagreeable, the delightful and
unsettling, into the murk of genuine evil; a lingering innocence
surrounds and hampers his true passion ("The Innocence of John
Updike," *Cweal*, LXXVII, 512-514). Michael Novak analyzes the
four-part story in *Pigeon Feathers* entitled "Packed Dirt, Church-
going, Dying Out, A Traded Car" as an effort to find images for
"that deep, serene, perennial way of looking at life which the secular,
active West has lost." Updike, he concludes, is succeeding; he is
beginning to make religion intelligible in America and to fashion
symbols whereby it can be understood ("Updike's Quest for Lit-
urgy," *Cweal*, LXXVIII, 192-195).

Lastly, Nathaniel West. David Galloway's excellent study,
"Nathaniel West's Dream Dump" (*Crit*, VI, iii, 46-64), finds
the dream as West's chief metaphor, and traces it in West's
Hollywood writings to show "the dream inevitably metamor-
phosed into nightmare." Noting West's friendship with Fitzgerald, he sees his art as an extension of Fitzgerald's vision
as enunciated in *The Great Gatsby*, and concludes that West in
The Day of the Locust and Fitzgerald in *The Last Tycoon* created
sympathetic macrocosms of a Hollywood world which distorts and
negates man's needs and desires, leaving him a senseless shell,
unable to fulfil his dreams. Daniel A. Carter compares early versions
of five chapters of *Miss Lonelyhearts* as published in periodicals
with the final printed novel to show how West experimented with
various techniques, and revised to secure greater unity, smoother
transitions, economy and clarity ("West's Revisions of *Miss Lonelyhearts*," *SB*, XVI, 11-20).

A final bibliographical note. Don't fail to miss the July number
of *Esquire* (L). Not only do William Styron and James Jones talk
over their work ("Two Novelists Talk It Over," pp. 57-59), but
Norman Mailer gives a rival's-eye-view of William Styron, James
Jones, James Baldwin, Saul Bellow, Joseph Heller, John Updike,

William Burroughs, J. D. Salinger, and Philip Roth ("Norman
Mailer vs. Nine Writers," pp. 63-69, 105) and Rust Mills presents a
chart of "The Structure of the American Literary Establishment"
(pp. 41-43) which the enterprising scholar can cut out and tack
onto his office wall and thus be able to tell at a glance who is where,
who is who, who writes for which publisher, and who is represented
by which literary agent. Priceless information.

14. Poetry: 1910-1930

Charles T. Davis

i. Robert Frost

What emerges clearly from an examination of the scholarly writing during 1963 on American poetry in the period from 1910 to 1930 is the quickened attention given to the life and the work of Robert Frost. Frost's death early in 1963 had everything to do with the publication of two editions of letters, since the poet during his life frowned upon personal revelations of this kind. Mr. Untermeyer's collection (*The Letters of Robert Frost to Louis Untermeyer*, New York, Holt, Rinehart, and Winston) and Margaret Bartlett Anderson's (*Robert Frost and John Bartlett: The Record of a Friendship*, New York, Holt, Rinehart and Winston) show in a remarkable way two quite different aspects of one man's nature. The rich harvest of the correspondence is yet to come, since the editions of this year are limited to the letters to two friends. The critical writing is another matter altogether. It has been a gradual development essentially unaltered by the limits of mortality. Books by Reuben Brower (*The Poetry of Robert Frost: Constellations of Intention*, New York, Oxford Univ. Press) and J. Radcliffe Squires (*The Major Themes of Robert Frost*, Ann Arbor, Univ. of Michigan Press) follow earlier serious attempts to examine Frost's literary ancestry, his technique, and his thought. These new works rest in part upon the rich experience in explicating individual poems in the 1950's. And they (especially Mr. Brower's study) rely too upon recent scholarly consideration given to English Romanticism, American Transcendentalism, the pastoral mode, and the use of dramatic conventions in verse.[1] Frost requires of his critics now the scrupulous attention to

[1] A partial list of titles would include the following: Robert Langbaum, *The Poetry of Experience* (New York, Random House, 1957); David Ferry, *The Limits of Mortality, An Essay on Wordsworth's Major Poems* (Middletown, Wesleyan Univ. Press, 1959); F. W. Bateson, *Wordsworth—A Re-Interpretation* (London, Longmans, Green, 1954); Stephen E. Whicher, *Freedom and Fate, An Inner Life of Ralph Waldo Emerson* (Philadelphia, Univ. of Pennsylvania Press, 1953); John F. Lynen, *The Pastoral Art of Robert Frost* (New Haven and London, Yale Univ. Press, 1960).

method and the careful regard for details that are demanded by
poems of Eliot, Pound, Stevens, and Crane. This has not always
boon co.

We observe then a shift in emphasis that points up the existence
of several traditions in American poetry since 1910, traditions that
are, finally, not closely related. The first, of course, is the revolution
in form and substance led by Pound and Eliot and involving as well
Stevens, Crane, Williams, MacLeish. Though the movement has
many sources, the chief defining characteristic seems to be the
European education—the poetry of the French Symbolists, the verse
of classical Greece and Rome, the achievement of Dante, and the
verbal music of the troubadors. Frost marked his difference when
he assessed his three years in England in a letter to Untermeyer in
1935: "I went as an exporter anyway, not as a self-accredited im-
porter of European art into our system" (p. 254). No less clear is
the form of a second tradition, one growing from native American
communities, sensitive to folk origins and permeated by Jeffer-
sonian and Populist political convictions. It is a continuity that
includes Sandburg, Lindsay, Masters, and Markham. A somewhat
hazier group is that formed by Amy Lowell, Edna Millay, Hilda
Doolittle, John Gould Fletcher, and others, characterized by more
limited intellectual perspectives, an appreciation for the poetic
image, and a refreshingly open attitude toward sense experience.
Unclassifiable are Frost, Robinson, Cummings and Aiken, who work
out in quite unique ways their own solutions to problems of source
and form. Scholarship in the 1960's continues to serve well the
"Pound gang," Frost's term of disrespect for a tradition not his. It
continues to ignore, in general, the native Americans and the so-
called "Imagist" group, for which Amy Lowell was an energetic
propagandist. The intensive study of Frost is the development in
scholarship that affirms seriously the fact of the complex and mul-
tiple tradition, and it leads to the hope that other poets may profit
ultimately by a more rigorous critical examination—perhaps Robinson or Aiken or H. D. or Lindsay.

Frost's letters to Louis Untermeyer extend from March 22, 1915,
to July 11, 1961, and they offer, perhaps, the most rewarding introduction to the poet published so far. Mr. Untermeyer's relationship
to Frost is not easily defined. The poet found in the critic an intelligent understanding of his work, a response deeply appreciated because it came early in Frost's career. By the 1930's Untermeyer had

become a force in forming poetic taste in America, and Frost's letters often deal with the problem of selecting the poems for anthologies that educated American students in impressive numbers. The letters to Untermeyer too were unfailing opportunities to indulge in literary small talk, something Frost enjoyed thoroughly. He passed judgment on his fellow poets—on Masters, Robinson, Eliot, Pound; he hailed, with sometimes questionable humor, his "rising contemptuaries" (p. 225), MacLeish, Jeffers, and Dillon, and he urged the publication of the verse of his students and disciples. He recorded with mixed amusement and annoyance his involvement with academic institutions and the Poetry Society of America. Frequently we find Frost's affection for word play and occasionally, but not as often as we might think, we encounter serious discussions of poetic theory, like that exploring the relationship between art and political revolution (p. 255).

What we miss, especially in the early letters to Untermeyer, is personal intimacy—that is to say, reference by Frost to difficult family problems and a sympathetic response on his part to the deeply felt needs of his correspondent. Mrs. Anderson's *Robert Frost and John Bartlett: The Record of a Friendship*, consisting in large part of letters from the poet, presents a relationship rich in human values. Bartlett and his wife were students of Frost when he taught at the Pinkerton Academy near the village of Derry in New Hampshire. The Bartletts were members of the class of 1910, graduating one year before Frost moved on to teach for a year at the Plymouth Normal School. The letters cover a period from 1912 to 1949, the year of Mrs. Bartlett's death (two years after her husband's). More than anything else Frost's letters reveal his anxieties about the health and the future of his family. We see the portrait of a protective parent, one, in John Bartlett's opinion, at least, always on the point of interfering with the development of his children. One of the virtues of Mrs. Anderson's book is that we come to know Frost's correspondent, Mrs. Anderson's father, almost as well as we know Frost. We can measure accurately in this way the poet's sympathetic concern for the young journalist who struggled to make his way, first in Canada, then in New Hampshire and Colorado. Frost offered advice on writing and, at times, more material support, and the Bartletts, in turn, ministered to Frost's daughter Marjorie when she was being treated for tuberculosis in Colorado. Though the friendship was personal, rather than professional or literary, it did stimulate in Frost, upon occasion, thoughtful comments on poetry. We find a revealing discussion of sound in a letter written from England in July, 1913. Here Frost says: "...If one is to be a poet he must learn to get cadences by skillfully breaking the sounds of sense with all their irregularity of accent across the regular beat of the metre..." (Anderson, p. 54).

Sound is the beginning point for Reuben Brower's study of Frost's poetry. Mr. Brower considers other formal elements, metaphor, voice, and dramatic progress, and he provides fresh and illuminating analysis even of such familiar pieces as "The Death of the Hired Man" and "West-Running Brook." He is expert in pointing to the classical qualities in Frost's technique—especially to connections with Virgilian pastoral. Explored with equal care is Frost's indebtedness to English and American Romanticism, the correspondences that link Frost to Wordsworth, Emerson, and Thoreau. Of primary concern are the attitudes toward nature and the conception of country people and country life. Mr. Brower is careful to note differences too. He is certainly right when he says that "In poetry that celebrates the making of a dream—truth in the act and the knowing of the act, Frost allies himself with James [William] and Charles Saunders Peirce" (p. 85). It is the pragmatic finally that counts for Frost. The critical study refers to echoes in Frost's verse that come from English poetry of the seventeenth and eighteenth centuries. Milton, Marvell, Pope, Swift, Smart, Gay, and Cowper have touched the form of Frost's poetry. Mr. Brower describes admirably Frost's position in the tradition of English poetry. He does not discuss with equal fullness, aside from the consideration of relationship to Emerson and Thoreau, Frost's place in an American continuity that would include, as well, Hawthorne, Melville, Emily Dickinson, Whitman, Robinson, and, perhaps, the contemporary poet, Richard Eberhart.

The Major Themes of Robert Frost is a study very different from Mr. Brower's. It lacks the analytic method, the historical perspective, and the scholarly precision that make the Poetry of Robert Frost the most rewarding of the critical examinations of Frost's verse. Mr. Squires finds Frost to be no "innovator" (p. 2)—and we think of Mr. Brower's discussion of Frost's use of the conventions of the pastoral and the masque (or, indeed, Frost's letter to John Bartlett on sound). Though he denies Frost originality in form, Mr. Squires, oddly, is essentially interested in Frost's separation from other modern poets, an apartness defined entirely in terms of ideas in the verse. Mr. Squires reconstructs the poet's metaphysical and religious vision, and in the process he runs the danger constantly of turning critical commentary into a testament of faith that owes as much to the recorder as to the subject testifying. Frost, more than other poets of our time, seems to invite this approach. One of the values of the study lies not so much in the demonstration of Frost's uniqueness but in the suggestion that other Americans before Frost have shared his problems. We find references to Hawthorne, Melville, Emerson, Emily Dickinson, Robinson, William James, and Henry Adams, though no thorough examination of Frost's relationship to any one literary figure.

Charles Anderson in "Robert Frost" (*SatR*, XLVI, Feb. 23, pp. 17-20) supports Brower rather than Squires on the problem of Frost as an experimenter in verse. He considers that Frost's ability to rework old forms, to move "easy in harness" (p. 18) is a valid claim to originality. Moreover, Frost exhibits the fine poet's power to think through his images, a power that Mr. Anderson illustrates by explicating "The Axe-Helve." John Frederick Nims, writing also in the *Saturday Review* ("The Classicism of Robert Frost," XLVI, Feb. 23, pp. 22-23, 62) explores in a general way Frost's "classicism," something that Mr. Brower has examined so rewardingly through formal comparison and analogue. Mr. Nims finds classical qualities in Frost's poetic manner—in the restraint, in the simplicity of a language that never descends to flatness, and in the shrewd economy in the use of metaphor. Affinities exist with Greek and Latin poetry without evidence of abundant allusion and without frequent citation of myths and fables. Establishing only a pattern of correspondence, not a source, Edward H. Rosenbery in "Towards Notes for 'Stopping by Woods': Some Classical Analogs" (*CE*, XXIV, 526-528) discovers an analogue for "Stopping by Woods" in the Twenty-Third Discourse in the Second Book of Epictetus. His justification—and it is partly Brower's too—is that a work of art is enriched when it acquires thematic perspective.

Reginald L. Cook, author of an earlier critical study of Frost's character and work, *The Dimensions of Robert Frost*, has Squires' concern for the form of Frost's vision in "A Fine Old Eye: The Unconquered Flame" (*MR*, IV, 242-249). He is struck by its "levelness"—by the delicate balance that the poet achieves between over and under exposure to dark realities and by the sure movement in the poems from the personal and the local to the public and the cosmic. W. R. Irwin in "Robert Frost and the Comic Spirit" (*AL*, XXXV, 299-310) accomplishes something similar when he defines the comic spirit in Frost's poetry and finds that the comic is the inverted expression of the tragic. Josephine Jacobsen is less concerned with balance than she is with affirmation in "The Legacy of Three Poets" (*Cweal*, LXXVIII, 189-192). The "Legacy of Three Poets" (Cummings and Williams, as well as Frost) is faith, but not easy optimism. Frost reveals to her something more than a grudging acceptance of the universe and a tendency to resolve pragmatically modern man's intellectual dilemmas. At the center of his poetry she finds, rather, belief in a hopeful design.

ii. E. A. Robinson

Louis Untermeyer has performed another commendable service for twentieth-century American poetry by writing *Edwin Arlington Robinson, A Reappraisal*, a pamphlet published by the Library of Congress in connection with an exhibit of Robinsoniana, displayed from April 15 to July 15, 1963. Mr. Untermeyer calls attention to Frost's great contemporary from New England in a year in which editors, biographers, and critics have devoted themselves, more intensively than ever before, to Frost. "Reappraisal" is perhaps too strong a word for what Untermeyer has done. He presents a biographical summary and he echoes the critical judgment, now long established, that Robinson was a "traditionalist": "Robinson was the first to acknowledge that he was no innovator, that he had no theories, no understanding of the creative impulse. He did not explore new methods of writing or new ways to be new" (p. 22). This opinion is not a fair estimate of Robinson. The author of "Captain Craig" certainly considered himself to be an innovator—in the use of dramatic conventions and in his diction and imagery as well. The letters written to his friends before the publication of the poem in 1902 (especially to Josephine Preston Peabody) indicate that he was fully aware of what he was about, even to the point of speculation upon theory. It is hard to see how we can "reappraise" Robinson without beginning with the same basic understanding of his poetic achievement that we have of the technical powers of Robert Frost. Appearing with Untermeyer's essay are a useful bibliography

of Robinson's "Separately Published Works," compiled by William
J. Studer, and Arthur G. Burton's "A List of Materials in the Edwin
Arlington Robinson Exhibit."

Ronald Moran in "*Avon's Harvest* Re-examined" (*CLQ*, VI, 247-
254) considers problems raised by two versions of Robinson's puz-
zling narrative. He concludes that one form invites a reading as a
ghost story and that the other, perhaps more serious in its artistic
intention, stands as a confession of a man overcome by guilt and
hallucination. Conrad Aiken seems close to the truth, in any event,
when he sees the poem as a Robinsonian caprice. Fred Somkin in
"Toqueville as a Source for Robinson's 'Man Against the Sky'"
(*CLQ*, VI, 245-247) uses evidence that points to parallels in image
and language involving the opening of the poem and a section taken
from the second volume of Toqueville's *Democracy in America*. We
must accept the new information on Robinson's sources in the light
of Robert Stevick's earlier claim ("Robinson and William James,"
UKCR, XXV, 1959, 293-301) that the poem was influenced by a
reading of James' *Human Immortality*. Mr. Stevick also cites parallel
phrases, and he has the advantage of knowing that Robinson had
read James carefully. One of the difficulties here in establishing
reliable sources is that a "public" poem like "The Man Against the
Sky" echoes so much in phrasing and in image of matter that forms
a part of the consciousness of the modern American. What we may
be acknowledging, in part, in these investigations is the extent to
which Toqueville and James have shaped our thinking.

Richard Cary's "E. A. Robinson as Soothsayer" (*CLQ*, VI, 233-
245) describes an element of Robinson's character that we know
little about. This is the "touch of the mystical" in the poet, evident,
according to Mr. Cary, in "his early claims to divination" (p. 233).
Robinson made predictions about the reputations of writers, the
reception of plays, the enduring importance of literary works, the
success of parliaments of nations, and the destiny of Adolf Hitler.
He seems to have been wrong as often as he was right, but he never
doubted the strength of his special power. We find signs of this
conviction in the poems and the plays. *Avon's Harvest*, we might
say, is the "touch" made heavy and sensational by the frame of the
popular mystery tale. Mabel Daniels in "Edwin Arlington Robinson: A Musical Memoir" (*CLQ*, VI, 219-233) documents in an
engaging manner Robinson's deep interest in music. Miss Daniels,

a composer, met Robinson at a music festival at the MacDowell
Colony in Peterborough, New Hampshire, and she became a friend
and admirer of the poet's. She recalls that Robinson loved opera—
especially Wagner and Verdi—Brahms symphonies, operettas by
Gilbert and Sullivan, old Scotch ballads, and blaring brass bands.
He despised jazz. She suggests that his knowledge of music has
contributed to the complex structure of *The Man Who Died Twice*.
Miss Daniel's memory of conversations with the poet when she was
setting to music parts of "Sisera" has interest because we see here
a poet completely dedicated to the integrity of his own verse.

iii. E. E. Cummings

A model of integrity, too, is E. E. Cummings as he emerges from
the letters published by Robert G. Tucker and David R. Clark in
MR, IV, 497-528. The letters, covering a period from February to
December, 1954, are a record of Cummings' reactions to the preparation, production, and ultimate shelving of a tape for Program 7
in "New England Anthology," a series produced by the Literary
Society of the University of Massachusetts for the National Association of Education Broadcasters. The NAEB objected to two poems
in a group selected by Cummings for his reading, "i sing of Olaf"
and "a politician is an arse upon," and Cummings, in response,
refused to accept any editorial cuts or deletions in the tape. There
the matter rested finally—an outraged and eloquent poet and an
unplayed tape (so far, at least, as the general radio public is
concerned).

John Clendenning in "Cummings, Comedy, and Criticism"
(*ColQ*, XII, 44-53) attempts to find a tradition for Cummings'
poetry. He sees Cummings as being uninfluenced by Eliot. He
finds part of the poet's originality to be derived from the tradition
of American humor, and he cites the poet's reliance upon a technique emphasizing surprise as supporting evidence. The technique
involves endings, grammatical shifts, and typographical arrangements. Mr. Clendenning recognizes that Cummings cannot be considered a modern poet by the definition supplied by Eliot's criticism
and practice, and he implies in this way that we must go to Eliot,
and, of course, then, to Pound, for the central development that is
modern American poetry.

iv. Pound

T. S. Eliot, by virtue of classification and citizenship in the annual MLA bibliography rather than by birth, is English, not American, and so does not fall within the scope of this review. Ezra Pound does, and the amount of scholarship devoted to the man and his work indicates the continued improvement of his reputation, despite his unhappy political history. It is even possible for George Dekker, author of a new study of the *Cantos* (*Sailing after Knowledge: The* Cantos *of Ezra Pound*, London, Routledge and Kegan Paul) to fear that "Pound is about to be enshrined along with Whitman—Whitman being the Homer, Pound the Dante of American Literature" (p. xvi).

Donald Gallup has supplied now a comprehensive and handsome *Bibliography of Ezra Pound* (London, Hart-Davis). The new book, one of the Soho Series that include bibliographies of Henry James, W. B. Yeats, D. H. Lawrence, and Virginia Woolf, builds on and supersedes *A Preliminary Checklist of the Writings of Ezra Pound*, published by John Edwards in 1953. Mr. Gallup has also had the assistance of Ian D. Angus's "A List with Descriptions of the Books of Ezra Pound for the Beginning of a Bibliography of Some Length," compiled in 1952, and of Myles Slatin's "More by Ezra Pound," published in the *Yale University Library Gazette* in 1955. *A Bibliography of Ezra Pound* includes a listing of the books and pamphlets written by or translated by the poet, the books and pamphlets edited by or with contributions by the poet, his contributions to periodicals, and the translations of his works. We find also a portrait of Pound at age thirty-five and the reproduction of three title-pages. Mr. Gallup's bibliography will be an indispensable tool for Pound scholars.

Louis Untermeyer, whose attention to Frost and Robinson has led during the year to important scholarly publications, has had something to offer too on Ezra Pound. Nine of Pound's letters to Untermeyer, serving again as a provocative correspondent, have appeared in a small volume edited by J. A. Robbins (*Ezra Pound to Louis Untermeyer*, Bloomington, Indiana Univ. Press). The first letter was written from London on January 8, 1914; the ninth from Rapallo, Italy, on July 13, 1931. There is a tenth letter of a later date (September 24, 1933), written also from Rapallo, but this has not been published. The most revealing is the fifth, presenting in 1930 the poet's illuminating summary of his own career. We find here also Pound's conviction that he had been rejected thoroughly by American publishers, universities, and various prize and fellowship committees (p. 19). Mr. Robbins' notes are useful, especially those documenting Pound's career as a student in American universities.

Four new books of Pound criticism have appeared during 1963. Two, George Dekker's *Sailing after Knowledge* and L. S. Dembo's *The Confucian Odes of Ezra Pound* (Berkeley, Univ. of California Press), present new evaluations of Pound's genius, estimates supported by analysis and informed taste. William Van O'Connor's *Ezra Pound* in the UMPAW (No. 26) and Walter Sutton's *Ezra Pound: A Collection of Critical Essays* (Englewood Cliffs, New Jersey, Prentice-Hall) in the series of Twentieth Century Views serve somewhat different purposes.

Mr. Dekker fails to find a principle of unity in the *Cantos*, though he grants the fact that certain continuities exist within the whole. One, examined perceptively in the study, is the theme of Eros, the conception of love that permits Pound to link Helen of Troy, Eleanor of Aquitaine, Mother Earth, and Elizabeth I. The legend of Cabestanh, a tale of revenge for adultery, offers the basis for another such continuity. To these and other directional lines in the *Cantos* Mr. Dekker brings a rewarding familiarity with Pound's sources—the verse of Propertius, de Gourmont's *Physique de l'amour*, the lyrics of the troubadours, the epics of classical Greece. He has read with profit other Pound scholars and he avoids much tedious repetition by the simple act of allusion. The problem that chiefly concerns him is the conflict in the *Cantos* between Pound's skill in reducing motley elements to pattern and the desire simultaneously "to honour the thing as it was at the point where it was captured" (p. 74).

Certain cantos (I, XXX, XLV, XLVII, XCI, for example) receive praise from Dekker, who maintains that these may be read without intimate knowledge of the others, though such knowledge would be useful as background. The Pisan sequence (LXXIV-LXXXIII) is held to be an exception to the general judgment that order is more accidental than necessary, "for there the cantos are so long, diverse and interrelated as to force one to view the sequence as a whole" (p. 140). Mr. Dekker alludes to Clark Emery's design for the *Cantos* in *Ideas into Action* (1958), but maintains that this map of relationships does not satisfy finally because it fails to take into account the vast difference in quality that may separate even cantos that stand by each other (to be specific, XLV and XLVI). The difference is not a matter of the poet's success or failure, but one that concerns "what is immediately apprehended as a poetic unit (not quite an independent poem) and what is, by courtesy, accepted as something more than a passage of prose"—and, Mr. Dekker adds, "the difference is absolute" (p. 140). Pound indicated once that he would supply an Aquinas-map for the *Cantos* for those who have trouble discovering a compelling order, but Dekker doubts that this would be more convincing than Emery's chart.

Mr. Dekker locates the source of Pound's difficulty in his method. It is a "translator's, not a poet's approach to the world" (p. 137), and trouble comes from Pound's obsession with the integrity of his materials. Though we may question how translation has contributed to the *Cantos*, we do not doubt the fact of the contribution, and we locate here a possible weakness in Dekker's argument. He does little with Pound's attention to Chinese writing. Pound derived from Confucian thought one of the important principles of unity in the *Cantos*.

L. S. Dembo does not measure Pound's indebtedness to Confucius in the *Cantos*; he concerns himself rather with evaluating Pound's skill in translating the 304 odes of the *Classic Anthology* as defined by Confucius. What Mr. Dembo has to say, however, directly concerns the *Cantos* since Pound found in the odes a way of linking art and history, a technique that made little distinction between poet and translator. The creator of the odes and Pound are both charged, according to Dembo, "with the almost divine mission of 'rectifying' language and bringing about the psychological and social renovation that would mark a new 'cultural synthesis' or 'paideuma'" (p. 2). Pound acquired from Confucius (or Kung) "the idea of an apocalyptic mode of communication, associated with Order, Beauty, and Truth, in contradistinction to a common or unenlightened mode, associated with chaos, corruption and illusion" (p. 2).

Mr. Dembo finds Pound's translations to be often brilliant, especially when the problem in restatement involves dramatizing emotions of the individual. There are less happy moments when Pound, not in the lyric mode, uses an irony that is inconsistent with the evident context of the odes. Dembo suspects the persistence in

Pound of the influence of Jules Laforgue, and the effect of the irony
in the odes of censure distorts the spirit of Kung: "Pound's aim is
simply to condemn or to achieve a general ironic effect, and there
is an unmistakable impression that whereas the Chinese has every
impulse to reeducate the criminal, Pound has every impulse to
destroy him" (p. 86).

Mr. Dembo's critical examination of Pound's Confucian odes
achieves several worthy ends. It describes the meaning of the
activity of "translation," as Pound understood it; illuminates, to a
degree, a system of references that is central to the progress of the
Cantos; aids in clarifying the purposes of the *Cantos*; and accounts,
once more, for the importance to Pound of the Chinese character,
the ideograph that weds "thing" and "act" and presents the "perfect
literary expression of the idea in action" (p. 23).

William Van O'Connor attempts in his *Ezra Pound* a task that
is close to the impossible. Within severely limited space he must
introduce a difficult and controversial poet to an audience only
sketchily acquainted with the man and his work. He constructs a
brief biographical sketch; discusses Pound's friends, associates, and
"discoveries"; and lists some of the literary influences (de Gourmont,
Browning, Henry James, Dante, Calvacanti, Propertius, Ovid, Confucius). The pamphlet has little to say about the technique of the
early verse or of the *Cantos*. Pound's prose is matter to be deplored,
in general, either for its excesses or its incoherence. Mr. O'Connor
sees the late cantos, except for the Pisan sequence, as demonstrations
contributing to the "spectacle of Pound's degeneration," to echo
Mr. Leavis's judgment.

Walter Sutton has provided another kind of introduction by collecting a number of important critical essays on Pound and his work.
We find here some indispensable statements—early estimates by
Yeats, Eliot, William Carlos Williams, and Leavis. Hugh Kenner,
who has done much to establish a basis for a rewarding analytic
study of Pound's poems, is represented by an essay on "Mauberly."
M. L. Rosenthal contributes a lucid description of the progress in
the *Cantos*, and Roy Harvey Peace a provocative comparison of two
masters of the epic, Whitman and Pound—on the surface, so different. We miss discussions from R. P. Blackmur, John Espey, and
Clark Emery, but George P. Elliot keeps us aware of the fact that
Pound is a problem as well as a poet.

G. P. Elliot begins his essay in the Sutton collection by praising the beauty of sound in Pound's poetry, yet, as William McNaughton indicates in "Ezra Pound's Meters and Rhythms" (*PMLA*, LXXVIII, 136-146), one important element of sound, meter, has received little scholarly study. Mr. McNaughton seeks to satisfy the need. He finds in Pound's critical pronouncements three statements of intention about meter: (1) "To break the pentameter..."; (2) "Poetry atrophies when it gets too far from music"; (3) "Metre is the articulation of the total sound of a poem" (p. 136). The essay examines Pound's studies and practice in terms of these principles, and it compares Pound's verse with models that come from Virgil, Arnaut Daniel, Shakespeare, Campion, Donne, Beddoes, Whitman, and T'ai Ch'ien. Concerned also with meter and rhythm is Edgar Racey, who compares the techniques of Pound and William Carlos Williams in "Pound and Williams" (*BuR*, XI, ii, 21-30). He finds differences in terms of accommodation to American speech when he examines closely passages from *Paterson*, Book II, and Pound's Canto XLV. As a consequence, he calls Williams a poet of personality and Pound a poet of culture.

Alan Holder in "The Lesson of the Master" (*AL*, XXXV, 71-79) attaches importance to Pound's high opinion of Henry James, and he thinks that Pound's attention to the speaking voice is an evidence of James's influence. The works given close scrutiny are a collection of stories by James, *Embarrassments*, and Pound's "Hugh Selwyn Mauberly." Myles Slatin, in "A History of Pound's Cantos I-XVI, 1915-1925" (*AL*, XXXV, 183-195), supplies a study of value to scholars undertaking a critical analysis of Pound's major work. Gordon K. Grigsby in "Newspeak in Pound's *Cantos*" (*SAQ*, LXII, 51-56) examines the method of the ideogram as Pound uses it in the *Cantos*. Mr. Grigsby finds weakness in Pound's nominalist bias. The completion of three doctoral dissertations on Pound, two of them on the *Cantos*, suggests no prospect now of any decline in scholarly interest; rather, the difficulties presented by the poet in matters of structure, diction, and allusion invite approaches that have become increasingly systematic.

v. Hart Crane

Though a primary task for the scholar must be discovering facts and methods to illumine a poet's art—especially if the art is demanding—a second responsibility exists too of fashioning an introduction to the art for the general reader. Only Mr. O'Connor has faced this problem in 1963 in Pound studies. On the other hand, Hart Crane, a poet almost as difficult as Ezra Pound is, has had the benefit during the year of two general introductions, Samuel Hazo's in the American Authors and Critics Series (*Hart Crane: An Introduction and Interpretation*, New York, Barnes and Noble) and Vincent Quinn's in TUSAS (*Hart Crane*, New York, Twayne). Mr. Hazo's has many virtues. For one thing, Hazo brings to his estimate of Crane a thorough familiarity with all the scholarly writing on the poems, and, for another, he offers a perceptive sensibility of his own that makes possible a rewarding discussion of Crane's lyrics. Mr. Quinn's introduction, though more ambitious in its effort to suggest Crane's intellectual background and to summarize the estimates of Crane's achievement made by leading contemporary critics, is often reductive and sketchy in approaching the lyrics. This fact becomes clear when we compare the discussions of "The Wine Menagerie." Moreover, Mr. Quinn is opinionated—perhaps misleading—at times. He dismisses the very considerable contribution that epic conventions make to *The Bridge*: "By far the most unfortunate remark made by Crane was that he was writing an epic" (p. 73).

Mr. Hazo's sympathetic rendering of Crane's life emphasizes the debt that we owe to Philip Horton's biography (1937). It remains the starting point for scholarly work on the poet. Despite the valuable beginning in Brom Weber's *Hart Crane* (1948), we are much less certain of the intellectual factors in Crane's background and of the traditions that shaped his work. Hazo uses the term "impressionism" to summarize the influences that we feel in the early lyrics; as a description of these forces "impressionism" is too amorphous and too general to have much value. He sketches a development in three stages of Crane's lyric talent, a development that seems arbitrary, since he does not demonstrate how Pound or Eliot or Laforgue or Jonson has had much to do with shaping or altering a line of Crane's verse. Mr. Hazo is more satisfying with Marlowe, since the rhetoric presents a discussion object of some firmness. Mr. Quinn is hardly more precise on this point since he resolves the problem by defining a tradition of visionary poetry that includes Blake, Coleridge, Poe, Emerson, Baudelaire, Rimbaud, and, of course, Crane (oddly, Whitman is not mentioned) and by describing the curriculum for poets prescribed by Pound and Eliot.

R. W. B. Lewis in "Hart Crane and the Clown Tradition" (*MR*, IV, 745-767) demonstrates one way in which the problem of determining significant intellectual factors in Crane's cultural environment can be solved. Mr. Lewis examines at depth one of Crane's poems, "Chaplinesque," with passing reference to "Black Tambourine," "Porphyro in Akron," "Praise for an Urn," and "My Grandmother's Love Letters." He connects Crane with Laforgue through the tradition of Pierrot and produces impressive evidence of the influence of Laforgue's *L'Imitation de Notre Dame La Lune.* Indeed, Crane translated three of Laforgue's sixteen "Locutions des Pierrots." Convinced that Crane's interest is not so simply explained, Lewis suggests a contribution from Whitman—the sketchy outline of the fool Yankee and the irreverent diction of *Leaves of Grass.* There is a rewarding discussion of why Crane became deeply interested in the figure of the clown. Crane was moved by Charlie Chaplin in "The Kid," and, beyond this, he saw the clown as the representation of the artist in a hostile contemporary world. It is a view, Mr. Lewis shows, that is shared in different ways by T. S. Eliot, Wallace Stevens, and E. E. Cummings, but only Crane, with his intense idealism, believed in the power of the clown to make "A grail of laughter of an empty ash can" (*The Complete Poems*, p. 78). Crane's art is a part of a continuity that leads to the fiction of Nathanael West and to many recent American novels that owe a spiritual debt to *Miss Lonelyhearts* and *The Day of the Locust.* Crane assumes here his proper position in the mainstream of the development of American poetry. Perhaps subsequent investigation, by Mr. Lewis and others, will relate other parts of the Crane canon to the important intellectual currents of the period.

The complexity of Crane's language, thought, and life presents a serious challenge to the scholar. David R. Clark in "Hart Crane's Technique" (*TSLL*, V, 389-397) discusses the poet's peculiar use of syntax and metaphor. He observes that defective syntax may be functional and proves his point by referring to "Voyages II." A second claim, that "Crane's chain-reaction series of metaphors may be effective without being analyzable in terms of concrete reference" (p. 391), requires more elaborate support. Mr. Clark analyzes the manuscript versions of the "Atlantis" section of *The Bridge* to trace the history of an image based on horseback riding. All that remains of the figure in its final form is the word "slit," but vestiges and overtones linger to enrich and heighten Crane's line, despite the process of drastic reduction. Gordon Grigsby in "Hart Crane's Doubtful Vision" (*CE*, XXIV, 518-523) maintains that ugly realities and negations have been inserted into *The Bridge* because the poet wished to keep his vision from being oversimple. The doubting sections of the poem, Mr. Grigsby suggests, owe something to Spengler. George Hendrick in "Hart Crane Aboard the Ship of Fools" (*TCL*, IX, 3-9) considers whether or not Crane is present as a character in Katherine Anne Porter's *Ship of Fools*. It is an opportunity for Mr. Hendrick to examine the friendship between the novelist and the poet and to comment upon the disintegration that seemed to be the fated end of many of Crane's close personal attachments.

vi. MacLeish, Lindsay, Masters, Markham

Archibald MacLeish, like Hart Crane, came of age as a poet in the 1920's. In 1963 MacLeish received the attention of scholars not so much for the books of poetry that appeared in the 1920's and the 1930's as for the verse play *J.B.* that became a successful production on Broadway. What has attracted examination especially is the philosophical or religious thought that stands behind the play rather than the novel or original form of the drama itself. Sheldon N. Grebstein in "*J.B.* and the Problem of Evil" (*UKCR*, XXIX, 253-261) compares *J.B.* and the story of Job and concludes that Mac-Leish denies the lesson of the Old Testament narrative by failing to affirm God. He offers instead, according to Mr. Grebstein, "human love and human awareness and the continuity of human existence" (p. 260). *J.B.* is a deeply religious work because it exalts man, not the God that man has risen above by the act of love.

Eleanor M. Sickels in "MacLeish and the Fortunate Fall" (*AL*, XXXV, 205-217) traces the emergence in MacLeish's poetry of his conception of the Fortunate Fall and explores the development of the idea in *J.B.* as it is applied to contemporary man. The works before *J.B.* that are important to her discussion are the early verse play *Nobodaddy* (1926), in which the poet first handles the myth of the lost paradise, *This Music Crept by Me upon the Waters* (1953), and *Songs for Eve* (1954). MacLeish's idea is made explicit in *Songs for Eve*: the Fall is "fortunate because without it man is a mere animal.... MacLeish's redemption is in all human good achievement, and in the very yearning for the infinite which caused the Fall" (p. 207). The form of the fall remains unchanged in *J.B.*, except that the emphasis here is not proudly humanistic, as in *Songs for Eve*, but upon a tragic reconciliation. J.B. accepts alienation and exclusion from Eden, and he comes to believe in man and in love—love not merely for his wife and children but for "all suffering humanity—and perhaps God as well" (p. 213).

Lindsay and Masters in 1963 seem no longer to be "new," though their voices were major ones in the so-called new poetry that received in 1915 the enthusiastic backing of Harriet Monroe, editor of *Poetry* magazine. Other poets, Pound, Eliot, Stevens, Frost, Williams, have been more fertile influences in the development of modern American poetry, and the revolt associated with the names of Lindsay, Masters, and Sandburg has become with the passing years less important. It may be true, as Lois Hartley maintains in "Spoon River Revisited," the first Ball State Monograph (Muncie, Indiana, Ball State Teachers College), that the *Spoon River Anthology* gave a much-needed shock to a large segment of the American reading public in 1915, but Masters' verse, in perspective, is less impressive as an achievement of high originality than the early volumes of Pound and Frost—and of Robinson, who preceded Masters by more than a decade.

Miss Hartley brings a care born of long acquaintance with and deep affection for the *Spoon River Anthology* and the Spoon River country. She identifies the models for characters, locates the towns and rivers that have provided details of scene, and assesses the influence of Bohn's *Greek Anthology* and the criticism of William Marion Reedy, editor of the St. Louis *Mirror*. She describes the circumstances of publication, summarizes the reception of the *Spoon River Anthology* at home and abroad, and records with sympathy Masters' futile efforts to have his work adapted for the movies. It is ironic that the current revival of interest in the *Anthology* should be linked to a successful dramatic production.

Affection, more accurately, nostalgia, is responsible for an edition by Mark Harris of *Selected Poems of Vachel Lindsay* (New York, Macmillan). Mr. Harris, an outstanding contemporary novelist, recalls in his introduction the circumstances surrounding his writing a biography of Lindsay in 1945. Lindsay's life then seemed to Harris to achieve a noble and pathetic fulfilment when the poet attempted to convert Americans by the hundreds of thousands to his gospel of beauty. Lindsay's death in 1931, actually a suicide, was for Harris the cruel price demanded of the artist by an unfeeling society.

Though his view of Lindsay's life in 1963 is somewhat less dogmatic, rather more tempered, Harris's appreciation of Lindsay's
poems has grown, if anything. The result of this renewal of faith
is a handsome and thoughtful edition of the poems, organized by
theme and fully representative of Lindsay's remarkable talents.

We find special pleading of a kind in the sympathetic evaluations
by Miss Hartley and Mr. Harris of poets no longer fashionable.
The cases they make for Masters and Lindsay are engaging, if not
altogether convincing. Nor is Louis Filler any more definitive or
persuasive in "Edwin Markham, Poetry and What Have You" (AR,
XXIII, 447-459) when he addresses himself to the problem of Edwin
Markham, a poet who, like Masters and Lindsay, "has not been well
remembered" (p. 447).

Mr. Filler says that Markham was "one of the great men of the
1900's" (p. 453), a popular poet who was America's conscience, a
pivotal figure in a period devoted to muck-raking and reform. We
should cherish Markham today because of the sad state of contemporary poetry. Ours is a period, according to Mr. Filler, for "private
worlds, sanatorium silence, all carefully supervised by a glossary of
criticism" (p. 456). The separation of poetry from the grass roots
of America occurred in 1910, and the process of disassociation has
continued since. Mr. Filler suspects now that we are back in the
1890's, at the end of a sterile journey to a culture no more attractive
or lively than the genteel world of Aldrich, Stedman, and Gilder.
Neither Miss Hartley nor Mr. Harris has assumed a position so
extreme as this one. Mr. Filler deplores all traditions in modern
American poetry and insists that the poet's primary task is "to begin
to consider ways back to people" (p. 458). There are few poets
and scholars who share his views. It is one that denies value finally
to all of the experimentation in technique and to all of the rich
explorations of contemporary man and his society that have been
characteristic of American verse since 1910.

Though no general estimate of the year's scholarly activity in
the period from 1910 to 1930 is possible or thinkable, what comes
close to providing a sober contemporary perspective for poetic
achievement in the two decades is "An Interview with Conrad
Aiken" (Shenandoah, XV, i, 18-40), a long and rewarding exchange
with Ashley Brown. Aiken recalled the literary enthusiasms that
were important in his young manhood: Whitman, both in his poetry

and his prose; Emily Dickinson, whose poems Aiken encountered in 1903; Francis Thompson, important because of his fine rhetoric; Santayana, with whom Aiken studied at Harvard when the philosopher was working out *Three Philosophical Poets*; William James, especially in *Varieties of Religious Experience*; Freud, in *Beyond the Pleasure Principle*. Aiken's critical judgments have unusual value for us. He deplored the "customs barriers" (p. 32) erected by Harriet Monroe to exclude English poetry; he pointed to the narrow range of Imagism in ignoring the cosmic and in restricting itself to no "more than one-fifth of potential poetry" (p. 33). He remembered the stimulating association with other poets and intellectuals of the *Harvard Advocate* (T. S. Eliot was one) and of the Poetry Bookshop in London. He spoke of rewarding exchanges of opinions and poems with Eliot and Pound. Robinson, Aiken connected with the "exciting" period in the popular arts that had its beginning in 1910. Though he thought that poetry in 1963 was less significant than it had been in other years, Mr. Aiken insisted that the "times [like the years after 1910] are propitious for great poetry" (p. 39).

15. Poetry: 1930 to the Present

Oliver Evans

i. General

Though several book-length studies of individual poets were published in 1963, no single book of importance appeared which discussed in general terms the current situation in American poetry. For overviews, therefore, one must consult either particular chapters in books devoted to broader subjects or articles in periodicals. None of these describes the total scene as objectively as did Donald Hall's excellent introduction to his anthology, *Contemporary American Poetry* (Harmondsworth, Penguin Books, 1962), but Randall Jarrell's "Fifty Years of American Poetry" (*PrS*, XXXVI, i, 1-27) is generally perceptive. Perhaps it no longer requires courage to suggest that Eliot, notwithstanding his theories about the relation of the poet to his art, may be regarded by the future as "one of the most subjective and daemonic poets who ever lived, the victim and helpless beneficiary of his own inexorable compulsions, obsessions." But to maintain nowadays that Williams' poems have been harmed by their "underemphasis on organization, logic, narrative, generalization" requires both courage and discernment. (Obviously Mr. Jarrell knows his Williams: one recalls that it was he who wrote the introduction, in 1949, to this poet's Selected Edition.) There are fine judgments of Stevens, Moore, Cummings, Jeffers, (Elizabeth) Bishop, Ransom, Warren, Roethke, Winters, Wilbur, Lowell, and Shapiro, as well as of poets whom one thinks of—not always very logically, in point of chronology—as belonging to an older generation, like Robinson, Sandburg, Pound, Lindsay, Aiken, and Frost. The weakness of the essay is that it is not really up to date, ignoring entirely such active younger talents as Duncan, Levertov, Bly, and Creeley. A strong anti-romantic bias is, not surprisingly, evident throughout, and in his blanket indictment of the poets whom he labels as Beatniks (without naming them) one suspects that he would include poets who, though definitely not members of "The Establishment," are not members of the Beatnik camp either, and that he is mindless not only of the differences that separate them from this camp, but also of the differences that separate them from one another.

Louis Simpson, in "Poetry Chronicle" (*HudR*, XVI, i, 130-140), is more respectful of the younger talents. He makes the point (and Mr. Jarrell's essay may well be proof of its validity) that our newest generation of poets lacks a critic, that the reason their work seems strange is that there was no preparation for it among the poet-critics who (like Mr. Jarrell) immediately preceded them: "The middle generation, the poets who came after Eliot, simply are not there as a critical force. One would be willing to be judged by Mr. Roethke, who doesn't; instead, we are judged by Miss Moore." Mr. Simpson claims that the poets of the twenties, engaged in active revolt against Victorian conventions, wrote in an atmosphere that was critically stimulating; the poets who followed them, however, did not revolt but imitated: "Is it any wonder," he asks rhetorically, "that the new poets seem to be making a complete break with the past, and that their poems are strange?" About the current scene he is generally optimistic: "There are many different kinds of poetry being written today, and ideas are flying about—as they were when Eliot and Williams began to publish."

For Stephen Spender, the problem of the modern poet is not that there is too little criticism, but too much. In an important article in *SatR* ("Poets and Critics: The Forgotten Difference," XLVI, Oct. 5, 15-18), he argues that the distinction between poet and critic has become blurred, and that there is "something healthy" about the dislike which such poets as Frost, Cummings, and Graves have felt for the critical process. The trouble with living in an age of criticism, he maintains, is that "only the work is appreciated which the current critical apparatus can deal with." Only those poets who share with the critics a high degree of intellectual consciousness will be admired; the others will be ignored "not out of malice, but simply because current criticism lacks the apparatus to say anything about poets who do not fit into their categories." The modern poet, he declares, must learn to defend his work against the current orthodoxy, which, because it confuses the critical with the creative faculty, encourages the manufacture of synthetic poetry. The critic's concern is with the precedented, while the genuine poet "stands partly on the ground of the precedented and partly on that of the life which has not yet been written in literature." Mr. Spender poses the problem in practical terms when he says: "If a poet writes an image and then attempts to judge the truth of his own lines, he does so by asking himself, 'Is this how I really saw or experienced it?,' not by asking, 'Is this how some other writer whom I approve of would have described it?'"

Somewhat similar views are expressed by Samuel Hazo ("The Poet's Cult," *Cweal*, LXXIX, v, 130-132) and Howard Nemerov ("The Muse's Interest," *Carleton Miscellany*, IV, ii, 83-90). Mr. Hazo claims that the emphasis in current poetry has shifted "from vision to craft." His praise of the New Critics, however, seems inconsistent with this thesis, for it is they who (if such a situation indeed exists) are usually held responsible for it. Mr. Nemerov insists that the poet's eye must be always on the poem, not on the audience for which it may be intended: properly speaking, it ought not to be *intended*, consciously and as such, for *any* audience. The peculiar power of the poet derives precisely from the fact that he does not, in the act of creation, aim at any "specific or immediate end other than the poem itself." One recognizes in this, of course, the influence of I. A. Richards. Robert Graves ("The Poet in a Valley of Dry Bones," *Horizon*, V, iv, 84-88) sees the poet's problem as primarily one of words: his first duty is to the *mot juste*, and in performing it he transforms the "valley of dry bones" (which is the world of dictionary meanings) into a place of life and beauty.

The formal aspects of modern poetry are discussed by J. V. Cunningham ("The Problem of Form," *Shen*, XIV, ii, 3-6) and Allen Tate ("Shadow: a Parable and a Polemic," *Carleton Miscellany*, IV, i, 61-64). Mr. Cunningham sees a paradox in the desire (which he says is a concomitant of the Romantic Revolution) of many poets to abandon form and "decorum"; "If informality and anti-formality are positive values, then the problem of form is how to get rid of it. But to do this we must keep it; we must have something to get rid of . . . . A generation of poets, acting on the principles of significant variation, have at last nothing to vary from. The last variation is regularity." The problem of the late eighteenth-century romantics, rebelling against octosyllabic and decasyllabic couplets, was by contrast relatively simple. Mr. Tate suggests a tripartite classification of poetry into abstract, formalistic, and expressionistic. With the exception of the abstract, all poets are always "partly formalistic, partly expressionistic." The increasing tendency toward expressionism he views as an attempt to create the content (the "formless Shadow Self") of the modern world.

The republication, with an introduction by Louis D. Rubin, Jr., of the Southern Agrarian anthology, *I'll Take My Stand* (New York, Harper), which was originally issued in 1930 and which contains essays by Ransom, Tate, (Robert Penn) Warren, and Davidson, provided the occasion for two articles concerned with the Fugitive group of poets who were associated with the Agrarian movement: "The 1930 Agrarians," by Edward M. Moore (*SR*, LXXI, i, 134-142), and "The Southern Phoenix," by Richard M. Weaver (*GaR*, XVII, i, 6-17). Only one of the original essays (Davidson's) dealt specifically with literary problems, and it is naturally dated; the chief interest that the book now has—and the reason for reprinting it— is that so many of its contributors have since distinguished themselves as poets and critics. Nevertheless, Mr. Weaver claims that it is "one of the great works of American social criticism." The Fugitives are also the subject of a chapter, "The Poetry of Agrarianism," in Mr. Rubin's *The Faraway Country* (Seattle, Univ. of Washington Press). Speaking of Ransom, Tate, Warren, and Davidson, he declares: "For all four poets, Agrarianism performed the function of a usable poetic myth." The essay is informative, though there are some controversial judgments (e.g., that Warren's poems are more private than Tate's) and a few faults of emphasis and proportion: a certain distortion occurs when poets as dissimilar—and as unequal by aesthetic standards—as Davidson and Ransom are analyzed exclusively in terms of their Agrarian affiliation. John M. Bradbury's *Renaissance in the South* (Chapel Hill, Univ. of North Carolina Press) also discusses the Fugitives, but its scope is of course broader, including, among the earlier moderns, John Gould Fletcher, (John Peale) Bishop, and George Dillon; and, among the newer talents, Karl Shapiro, who, though he was born in Baltimore, one seldom thinks of as a Southern poet; Randall Jarrell; Byron Herbert Reese; and George Scarbrough. Mr. Bradbury has, in fact, tried to leave almost no one out, and his desire to do everyone justice sometimes results in a loss of focus.

The idea (which one associates with Agrarianism) that a mechanical civilization is inimical to the interests of poetry is attacked by Martin S. Dworkin in "Poetry and the Machine" (*DR*, XLII, iv, 445-451). There is, he maintains, nothing either in the nature of machines or in the chaos that may result from their misapplication that unfits them for poetic material, since poetry has to do with things, and with situations, only in the way they may be used by the poet's shaping imagination: "If there is a 'problem' of modern poetry, it is one of poets." The first duty of the poet, he asserts, is to be honest, and if he ignores the materials with which his age supplies him he is acting dishonestly. If the experience of his age seems incoherent, if he can make no "sense" out of it, he must remember that coherence itself "is not static, but dynamic—changing as we change, needing always to take new bearings on new landmarks of meaning on the shores of civilization." And there is, for the genuine poet, a certain value even in chaos: "Let poets only honestly despair of clarity, and write their despair honestly, and they will never be more clear—though all coherence goes but that which men make by their art."

The Sullen Art (New York, Corinth), edited by David Ossman, consists of a series of interviews with such newer poets as, among others, Blackburn, Carroll, Bly, Sorrentino, Creeley, Merwin, Logan, Levertov, (LeRoi) Jones, and Ginsberg. (Rexroth, older than any of these, is included on ideological grounds.) The title, of course, is an allusion to Thomas's poem, "In My Craft or Sullen Art," and Mr. Ossman is careful to state in his introduction that he is not using the word *sullen* pejoratively but in its original sense of *solitary* (from Latin *solus*). He also exposes the popular error that these poets are divided from "The Academy" and "The Establishment" by an irreconcilable breach: some of them, he points out, are or have been teachers; one of them was, and another is now, Poetry Editor of the *Nation*; and their work has appeared elsewhere than *Evergreen Review, Big Table, Black Mountain Review,* and *Jugen.* That we find one of them (Logan) quoting John Crowe Ransom approvingly and another (Levertov) quoting Eliot with equal approval would seem to prove his point. (Pound and Williams, of course, are cited throughout.) Actually at least three groups are represented (Black Mountain, San Francisco, and *Big Table*), and there is only one poet who is, properly speaking, a Beatnik: Ginsberg.

As is only to be expected from such a variety of affiliations, a number of divergent opinions are expressed, but several dominant ideas recur, among them the belief, inherited from Pound via Rexroth, in the importance of translations (Rexroth, Rothenberg, Bly) and in the value of "depth imagery" (Rothenberg, Kelly, Bly).

Rothenberg, who regards the new poetry as the legitimate heir of Surrealism, says that what the Surrealists, both in Europe and America, evolved was "not a poetry which obscures communication, but a poetry of the most direct communication possible—that is, an exploration of the unconscious region of the mind in such a way that the unconscious is speaking to the unconscious." Bly, who believes that the language of poetry has begun to "dry up" because of the poet's concern with "the surface of life," is in essential agreement: "Unless English and American poetry can enter, really, an inward depth, through a kind of surrealism, it will continue to become dryer and dryer." The most effective poetry being written today, he argues, "simply disregards the conscious and the intellectual structure of the mind entirely, and, by the use of images, tries to bring forward another reality from *inward* experience."

There are a few exaggerations and absurdities. Noting the influence of Olson upon Creeley, Sorrentino says calmly, "Everyone in the world today who cares for poems has learned from Olson." And here is Ginsberg on his experience with laughing gas: "Every time I go to my cousin—he's a dentist—he gives it to me for working on my teeth. Then I wake up and write down whatever I can about it. Sometimes it's very funny. Sometimes they're incomprehensible— like the last thing I wrote, 'Stick your finger up your knows and you'll know what I mean by one Cosmos.' That's very good, I think. I'd put that into a poem, if I had a poem to put it into. I keep getting strange images under it." But even Sorrentino admits, "Nine out of every ten poems I write I just chuck out," and the contrast which he draws between the styles of Creeley and Ginsberg is exactly right. Of the few books published in 1963 which deal specifically with theories of modern poetry, *The Sullen Art* may well be the most important. Unfortunately it is not indexed and shows evidence of having been carelessly proofread (in the captions, *Creeley* is misspelled *Greeley* for the length of seven pages).

ii. Individual Poets: Stevens, Williams, Moore, Ransom, Tate, Lowell

a. **Wallace Stevens.**   Interest in this poet, as evidenced by recent critical activity, is mounting steadily: obviously, 1963 was a "Stevens year." There were two important book-length studies, *The Comic Spirit of Wallace Stevens,* by Daniel Fuchs (Durham, Duke Univ.

Press) and *Wallace Stevens: A Collection of Critical Essays*, edited
by Marie Borroff (New York, Prentice-Hall); a giant-sized *Concordance to the Poetry of Wallace Stevens*, by T. F. Walsh (University Park, Pennsylvania State Univ. Press), handsomely bound
and printed; a book-length bibliography, *A Checklist of Stevens
Criticism*, by S. F. Morse, J. R. Bryer, and J. N. Riddell (Denver,
Swallow); miscellaneous essays in books and periodicals; and no
fewer than six doctoral dissertations. Few poets present such a
challenge to the explicator, and (though analyses of individual
poems are not included in this survey) the explicators have responded gallantly, and in some cases nobly, to the challenge.

Mr. Fuchs's study is, as its title indicates, limited in its scope,
and it is only the comic poems which are discussed in any detail.
However, as Mr. Fuchs points out, the comic spirit in Stevens is
essential, and "without a sense of it, there is no true understanding
of Stevens." And the poems which are explicated are done so with
a thoroughness and an honesty which make this book an indispensable aid to the teacher of contemporary poetry. Mr. Fuchs is never
guilty, as are so many commentators, of explaining the obvious and
ignoring the difficult, a practice which—when the difficulty is central, as it often is in Williams—can be maddening. (A classic case is
Kermode on "Notes Toward a Supreme Fiction": "I will not disgrace Stevens' greatest poem by plodding commentary.")

Miss Borroff's anthology, with its interesting introduction, collects ten essays (of which all but one, "'Notes Toward a Supreme
Fiction': A Commentary," by Harold Bloom, have been previously
published) dealing with Stevens' art; there is also one of Stevens'
own essays ("Three Academic Pieces: I") reprinted from *The
Necessary Angel*. It is a discriminating selection. Miss Borroff has,
for the most part, wisely chosen essays whose concern is with
Stevens' total significance rather than with narrowly specialized
aspects of his work. Roy Harvey Pearce's "Wallace Stevens: The
Life of the Imagination" and Northrop Frye's "The Realistic Oriole:
A Study of Wallace Stevens" are particularly discerning.

Glauco Cambon's chapter on Stevens in *The Inclusive Flame*
(Bloomington, Indiana Univ. Press) is a brilliant poem-by-poem
commentary on "Notes Toward a Supreme Fiction." Mr. Cambon is better qualified than most critics to see the debt (and it
is a heavy one) that Stevens owes to European, and particularly
Continental, literature and philosophy. In his analysis of "Notes,"

he traces the influence of Plato and Ovid ("Stevens," he remarks, "is never very far away from Ovid anyway, with his predilection for each thing's secret metamorphoses") and also suggests an affinity with Martin Heidegger. The poem, he says, is a "grand rehearsing" of Stevens' major themes and, as such, is "a milestone in modern American and Western poetry."

Of the articles in periodicals, two of the most important are Cleanth Brooks's "Wallace Stevens: An Introduction" (*McNeese Review*, XIV, 3-13) and Richard Gustafson's "The Practick of the Maker in Wallace Stevens" (*TCL*, IX, 83-88). Mr. Brooks observes that Stevens' concern with "elegant trifles," and his reputation as a dandy and connoisseur, have deceived many readers into underestimating his essential seriousness. The various masks he has adopted cannot, however, conceal the fact that he is one of the major poets of the twentieth century. Mr. Gustafson views Stevens as a master craftsman, a "maker" not only in the technical sense but also in the sense that he is capable of creating a transcendent reality. Both critics agree that his theme is the ability of the human mind to impose its own patterns upon the universe.

Thomas Whitbread (*TSLL*, IV, 465-480) shows how four of Stevens' poems ("The Poem that Took the Place of a Mountain," "Flyer's Fall," "The Owl in the Sarcophagus," and "Final Soliloquy and the Interior Paramour") illustrate his conception of poetry as the final measure of man's stature. Such poems, he says, go the limit in asserting the powers of the poetic imagination: the statement (in "Final Soliloquy") that "God and the imagination are one" represents the culmination of this effort. Richard Eberhart's comparison of Stevens and Emerson in *LitR* (VII, 51-71) suggests that there is no essential difference in the quality of transcendentalism that is present—explicitly in Emerson and by implication in Stevens—in both poets. And Howard Nemerov, in "Wallace Stevens and the Voices of the Imagination" (*Carleton Miscellany*, IV, ii, 90-97), makes the point, which many readers will concede reluctantly if at all, that Stevens' poetry is neither philosophical nor intellectual, that his final concern is with "expressiveness." The one dissenting voice in this chorus of praise is that of Morris Greenhut ("Sources of Obscurity in Modern Poetry: The Examples of Eliot, Stevens, and Tate," *CRAS*, VII, 171-190), who, though he concedes that obscurity was not a deliberate aim with Stevens, finds that, because

of their ambiguities, "The Idea of Order at Key West" and "Peter
Quince at the Clavier" are "failures in communication."

b. **William Carlos Williams.** This poet's death in 1963 was the
occasion for several tributes on both sides of the Atlantic. Denise
Levertov, who knew him well, observes (*The Nation*, CXCVI,
230) that more than any other poet he exploited in his work the
rhythms of everyday life, and that his greatest poems were written
in his old age. In *Shen* ("WCW," IV, iv, 3-10) Jack Hirschman
says very much the same: "In our century only Yeats was able to
go on singing brightly and clearly right up to the very end. And
now there is Williams." (There was, of course, also Hardy.) Mr.
Hirschman claims that Williams' greatest achivement was that he
wrote in the "American Idiom" (which he says, inaccurately, that
Frost was unable to do). The poet with whom he had most in
common, he declares, was Whitman; unlike Whitman, however, he
was able to risk sentiment without "wallowing." Mr. Hirschman
also discusses the powerful influence that Williams has exerted upon
Levertov, Olson, and Creeley. Williams' affinity with Whitman is
also noted by Hugh Kenner ("William Carlos Williams: In Memo-
riam," *National Review*, XIV, 237). "American poetry," he declares, "groups itself around two peaks, Williams and Whitman."
Williams, he maintains, thought of himself as a physician first and
as a poet secondarily, but one wonders if there is any more truth
in this than in the notion (in which there is very little) that Stevens
thought of himself primarily as a businessman. Yet a third comparison with Whitman is suggested by Charles Angoff in "Three
Towering Figures: Reflections upon the Passing of Robert Frost,
Robinson Jeffers, and William Carlos Williams" (*LitR*, VI, 423-
429), who mourns the demise of these three "Yea-sayers" to life.
His attempt to classify the misanthropic Jeffers as a Yea-sayer, however, is not altogether successful.

The most substantial treatments of Williams were John Malcolm
Brinnin's *William Carlos Williams* (Minneapolis, Univ. of Minnesota Press), which is the twenty-fourth in the series of the
University of Minnesota Pamphlets on American Writers, and which
in forty-eight pages admirably synthesizes the prevailing critical
opinion of Williams; and Glauco Cambon's fine study (which appears as a chapter in *The Inclusive Flame*) of *Paterson*, in which
he concludes that Williams, in this poem, "achieved a high degree

of integration between the hard, masculine half of his spiritual world and the atmospheric, fluid, feminine one, which is of course the 'marriage' ['The rock / Married to the river'] that *Paterson* invokes."

Edward F. Racey's essay, "Pound and Williams: the Poet as Renewer" (*BuR*, XI, ii, 21-30), relates Pound's concern with economic justice to Williams' concern with aesthetic honesty. Comparing Pound's line, "With usura hath no man a house of good stone" with Williams' "Without invention nothing is well spaced," he concludes that both poets in their separate ways deplored the divorce of words from things, and sought to "slough off the cliché forms which distort the poet's perception of things," thereby renewing the integrity of the language. Another comparison is made by Frederic Franklyn ("The Truth and the Poem," *Trace*, No. 48) between Williams and John Cage, the contemporary composer. Mr. Franklyn sees an analogy between Williams' use of the variable foot and Cage's use of "silence stresses": "Cage's silence is the recognition of unpremeditated noise-intervals he provides for in irregularly interrupted intervals of musical composition. Williams gives a similar value to pauses at the ends of some lines, where his ear informs him they are naturally dictated." Other interesting items are Alan Stephens' review ("Dr. Williams and Tradition," *Poetry*, CI, 360-362) of *Pictures from Breughel and Other Poems*, S. F. French's review of the same book in *WSCL* (IV, 373-374), and the recent all-Williams number of *Agenda* in which Peter Whigham (III, ii, 25-32) acclaims him "a poet of warm, penetrating, and, at his greatest, tragic humanity" and which reprints "Asphodel, that Greeny Flower" for British readers.

c. **Marianne Moore.** Indispensable to Moore scholarship is the *Paris Review* interview reprinted in *Writers at Work* (New York, Viking). In the case of so reticent a poet as Moore, who has theorized so little about her methods, the directness of the question-answer approach has particular advantages. Her remarks on the relation of art to morality and to science are extremely interesting, as are also the judgments of her own work. (Of "In Distrust of Merits" she says, "It is sincere but I wouldn't call it a poem.") The portrait of the artist which emerges from this interview is one of unusual generosity (to other poets and critics), humility, and dedication.

Sister Mary Cecilia's essay, "The Poetry of Marianne Moore"

(*Thought*, XXXVIII, 355-374), examines Moore's various themes, particularly the one which she finds to be most pervasive: the need for moral courage. She maintains that the affirmative quality of her work is owing to her religious convictions, which the secular spirit of our time has not succeeded in shaking. Sister Cecilia somewhat overestimates the "serenity" of this poet (after all, she *did* write "In Distrust of Merits"—whatever her opinion of *its* merits) and is generally on safer ground when she states: "The fullness of her aesthetic reputation relies upon the complexity of a technique that is fundamentally dictional." While it contains valuable insights, Sister Cecilia's essay betrays some of the weaknesses of institutional criticism. Bernard F. Engle ("Marianne Moore and Objectivism," *PMASAL*, XLVIII, 657-664) accounts for Moore's interest in paradox by suggesting that she has two commitments—one to ethical values and the other to Objectivism, "concentration on the thing itself."

In a very knowledgeable review of *A Marianne Moore Reader*, Hugh Kenner notes ("Meditation and Enactment," *Poetry*, CII, 109-115) that, in an age of explication, Moore's poems have been left "approvingly uninvestigated." The reasons for this neglect are certainly curious: her importance is universally acknowledged, and it may be that hers is such a case as Spender had in mind when he wrote, in the article previously mentioned, that modern criticism is sometimes speechless because it "lacks the apparatus to say anything about poets who do not fit into their categories." According to Mr. Kenner, we have "hardly begun" to appreciate Moore's work: not only is she the "greatest living observer," but also a great virtuoso of form and tone.

Moore's brilliant editorship of the *Dial* is the subject of a study by William Wasserstrom ("Marianne Moore, *The Dial*, and Kenneth Burke," *WHR*, XVII, 249-262). She had, he observes, two important characteristics of a successful editor: restraint and variety. The former was illustrated by her rejection of Joyce's "Anna Livia Plurabelle"; the latter, by her promotion of Kenneth Burke and other relatively unknown (at the time) critics. Under her influence, the *Dial* became an important part of American literary history.

d. **John Crowe Ransom.** The quiet, unostentatious talent of John Crowe Ransom, who was seventy-five in 1963, was honored in a special issue of *Shen* (XIV, iii) by Robert Penn Warren (19-21), Allen Tate (5-8), Cleanth Brooks (50), Francis Fergusson (13-14),

and John Stewart (33-48). The most thorough appreciation is that
of Mr. Stewart (author of the pamphlet *John Crowe Ransom*
[Minneapolis, Univ. of Minnesota Press, 1962]), who finds the
source of Ransom's characteristic melancholy is an anxiety which
appears in his preoccupation with mortality and in his treatment
of the sexual passion. In his poems (as in the novels of Carson
McCullers) love on the physical level is invariably doomed to dis-
appointment: "The happy people of the poetry and of the ideal
world are either sexless or so young that desire is weak and their
feelings for one another are more like those between siblings than
those between adult lovers. Physical desire is represented as selfish
and destructive." He observes shrewdly that the anti-romanticism
of the poetry "may be a means of protecting the imagination against
the emotional demands of a romantic commitment to absolutes
which, by their nature, ask more of man than all his energy and
sacrifice can promote." And he claims that Ransom, like Stravinsky,
mastered the conventions of earlier periods and assimilated them
into a style "so bold and original that it creates its own meaning and
discovers new meaning in ours." For Mr. Warren, Ransom's dominant characteristic is not melancholy but charity: "This charity may
not be Christian, but if not it shows us, in these poems of devoted
discipline, a world redeemed by, at least, natural love, and somehow
sweetened by the pathos of a love that is only natural." Warren
acclaims Ransom as a "master of the last line, of the withheld
effect, that turns upon the poem and, in a flash, alters all," and
observes: "We find here that rare thing, a sense of vital continuity
of the *sayer*, the *saying*, and the *said*." Mr. Tate concludes an affectionate reminiscence of the days when he was a student of Ransom's at Vanderbilt by fulminating: "I consider him now, since the
death of Stevens and Frost, the dean of American poetry, whose
poetry can scarcely be read by a young, coarse, and ignorant generation; whose poetry can therefore have little influence on the young
and cannot found a school." Mr. Brooks claims that this poet taught
a whole generation of poets and critics the importance of tone: "The
theme of so many of his poems is the modern war between the head
and the heart but the poems themselves exemplify their own kind
of reconciliation in which intellect is married to emotion." And Mr.
Fergusson, in a discussion of Ransom's style, which he identifies as
Neoclassic, comments: "The human figures in these poems are
mythic . . . they cannot be placed accurately in time; they inhabit
a world at least as old as Dryden."

A second revised and enlarged edition of Ransom's *Selected Poems* (New York, Knopf) also appeared in 1963. It contains a total of fifty-three poems, one of which, "Prelude to an Evening," a revision of an earlier poem, is accompanied by the poet's own explication. (This item originally appeared in *KR*, XXV, 70-80, under the title "'Prelude to an Evening': A Poem Revised and Explicated.")

e. **Allen Tate.** This controversial poet is the subject of a book-length study by R. K. Meiners, *The Last Alternatives* (Denver, Swallow), which examines his total career and which considers him in his triple role as poet, critic, and novelist. (It is often forgotten that Tate wrote one of the best novels to come out of the South in the thirties: *The Fathers.*) Mr. Meiners traces the influence of Longinus, Eliot, Ransom, and Maritain in the shaping of Tate's ideas. All his literary efforts, he observes, have been "that of one who looks for unity in a grossly disunited world," and his poetry has always been intensely personal. *The Last Alternatives* is likely to be the definitive book on Tate for some time to come: it is intelligent, thorough, and well written. It is good to see *The Fathers* done proper justice at last, and though few readers will agree with all of Mr. Meiners' judgments, one is compelled to respect them: they belong to a man who is well acquainted with his subject. The last chapter is an explication of what he regards Tate's finest poem, "Seasons of the Soul." (The poem is, conveniently, reproduced in an Appendix.) The book contains a selective bibliography, both of works by and about Tate, and is well indexed.

Morris Greenhut (see the section on Stevens), in an examination of "Ode for the Confederate Dead," proclaims the poem a failure. Using Tate's own explication of it in the essay "Narcissus as Narcissus," he declares that the poet failed of the effects that he was interested in securing. The essay, he says, is a revealing account of "a poet's struggle to escape solipsism by means of an anti-rationalist theory of poetry which closes all doors of escape, which with its categorical imperative against communication demands the use of desperate strategems for evading direct statement and logical progression." A weakness of Mr. Greenhut's essay is that he conceives of communication almost exclusively in terms of the conscious mind.

f. **Robert Lowell.** Hugh Staples' *Robert Lowell: The First Twenty Years* (New York, Farrar, Straus, and Cudahy, 1962) was reviewed by O. B. Hardison in *Shen* (XIV, ii, 24-32) and Robert L. Weeks in *PrS* (XXXVII, 185-186). Mr. Hardison observes that Lowell attempts to reconcile his desire for a personal catharsis (in poems of "confession and rebuke") with his desire for universality (in poems whose themes are of more general significance). His special talent, he claims, is his ability "to achieve artistic universality through meticulous, often merciless examination of his own experiences." Mr. Staples considers *The Mill of the Kavanaghs* Lowell's weakest book. Of *Imitations* (his latest, which met with a mixed reception) he says: "For most poets writing today it would be a major achievement; but for Lowell it is only a qualified success." No evidence exists, he maintains, for believing that this poet's talent has weakened. Mr. Weeks, in his review, regrets that Mr. Staples has not made the most of the opportunities for biographical criticism that his subject afforded him. "I have always assumed," he writes, echoing Kenneth Burke, "that anyone interested in the creative process wants to know everything he *can* know about the *total* process." In the case of a poem such as "Skunk Hour," he declares, such information (lacking in Mr. Staples' discussion of the poem) is particularly relevant.

A severe criticism of Lowell's translations and paraphrases in *Imitations* is made by C. Chadwick (*EIC*, XIII, 432-434). Mr. Lowell, he claims, has missed the point of three important poems: Baudelaire's *Le Cygne*, Rimbaud's *Bateau Ivre*, and Mallarmé's *Toast Funèbre*. The distinction between *meaning* and *tone*, which Lowell makes in his introductory note to the collection, is, Mr. Chadwick maintains, false: "The two things are so inextricably bound together that failure to grasp the one inevitably leads to failure to convey the other."

The recent rumor that this poet in his later work has been influenced by William Carlos Williams (*vide* Donald Hall, *op. cit.*, "When he wrote *Life Studies* Robert Lowell sent his muse to the *atelier* of William Carlos Williams") is denied by Lowell himself in "A Conversation with A. Alvarez" (*Review*, No. 8, pp. 36-40). In this interview he declares that he has remained loyal to the tradition of French symbolism as it was inherited by Tate and, to a lesser extent, Ransom. Questioned about the Beatniks, he says that though some of them are good poets the movement as a whole has been of little importance. French symbolism is still the biggest "influence" at work in modern poetry.

16. Drama

Malcolm Goldstein

i. Texts, Bibliography

The first four volumes of the America's Lost Plays series, originally published by the Princeton University Press and long out of print, have been reissued in two double volumes by the Indiana University Press. Volume I of the series as reissued includes six plays by Dion Boucicault and two by William Dunlap; Volume II includes three by George Henry Boker and one each by J. J. McCloskey, Lester Wallack, Frank Murdoch, G. H. Jessop, and Leonard Grover. It is to be hoped that the reappearance of the series will stimulate studies in American drama before the twentieth century, a field which at present tempts few scholars.

Stephen Crane's *Drama in Cuba*, a short play of the Spanish-American War, has been edited by Robert W. Stallman (*BNYPL*, LXVII, 498-511). In an accompanying essay, "Stephen Crane as Dramatist" (*BNYPL*, LXVII, 495-497), Stallman describes this as Crane's best play. The essay includes comment on Crane's other efforts in drama and his unsuccessful attempts to have the plays produced. The play is reprinted in *The War Dispatches of Stephen Crane*, R. W. Stallman and E. R. Hagemann, eds. (New York, New York Univ. Press, 1964), pp. 318-334.

New volumes of selected works by two twentieth-century writers make available a total of ten pieces useful to students of social theater. Langston Hughes' *Five Plays*, ed. Webster Smalley (Bloomington, Indiana Univ. Press), includes *Mulatto, Soul Gone Home, Little Ham, Simply Heavenly,* and *Tambourines to Glory.* Hughes, the regional dramatist of Harlem, has worked ardently in the cause of Negro drama toward both the development of a repertory and the establishment of acting companies. A militant social dramatist in the 1930's, in more recent years he has written two well-received urban folk dramas with song. The editor's introduction provides biographical data and concise analyses of the plays. Smalley also remarks on Hughes' preference, as a playwright, for the ordinary citizens of Harlem (*Mulatto* is an exception) over the affluent, and therefore special, members of his race.

Paul Green, also a superior regionalist, is represented by *Five Plays of the South* (New York, Hill and Wang), including *In Abraham's Bosom, The House of Connelly, Johnny Johnson, Hymn to the Rising Sun,* and *White Dresses.* A short introduction by John Gassner includes a biographical sketch with comments on Green's work at the University of North Carolina and his perennially repeated pageant plays. In his suggestions toward an evaluation of the playwright's accomplishment, Gassner emphasizes Green's democratic, humanitarian views. *The House of Connelly* as printed in this volume has Green's original harrowing final scene, not the optimistic ending used for the Broadway production in 1931.

Heinz Kosok's "Thornton Wilder: A Bibliography of Criticism" (*TCL*, IX, 93-100) provides the evidence that Wilder's plays and novels have enjoyed a steady following, but reveals on the other hand that they have seldom been appraised by critics of the first rank. Kosok's painstaking bibliography is a valuable guide toward the study of an important writer.

ii. Scholarship and Criticism

a. **Nineteenth century.** Curtis Dahl's *Robert Montgomery Bird* (New York, Twayne) is a reminder of a playwright long ignored. Bird, a man of many professions, wrote for the stage from 1826 to 1834. An unhappy association with Edwin Forrest, beginning in 1830, caused him ultimately to break with the theater; when it became apparent that the actor had no intention of fulfilling his financial obligations to him, Bird turned to the writing of fiction. After acknowledging in his introduction that Bird's work cannot be called great, Dahl provides a well-documented biographical chapter and a comprehensive analysis of the plays and novels. He holds that a study of Bird's life throws light on the problems of the man of letters in nineteenth-century America; certainly his account of Bird's difficulty in extracting payments from Forrest supports the assertion. In commenting on Bird's plays, Dahl sorts them into three groups: patriotic plays, plays of Indian life, and plays of home life. Those in the first category are the most interesting to him; *The Gladiator,* a dramatization of the revolt of Spartacus, is of particular importance. A superb vehicle for Forrest, it was the most popular tragedy of its time. A chapter on "Bird's Theories of Drama" is a well-written essay on the playwright's sense of theater and avoidance of closet drama, but the discussions of the plays, which include samples of Bird's blank verse and extended summaries, proceed to almost wearisome length; a mediocre writer does not deserve, either as reward or as punishment, treatment quite so detailed.

John Howard Payne, Bird's contemporary, is the subject of two essays: Thurman Wilkins's "John Howard Payne: Friend of the Cherokees" (*CLC*, XII, i [1962], 3-11) and Grace Overmyer's "The Baltimore Mobs and John Howard Payne" (*MdHM*, LVIII, 54-61). Both writers describe incidents in Payne's political life, but without relation to his career in the theater.

b. **Twentieth century.**   Arnold T. Schwab's *James Gibbons Huneker: Critic of the Seven Arts* (Stanford, Calif., Stanford Univ. Press) presents a full-scale biography of the essayist and novelist. A pioneering American commentator on the new European drama of the late nineteenth and early twentieth centuries, Huneker served as critic for several leading New York papers. He wrote in praise of Ibsen and was, with some reservations, an admirer of Shaw, "the Irish Ibsen," whose reviews he edited for publication in book form. For students of the theater, the pages devoted to his relations with and letters from and to Shaw will be of particular value. As Schwab demonstrates, Huneker's interest in late developments in the theater continued throughout his life; toward its end he found occasion to praise the Washington Square Players, forerunners of the Theatre Guild. The book takes up, in passing, the entire range of the arts in Huneker's time. It offers evidence that he was among the most intelligent spokesmen for drama the country had produced before World War I. Unquestionably, his work did much to prepare the way for the ambitious playwrights of the 1920's.

The widely held opinion that American drama came of age with the emergence of Eugene O'Neill after World War I is reflected in the swelling run of essays on the playwright. Many are characterized by prudence; despite their willingness to praise, the writers are in general agreement that the number of great works in O'Neill's long list of plays is relatively small. His primacy in the American theater is, however, taken for granted, and because evaluations of his work, though continuing, are no longer urgently needed, a search for sources of the individual plays is underway.

The year's only book-length study of the playwright comes, indirectly, from Britain. Clifford Leech's *Eugene O'Neill* (Edinburgh, Oliver and Boyd; New York, Grove Press) will be of greater service to British readers than to Americans, who are likely to be familiar with most of its material. Leech offers few fresh insights and for factual details draws chiefly upon Barrett H. Clark and Agnes Boulton. As a succinct general commentary, however, the book has a modest usefulness. The keenest observations are those on O'Neill and expressionism.

Edward T. Herbert in "Eugene O'Neill: An Evaluation by Fellow Playwrights" (*MD*, VI, 239-240) gathers up some brief remarks by Paul Green, Thornton Wilder, Sean O'Casey, Arthur Miller, and Clifford Odets. All admire O'Neill, but Green is alone in admitting to a direct influence, and that only on *In Abraham's Bosom.*

William H. Davenport in "The Published and Unpublished Poems of Eugene O'Neill" (*YULG*, XXXVIII, ii, 51-66) writes entertainingly on a little-known part of O'Neill's work. Davenport relates the poems to the plays and gives something of the circumstances under which they were written. It will not come as a surprise that the late-romantic flourishes present in O'Neill's dramatic dialogue are to be found in the poems as well.

Writing at considerable length, Joseph P. O'Neill, S.J., in "The Tragic Theory of Eugene O'Neill" (*TSLL*, IV, 481-498) attempts the impossible: an exposition of the playwright's general method through the analysis of only one play. The choice is *Mourning Becomes Electra*, which, because it has a direct literary source, would seem to reveal the author's shaping hand quite clearly. Yet the critic, despite the closeness of his examination of the play's deviations from the plot line of the *Oresteia*, does not succeed in demonstrating a "theory."

Studies in the sources have turned up some interesting details. Doris Alexander in "Eugene O'Neill and Charles Lever" (*MD*, V, 415-420) establishes that one important source of *A Touch of the Poet* is Lever's popular novel, *Charles O'Malley, the Irish Dragoon.* O'Neill appears to have drawn upon the novel for the background of his tortured hero, Con Melody, as well as for certain elements of the play's language. According to Mordecai Marcus in "Eugene O'Neill's Debt to Thoreau in *A Touch of the Poet*" (*JEGP*, LXII, 270-279), Melody himself closely resembles the unfortunate Hugh Quoil described by Thoreau in both *Walden* and the *Journal.* Marcus also finds that Simon Harford, mentioned in the play but not brought on stage, bears a partial resemblance to Thoreau and that Deborah Harford, Simon's mother, is modeled in part on Thoreau's own mother.

Doris V. Falk in "That Paradox, O'Neill" (*MD*, VI, 221-238) provides a coda to her *Eugene O'Neill and the Tragic Tension*. She shows that, O'Neill's tendency to take himself and his work "with overwhelming seriousness" notwithstanding, the plays reveal his use of numerous inartistic materials. That he should resort to them she relates to his sense of the dualistic nature of man, in which the vulgar is coupled with the heroic, and to conflicting desires both to reveal and to conceal his own personality. Buried at various levels in the plays are the popular song (*All God's Chillun Got Wings*), the dirty joke (*The Iceman Cometh*), and the plot of a popular melodrama (*Desire under the Elms*). The six pages on the relation of *Desire under the Elms* to Denman Thompson's *The Old Homestead* are an impressive contribution both to O'Neill studies and to research in the popular stage of the late nineteenth century.

Of the many other writers whose first successes occurred in the 1920's, five are the subjects of new essays. B. R. McElderry, Jr., in "Thomas Wolfe: Dramatist" (*MD*, VI, 1-11) describes Wolfe's plays, published and unpublished. In his opinion, recognition of Wolfe's talent as a dramatist would affect criticism of the novels by calling attention to his humor and his ability to compose the stirring, "dramatic" episode. Howard D. Pearce's "Job in Anderson's *Winterset*" (*MD*, VI, 32-41) is an attempt to find a parallel to the book of Job in the tragedy. Pearce presents the evidence carefully, but the task of stimulating interest in Maxwell Anderson's prolix play, whether by this means or any other, is surely thankless. George Freedley's "George S. Kaufman: 1889-1962" (*MD*, VI, 241-244) is part memoir, part appreciation. Writing on "The Kelly Play," Arthur Wills (*MD*, VI, 245-255) notes the narrow compass of George Kelly's work, his dependence upon the well-made form, and his inclination to stress weakness in character over weakness in the social order. Wills draws not only upon the familiar plays, but also upon the unpublished "Maggie the Magnificent" and plays of 1949 and 1951 that have been neither published nor produced. Walter J. Meserve in "Sidney Howard and the Social Drama of the Twenties" (*MD*, VI, 256-266) comments on Howard's position in the development of post-Ibsenite realistic drama in America and observes that although only *They Knew What They Wanted* and *The Silver Cord* are notable achievements, the playwright deserves acclaim for giving status to social drama and for courageously expressing his social views.

Three essayists examine special topics of the theater between the wars. John C. Wentz in "American Regional Drama, 1920-1940: Frustration and Fulfillment" (*MD*, VI, 286-293) canvasses the major "folk" or regional plays of the period. Noting that the plays reflected current national concerns, he suggests that their immediate theatrical value lay, nevertheless, in their respectful presentation of regional feeling. Figures on the plays' Broadway runs are given to indicate the modest commercial success of the movement. A perplexing, inadequately pointed article is Winifred L. Dusenberry's "Myth in American Drama between the Wars" (*MD*, VI, 294-308). The author shows the extent to which archetypal patterns are detectable in the plays of Maxwell Anderson, Philip Barry, Sidney Howard, Robert E. Sherwood, and Elmer Rice. On her evidence, however, the authors' employment of myth was so inconsistent and imprecise that it cannot have been a matter of much importance to them. Donna Gerstenberger in "Verse Drama in America: 1916-1939" (*MD*, VI, 309-322) begins with the observation that although verse drama persisted in America between the wars, it had virtually no influence on native drama in general. She points to two reasons for its ineffectuality: first, the lack of a vital American tradition of verse drama, and second, the domination of the stage by realism when, after World War I, the American theater came unequivocally of age. The author focuses on the plays and theories of Wallace Stevens, Edna St. Vincent Millay, Maxwell Anderson, and Archibald MacLeish. She contends that MacLeish is the most accomplished writer of poetic drama in the period, and indeed the only one to understand its special problems.

The span of years from the crash of 1929 to the outbreak of World War II is currently more attractive to critics of drama than the 1920's. In 1963 two books and six articles on the period were published, and it appears likely that others will follow.

The more ambitious of the books is M. Y. Himelstein's *Drama Was a Weapon* (New Brunswick, N.J., Rutgers Univ. Press). Subtitled "The Left-Wing Theatre in New York 1929-1941," it is an examination of the plays offered by the major producers of social drama. Himelstein brings together a mass of material from news-

papers, magazines, and Congressional hearings, the primary sources
of his study. For the numbers of performances given and the reactions of the leftist press, his work is entirely trustworthy. On the
other hand, so important a subject deserves a more readable treatment than Himelstein has provided. The style is wooden and humor-
less, and nothing is present of the excitement felt daily by the
participants in the theatrical events described. Nor does Himelstein appear to have studied closely the political situation which
gave rise to and sustained the producing units. Moreover, by no
means all the plays or companies mentioned fit comfortably under
the "left-wing" designation.

Like Himelstein's book, R. Baird Shuman's *Clifford Odets* (New
York, Twayne) originated in a dissertation. Though no doubt revised to conform to the pattern established for the Twayne United
States Authors Series, it is equally dense in style. Nor may the book
be used with confidence, for the most important section, the biographical chapter, is inadequately documented. Documentation,
indeed, is a problem throughout; there seems to be no system in
the author's mind for footnoting the sources. Some quoted comments receive notes, and others do not. In his chapters on the plays,
Shuman summarizes the plots to uncomfortable length. Finally, it
must be said that Shuman, again like Himelstein, has not informed
himself sufficiently on political and social background.

Several articles on Odets and a transcription of an interview
with him have also appeared. Catherine Hughes in an obituary,
"Odets: The Price of Success" (*Cweal*, LXXVIII, 558-560), reviews
his career and concludes that in view of his early success and quick
neglect, Odets was a prototypical American figure. Charles Kaplan
in "Two Depression Plays and Broadway's Popular Idealism" (*AQ*,
XV, 579-585) notes that *Awake and Sing* and *You Can't Take It with
You*, George S. Kaufman and Moss Hart's popular comedy, have
much in common as portraits of middle-class family life; both, albeit
in quite different ways, support American idealism in the face of
excessive materialism, another quality of American life. In "Clifford
Odets and the American Family," Michael J. Mendelsohn (*DramS*,
III, 238-243) argues that the gradual lessening of the playwright's
rebelliousness is reflected in his treatment of family relationships,
which are shown as mirrors of society in all the plays. Mendelsohn's
taped interview with the playwright, "Odets at Center Stage" (*TAr*,
XLVII [May], 16-19, 74-76; [June] 28-30, 78-80) provides Odets'

own estimate of his work and his thoughts on the personal and social motives behind it.

Three additional articles treat other writers and theatrical phenomena of the 1930's. In "The Social Critics on Stage," Michael J. Mendelsohn (*MD*, VI, 277-285) comments briefly on the work of the depression dramatists, with emphasis on Odets, John Howard Lawson, and Elmer Rice. The "house organ," so to speak, of the most militant of the producing units is analyzed by Eleazer Lecky in *"New Theatre"* (*MD*, VI, 267-276). Under various titles this journal of the New Theatre League ran from April, 1931, to April, 1937. Perhaps to spare the feelings of the contributors, many of whom were only slightly left of center, Lecky does not indicate that the journal was well within the orbit of the Communist party. Strangely, he neglects to mention *Theatre Workshop* and *New Theatre News*, also published by the League. Malcolm Goldstein's "Drame et danse révolutionnaire aux États Unis: 1926-1935," trans. Maurice Jonas (*RHT*, XV, 285-293), attempts to trace the development of "agitprop" drama from Michael Gold's *Strike* in 1926 to Archibald MacLeish's *Panic* in 1935, along with the corresponding development in the programs devised by the leading leftist dance troupes.

Among post-World War II playwrights, Tennessee Williams and Arthur Miller are still the most highly regarded. Others whose work is considered in the year's essays are MacLeish (for *J.B.*, a product of the 1950's) and the young generation of playwrights often identified with the "Theater of the Absurd."

Colin C. Campbell's "The Transformation of Biblical Myth: MacLeish's Use of the Adam and Job Stories" (*Myth and Symbol*, ed. Beatrice Slote, Lincoln, Univ. of Nebraska Press, pp. 79-88), Eleanor M. Sickels' "MacLeish and the Fortunate Fall" (*AL*, XXXV, 205-217), and Sheldon Norman Grebstein's "*J.B.* and the Problem of Evil" (*UKCR*, XXIX, 253-261) are primarily concerned with the humanist arguments of *J.B.* Campbell and Sickels also refer to MacLeish's early *Nobodaddy*.

Of the studies in Tennessee Williams, three are reviews of the work as a whole and three are interpretations of specific plays. John Buell in "The Evil Imagery of Tennessee Williams" (*Thought*, XXXVIII, 167-189) accounts for the shock effect of the plays with the reminder that tragedy is always shocking to its immediate audience. He further observes that brutality and gentleness coexist in

the plays, but that the closer Williams' gentle characters come
toward happiness, the more they are brutalized; to be oneself, then,
as each of the gentle characters endeavors to do, is to put oneself
open to victimization. Esther M. Jackson in "Music and Dance as
Elements of Form in the Drama of Tennessee Williams" (*RHT*, XV,
294-301) discusses the plays in terms of "plastic theater" (Williams'
phrase), which is a synthesis of music, dance, and dialogue. She
discerns three stages in Williams' development. Music and pat-
terned movement are common to all three, but their employment
alters. In the early one-act plays the relation to dance is very close,
but in the long plays through *The Rose Tattoo* music, aural effects,
and verbal images take a greater part. Finally, in *Camino Real*, symbolic characters appear within a kind of dance drama. Except for
brief mention of *Cat on a Hot Tin Roof*, she does not discuss later
plays. Marion Magid in "The Innocence of Tennessee Williams"
(*Com*, XXXV, 34-43) writes wittily of the childishness of Williams's
male characters in regard to sex. From their behavior arises a confusion of male-female relations: they are muscular, apparently
sensual, and pursued by women, yet reluctant—thus the roles of
the sexes are reversed. Such men are pure in heart, still suffering
from the "wounds and desolation of childhood."

Essays on individual plays are somewhat less stimulating. Sam
Bluefarb in "*The Glass Menagerie*: Three Visions of Time" (*CE*,
XXIV, 513-518) discusses the three Wingfields in relation to the
special sense of time which each possesses—for Amanda, the past;
for Tom, the future; for Laura, in effect, no-time. Joseph N. Riddel
in "*A Streetcar Named Desire*—Nietzsche Descending" (*MD*, V,
421-430) interprets the play in terms of the Apollonian-Dionysian
synthesis and finds that Williams has put too great an emphasis on
the Dionysian rhythm, whereas Nietzsche conceived of an ideal
blend of Dionysian energy and Apollonian restraint. Bernard F.
Dukore in "The Cat Has Nine Lives" (*TDR*, VIII, i, 95-100) argues
that the theme of *Cat on a Hot Tin Roof* is neither homosexuality
nor mendacity, as sometimes claimed, but the process of living.
That Brick, the protagonist, is reluctant to fulfil his marital obligations is evidence, in this view, not of homosexuality, but of an
unwillingness to enter adulthood, which is a stage on the way to
death.

Though mindful of the playwright's skill, many of Arthur Miller's
critics point to weaknesses. Arthur Ganz in "The Silence of Arthur

Miller" (*DramS*, III, 224-237) notes two characteristics of the plays which suggest a deficiency of thought. The first is the imprecision of Miller's complaints against the social order and of his ideas about individual man in relation to it. Second, Ganz cannot agree with Miller that the acquisition of self-knowledge is sufficient in itself to elevate a man to tragic stature, as it does with most of Miller's heroes. In "Arthur Miller and the Impasse of Naturalism," Joseph A. Hynes (*SAQ*, LXII, 327-334) registers a sharper complaint. According to his argument, Miller's predilection for naturalism lessens the value of his plays insofar as it permits him to escape responsibility; that is, the playwright merely presents a distressing case and, having done so, discharges his duty to the cause of good theater and social improvement without judging the merits of his characters, who are, indeed, "mentally halt and lame." On the other hand, Paul West in "Arthur Miller and the Human Mice" (*HJ*, LXI, 84-86) contends that the Miller hero is an Everyman who expresses the playwright's great concern for humanity.

Balancing these general estimates are three on individual plays. James W. Douglass in "Miller's *The Crucible*: Which Witch is Which?" (*Ren*, XV, 145-151) points to the obvious discrepancies between the incidents of the play and the situation in Salem to conclude that Miller wrote out of an a priori conception of the trials and the attitudes of those conducting and supporting them. In a somewhat loosely constructed essay, "*Death of a Salesman*: Tragic Myth in the Modern Theatre," Esther M. Jackson (*CLAJ*, VII, 63-76) describes the play's structure as a theatrical realization of stream of consciousness in which Willy Loman proceeds from ignorance to enlightenment, winning virtue at the close. The most unexpected item among Miller essays of the year is John V. Hagopian's "Arthur Miller: *The Salesman's* Two Cases" (*MD*, VI, 117-125). The author asserts that the central character is not Willy but his son Biff. The play, in this argument, is an investigation of Biff's struggle for personal development, and as such it falls short of tragedy. Nor, for Hagopian, does Willy's career rise above pathos, since the salesman goes to his death unchanged.

Controversies of greater intensity than Williams and Miller have provoked now rage over the so-called "absurdists" of the American theater. Although it is too early to predict whether they will develop into major talents, their plays—still a small body of work—have received close attention. George E. Wellwarth's "Hope Deferred:

The New American Drama. Reflections on Edward Albee, Jack Richardson, Jack Gelber, and Arthur Kopit" (*LitR*, VII, 7-26) is a general introduction to the new writers. Despite strenuous objections to Gelber, Wellwarth finds that their efforts on the whole are superior to the work of the English "angry young men." Directing his essay to readers who may be unfamiliar with the plays, Wellwarth describes them in detail and comments on the writers' themes. L. E. Chabrowe in "The Pains of Being Demystified" (*KR*, XXV, 142-149) is less enthusiastic. Objecting to the absurdists' emphasis on "didactic alienation," he proposes a drama of the inner life resembling the productions of O'Neill, Robert Edmond Jones, and Kenneth Macgowan in Greenwich Village during the 1920's. Edward Albee, no longer "absurd," is the most embattled of the new writers, because the most successful. Alfred Chester in "Edward Albee: Red Herrings and White Whales" (*Com*, XXXV, 296-301) asserts in sardonic prose that Albee gives little pity to the characters of *Who's Afraid of Virginia Woolf?*—that, indeed, he hates them. Richard Schechner in "Who's Afraid of Edward Albee?" (*TDR*, VI, iii, 7-10) expresses his disapproval of the rapid acceptance of the writer. Describing the play Holden Caulfield–fashion as "phony," Schechner complains of the metaphor of the non-existent child, the inordinately long playing time in relation to ideas and action, and the lack of taste evident to him in Albee's use of sexual innuendo. Alan Schneider, the play's director, offers a reply titled "Why So Afraid?" (*TDR*, V, iii, 10-13). Proclaiming his confidence in the play, Schneider defends the metaphor as evidence of the characters' weakness and maintains that Albee is too serious a writer to employ sexual references for the mere titillation of the audience. Such an exchange indicates that for the present Albee is in no danger of being ignored.

Finally, a word of praise must be given to Elmer Rice for his revealing autobiography, *Minority Report* (New York, Simon and Schuster). Though seldom a profound writer, Rice has contributed steadily to Broadway over a fifty-year period. His own account of the writing and staging of his works—crime melodramas, romantic comedies, and plays of social protest—should prove a document of value to researchers in the history of the twentieth-century American theater.

17. Miscellaneous

Harry Finestone

To discover some consistent principle of unity and order among the "miscellaneous" listings in the *PMLA* bibliography was, as it turned out, a feat impossible for the present reviewer to perform. Rough categories did suggest themselves, however, based largely on certain recurring themes.

Critics and scholars have continued the task of reassessing those two curiosities, the 1920's and the Southern literary renaissance, while some have begun to find it possible to observe the thirties with equanimity and detachment. An unwillingness remains to consider the leftist literary movement of the thirties as literature, but writers in what is often referred to as our age of conformity look back nostalgically to those polemical times. Meanwhile impetus from the integration movement has no doubt prompted a number of studies of Negro writers which may in turn provide a polemic for our time.

As though to counterbalance these political and social concerns, an attempt to recover works by the conservative New Humanists or Agrarians is much in evidence, while the urge for re-evaluations has taken another group perhaps similarly prompted by conservative motives back to the Gilded Age.

If many works in the bibliography can best be characterized by a desire to recover, recall, or reassess, other works try to interpret the present and predict the future, as they speculate on the present state of American fiction, criticism, or as they attempt to assess the world status of American literature.

i. The Twenties

As evidence for continued interest in the 1920's, note *A Dial Miscellany* (Syracuse, N.Y., Syracuse Univ. Press), for which William Wasserstrom, the editor, has provided an extremely informative introduction. Wasserstrom recalls the purchase in 1919 by Scofield

Thayer and James Sibley Watson, Jr., of the magazine, which had
been in existence on and off since 1840. He explains the circumstances which have combined to delay an anthology of the *Dial*
until 1963, recounts the appointment in 1925 of Marianne Moore as
the second editor, and follows the history of her tenure until the
magazine's demise in 1929 as well as the major role played by
Kenneth Burke on the staff. He notes Thayer's policy of establishing
the magazine as a symbol of "the highest imaginable art" and
records the attacks by William Carlos Williams in 1921, by the
editors of the *New Republic* in 1927, and by Ezra Pound toward
the end of the magazine's publication. All scholars and critics interested in a sampling of the best international literature of a very
internationally minded decade will welcome this volume as much
as they will be puzzled by *The Time of the Dial* (Syracuse, N.Y.,
Syracuse Univ. Press), also by William Wasserstrom. The founders
of the 1920's *Dial* wished to establish a magazine as part of a movement to help save civilization not by democracy, but through art.
Wasserstrom describes this belief that art alone could help men
perfect society as "the prophetic imagination." In order to discuss
the time of the *Dial* he describes the chief manifestations of the
prophetic imagination from 1910 until 1960.

Ezra Pound, Alfred Stieglitz, the founders of the *Dial*, Thayer
and Sibley, William Carlos Williams, Marianne Moore, Henry Miller
—these are all key figures in the movement to assert aesthetic
domination over the affairs of men. The chapters devoted to each
embrace a vast array of allusions to other writers and artists which
tend more to thicken and muddy the author's argument than to
illuminate it.

Edward Dahlberg's "The Expatriates: A Memoir" (*TQ*, VI, ii,
50-55) follows an appreciative article on Dahlberg in the same issue
by Jonathan Williams, "Edward Dahlberg's Book of Lazarus." The
memoir recalls with poignant clarity the American expatriates in
Europe, Ernest Walsh, Hart Crane, and chiefly Ethel Moorhead,
who published Dahlberg's work in *This Quarter*.

Paul S. Boyer in "Boston Book Censorship in the Twenties" (*AQ*,
XV, 3-24) traces the beginnings of the New England Watch and
Ward Society, founded in the late nineteenth century by Dr.
Frederick Baylies Allen, a leading Boston Episcopalian, which drew
its support from the wealthy and socially prominent of Boston. The
society was at first considered an important adjunct to the reform

movement in Boston, and in 1911 the newly retired President Eliot of Harvard described the society as a "thoroughly scientific charity." Unfortunately it outlived its years of reformism and found itself confronted with the Roaring Twenties, at which time it was abetted in its activities by the strong Boston Catholic public opinion, largely influenced by papal attacks on modern indecent literature and by the Irish Free State legislature's investigations into "evil literature." Although during the twenties the society became increasingly a coercive censor of books and drama, its power was eventually broken and its duties were assumed by the *Pilot*, the official diocesan weekly of the Catholic church.

Boyer asserts that the feeling of anti-censorship which developed, "with strains of academic superiority, nativism, and Know Nothingism was to plunge the issue into a maelstrom of bitterness and social tension."

Much of the excitement of the period is reflected in Reed Whittemore's *Little Magazines*, UMPAW, No. 32 (Minneapolis, Univ. of Minnesota Press). See also Jack Lindemann and others in "Little Magazines: A Symposium" (*Mainstream*, XV, xii, 1962, 37-52).

ii. The Thirties

Writers on the Left (New York, Harcourt, Brace and World, 1961) is by Daniel Aaron. Subtitled "Episodes in American Literary Communism," it is a volume in the series "Communism in American Life," under the general editorship of Clinton Rossiter. A chronicle of the Left Wing from 1912 to the early 1940's, this excellent study concentrates mainly on the crucial period of the 1930's, tracing the rise and fall of the Popular Front and its effects on writers.

Since the tone of most books dealing with the relationship of writers to the communist movement is generally either hostile or overly apologetic and sentimental, a work of such objectivity as *Writers on the Left* is welcome. It traces the general drift of most American writers to the leftist camp, noting various gradations of attachment, and the complex process of disillusionment and disengagement which followed the Moscow trials, the revelations of Stalinist betrayal in Spain during the Civil War, and the Nazi-Soviet Pact. Relying to a great extent on letters, private conversations, and memoirs, Aaron recounts the organization of the various

writers' congresses, the controversy over the *Partisan Review* in the
New York John Reed Club, the battle between the leftists and the
New Humanists, the relations between orthodox leftists and sympathetic, liberal middle-class writers, the bitter personal and ideological feuds such as the attacks by Michael Gold on Thornton
Wilder. Edmund Wilson, Malcolm Cowley, Kenneth Burke, Granville Hicks, Joseph Freeman, Max Eastman, Theodore Dreiser—
these are only a few of the names whose relationship to the leftist
movement is closely followed.

For further evidence of renewed interest in the 1930's witness
The Anxious Years (New York, Putnam), an anthology comprised
of stories, poems, essays, and selections from novels. In a long
introduction Louis Filler discusses with sympathy the emotional
and intellectual currents of that highly political decade. Many of
the selections have more historical than literary worth, but one gets
from the anthology a general impression of the liveliness and heat
of feeling which characterized the arguments of the time.

Charles Angoff, whose life has bridged a large portion of the
radical movement, recalls one of its founders in "Oswald Garrison
Villard and the *Nation*: A Memoir" (*AR*, XXIII, 232-240). A valuable bibliographical tool is provided by Walter Goldwater's "Radical
Periodicals in America 1890-1950: A Bibliography with Brief Notes"
(*YULG*, XXXVII, 133-177). For an account of Marxist literary
criticism, see Rudolph Sühnel, "The Marxist Trend in Literary Criticism in the USA in the Thirties" (*JA*, VII, 1962, 53-66).

Irving Howe is a writer who has inherited from the period of
literary radicalism a real gift for polemic. *A World More Attractive*
(New York: Horizon Press), which bears the subtitle, "A View of
Modern Literature and Politics," shows the flavor of partisanship.
The collection contains in general three types of essays: those which
view literature from the social or political context ("Mass Society
and Post-Modern Fiction," "Black Boys and Native Sons," "A Quest
for Peril: Norman Mailer," are examples); those of a purely literary
nature, such as the essays on Whitman, Frost, and Wallace Stevens;
and those which survey modern society from Howe's neo-Marxist
viewpoint. The essays in this last category are frankly the most
successful. For example, "A Mind's Turnings," "God, Man, and
Stalin," and "Edmund Wilson and the Sea Slugs" analyze, in all
their subtle complexity, many of the dilemmas which confront
modern intellectuals. Most of the essays, which range in date of

composition from 1950 to 1963, demonstrate the truth of an observation made about Howe's other writing: his major contributions are in his stimulating political insights; his efforts in a purely literary vein are often either tedious or deal with ideas better stated elsewhere; for example, compare his competent essays on Whitman and Frost with the brilliant studies by Randall Jarrell in *Poetry and the Age*.

iii. The South

A significant example of combined interest in the 1930's and the South can be seen in the reissue of *I'll Take My Stand* (New York, Harper, 1962), the Agrarian statements by John Crowe Ransom, Donald Davidson, Stark Young, Allen Tate, Robert Penn Warren, and others of the Vanderbilt group, which originally appeared in 1930. Louis D. Rubin, Jr., has provided an introduction and Virginia Rock biographical sketches for each of the twelve contributors. Rubin points out that the South has obviously not followed the various paths of action offered by the Agrarian group and that, furthermore, one might expect today to find surviving Agrarians sharply divided on the issue of desegregation. Why then does the book continue as an influence and why has a new edition come into being? To answer this question Rubin stresses the book's poetic or metaphoric nature. The Agrarians speak to us through their vision of the good life, which was at the same time a critique of the modern world, with its false gods of materialism and progress and its fragmentation of modern man. Although we are reminded that social analysts such as Reisman, White, and Packard have largely confirmed the validity of the Agrarian attack on our business civilization (by the same logic may they not also be said to have confirmed Lenin's quite dissimilar attacks on our business civilization?), Rubin urges us to read the book not as a program for economic or political action or regional planning, but as a commentary on the nature of man. But surely such a view is to deny the authors' intentions, which were precisely to offer a positive and coherent social program. Subsequent history has shown that the Agrarian program would have proved unfeasible, based largely as it was on a nostalgic and essentially inaccurate notion, not only of the economic conditions of the South, but of the needs of its people as well. To be critical of materialism, one need not accept the

Agrarian dream. Remembering Robert Penn Warren's rejection of his own essay in the volume, "The Briar Patch," which was a youthful defense of conventional Southern attitudes toward the Negro, one wonders whether interest in *I'll Take My Stand* does not continue primarily because its authors were to write some of the best poetry and fiction in our time.

Edward M. Moore's "The Nineteen-Thirty Agrarians" (*SR*, LXXI, 133-142) and Richard M. Weaver's "The Southern Phoenix (*GaR*, XVII, 6-17) are both review articles on the reissue. For another essay on the movement, see Thomas Lawrence Connelly's "The Vanderbilt Agrarians: Time and Place in Southern Tradition" (*THQ*, XXI, 22-37).

The South since 1865 (New York, Macmillan) by John Samuel Ezell contains two chapters which deal with subjects of interest to students of American studies. "The Southern Literary Renaissance" records the blossoming of literature in the South which began with Ellen Glasgow. The author discusses obvious major figures, Wolfe and Faulkner, for example, but what is one to say of an account of a renaissance in Southern writing which notices Margaret Mitchell, Julia Peterkin, Lula Vollmer, and Hatcher Hughes, with a paragraph on T. S. Stribling, but which fails altogether to mention Carson McCullers, Lillian Smith, Flannery O'Connor, James Agee, Truman Capote, Peter Taylor, Karl Shapiro, or William Styron? The chapter entitled "Other Aspects of Southern Culture" does point out that most of the monuments in Richmond, Virginia, contain second-rate statuary.

A similar work, *Renaissance in the South: A Critical History of the Literature, 1920-1960* (Chapel Hill, Univ. of North Carolina Press), by John M. Bradbury, is a thorough study of Southern writers, with an appendix listing, by state, the Southern renaissance authors. Although Bradbury comments on almost every literary work produced by a Southerner since 1920, he fails to discuss the brilliant volume *Red Wine First* by the Georgian Nedra Tyre.

The Faraway Country: Writers of the Modern South (Seattle, Univ. of Washington Press) by Louis Rubin, Jr., is a study of the paradox of the Southern literary renaissance, whose writers are nurtured by their heritage, but are unable to continue to live there in their maturity unless they retreat into the "faraway country" of their poetic imagination. Rubin contrasts writers of the modern South who are alienated from conventional Southern attitudes with those writers of the ante-bellum South who did, indeed, identify with its regional aims. A perceptive essay on George W. Cable, perhaps the first alienated Southern writer, and his neglected novel *John March, Southerner*, follows the general introduction, with additional essays on the fiction of Robert Penn Warren, Faulkner, Wolfe, Eudora Welty, the poets of the Agrarian movement. A postscript, the final chapter, reflects on the loss to the Southern renaissance incurred by the death of William Faulkner and speculates on the direction of Southern letters in the post-Faulkner world.

Ante-Bellum Southern Literary Criticism (Athens, Univ. of Georgia Press, 1962) by Edd Winfield Parks is the culmination of many years of work in this field which began in 1935 when the author included a section on poetic theory in his book *Southern Poets*. Professor Parks presents an intellectual and literary history of the South from 1785 to 1861, tracing the shift from Classicism to Neo-Classicism to Romanticism, demonstrating particularly the influence of the English Romantic poets and Walter Scott on Southern literary theory and taste. The book begins with a chapter on Thomas Jefferson which illuminates his contribution as a commentator on literature. Although many of the critics discussed in subsequent chapters will be unknown to all but specialists in the field of Southern letters, chapters on William Gilmore Simms, Thomas Holley Chivers, Henry Timrod, and Paul Hamilton Hayne, and a chapter on Southern humorists are indispensable. Of especial interest is the chapter entitled "Thomas Holley Chivers: Mystic," with its analysis of the complex relation of Chivers to Poe. It includes Chivers' annoyed response to Poe's praise of Tennyson, whose poems Chivers felt were "as effeminate as a phlegmatic fat baby."

While it is not one of his primary intentions, Parks makes evident the painful dilemma of the Southern writer, bound to his society but largely ignored by it, and the chapter "Henry Timrod: Traditionalist" illustrates the Southern writer's ambivalent feelings for his region. A prodigious amount of first-rate scholarship underlies this work. The meticulous notes further enhance and illuminate many of the ideas in the body of the text.

Literary Wise Men of Gotham: Criticism in New York, 1815-1860 (Baton Rouge, Louisiana State Univ. Press) by John Paul Pritchard covers a period similar to that of Parks' study. Seen together the books offer a survey of two-thirds of the American literary mind. Both works also of necessity reveal the New England third which loomed so large, both for the Southerner and the New Yorker, and with which they were so often in conflict. Both books also treat the ambiguous drive for cultural independence from New England and Europe by Southern and New York writers. Pritchard discusses problems of importance to the New York critics, the relation of the author to his work, the nature of poetry and fiction, and the very concept of the nature of literary criticism. Several chapters contain an historical study of the key figures and the major forces at work in the critical world of New York in such journals as the *Knickerbocker, Arcturus, Putnam's,* the *New York Review,* the *Mirror* and the *Democratic Review.*

Other works on the South worthy of notice are Loren J. Kallsen, editor, *The Kentucky Tragedy: A Problem in Romantic Attitudes* (Indianapolis, Bobbs-Merrill), a source book containing documents pertaining to the murder of Colonel Solomon Sharp by Jereboam O. Beauchamp, a story used by eight American authors from Thomas Holley Chivers to Robert Penn Warren; William R. Linneman, "Southern Punch: A Draught of Confederate Wit" (*SFQ,* XXVI, 1962, 131-136); Ray M. Atchison, "*Our Living and Our Dead*: A Post-Bellum North Carolina Magazine of Literature and History" (*NCHR,* XL, 423-433); and Susan B. Riley "The Hazards of Periodical Publishing in the South During the Nineteenth Century" (*THQ,* XXI, 1962, 365-376).

iv. The Negro

In three short articles (*SatR,* XLVI, 20 Apr., 19-21, 40) Langston Hughes, LeRoi Jones, and John A. Williams discuss problems of the Negro writer. "The Bread and Butter Side" by Hughes is a somewhat superficial statement concerning the limitations and restrictions which a Negro writer must undergo because of his race.

LeRoi Jones' "The Myth of a Negro Literature" with more feeling than logic states that there is no Negro literature, merely copies of middle-class, middle-brow white American literature. Wright, Ellison, and Baldwin are comparable to Maugham, hardly to Joyce or Melville. He asserts that high art arises from the legitimate emotional resources in the soul and cannot be produced by evading these resources or pretending that they do not exist or by expropriating the withered emotional responses of some strictly social idea of humanity. The Negro writer on Negro life in America, he says, invents a Negro life and an America to contain it. The Negro writer who has escaped into the university is no better off since the academy is "perhaps the most insidious and clever dispenser of middle-brow standards of excellence" in this country. The real contribution from the Negro has come in the field of music.

"The Literary Ghetto" by John A. Williams claims that critics and publishers too often consider the Negro writers as a group. The essay by Jones is the only provocative one in the brief symposium.

Soon, One Morning: New Writing by American Negroes 1940-1962 (New York, Knopf) is an anthology edited by Herbert Hill, who in his introduction asserts the present need to judge Negro writers only by the criteria of art and literature. The high quality of much of this generous selection would seem to contradict LeRoi Jones' argument in "The Myth of a Negro Literature," in the *SatR* symposium.

Other items dealing specifically with the Negro in American literature are: Catherine Juanita Starke, "Negro Stock Characters, Archetypes and Individuals in American Literature" (*DA*, XXIV, 288); Hannah S. Goldman, "The Tragic Gift: The Serf and Slave Intellectual in Russian and American Fiction" (*Phylon*, XXIV, 51-61); James A. Emanuel, "The Invisible Men of American Literature" (*BA*, XXXVII, 391-394); Nick Aaron Ford, "Walls Do a Prison Make: A Critical Survey of Significant Belles-Lettres by and about Negroes Published in 1962" (*Phylon*, XXIV, 123-134); and Howard Levant, "Aspiring We Should Go" (*MASJ*, IV, ii, 3-20).

v. The Nineteenth Century Revisited

An unexpected glimpse of nineteenth-century worthies is found in Samuel Shapiro's "Fidel Castro and John Brown" (*CUF*, VI, i, 22-28), which compares the period of violent change in the U.S. in the 1850's and Latin America in our own times. He says that just as John Brown was a rallying point for abolitionists, so may the way of Fidel Castro inspire change in Latin America. He points out that just as Southern intransigents learned little from Brown's attack, the Latin American oligarchy and the U. S. government seem to have learned little about the nature of the revolutionary mood in Latin American countries today.

He further compares C. Wright Mills', Hemingway's, and Mailer's defense of Castro with the defense of Brown made by Howells,

Whittier, Thoreau, Emerson, Longfellow, Bryant, and Lowell. Similarly, Victor Hugo's interest in Brown is compared with that of
Sartre and Pablo Neruda in Castro.

Shapiro points out that in moments of historical crisis and violent
change the men who become critical figures are not necessarily
pleasant and agreeable, but are characterized by fanaticism and a
supreme conviction of the morality of their actions.

Carl Bode, "Columbia's Carnal Bed" (*AQ*, XV, 52-64), provides
us with a fascinating discussion of early literary pornography and
offers new light on a little-known aspect of the Victorian mind.

The Gilded Age, A Reappraisal (Syracuse, N.Y., Syracuse Univ.
Press), edited by H. Wayne Morgan, contains essays on American
culture, politics, business, and labor, which re-evaluate the Gilded
Age in order to elevate it. H. Wayne Morgan's introductory "An
Age in Need of Reassessment: A View Beforehand" points out, for
example, the largely negative influence of Parrington and Charles
Beard on all subsequent attempts to look at the period with objectivity. In their zeal to rehabilitate the period, the essayists tend to
overlook or blur into indistinctness many of its social, political, and
economic disgraces. Of particular value to the field of American
Studies are the final three chapters, "Gilt, Gingerbread, and Realism: The Public and its Taste" by Robert R. Roberts; "The Search
for Reality: Writers and Their Literature" by Robert Falk; and
"New Men and New Ideas: Science and the American Mind" by
Paul F. Boller, Jr.

Note also for this era Ray Frazer, "Looking Backward: Books
in the '80s" (*ClareQ*, X, iii, 29-33).

American Prose Masters (Cambridge, Mass., Harvard Univ.
Press, Belknap), edited by Howard Mumford Jones, contains evaluations of Cooper, Hawthorne, Emerson, Poe, Lowell, and Henry
James, written by the forerunner of the New Humanist movement,
William Crary Brownell. The essays were printed separately from
1905 to 1909, and the book was published in 1909 by Charles Scribner's Sons, for whom Brownell was chief literary adviser for forty
years. Several of the essays republished here are valuable contributions to American criticism, particularly those on Cooper and
Emerson, and Professor Jones' introduction accurately sets forth
Brownell's position as a critic. Excellent notes and annotations are
also provided.

A companion volume to Professor Jones' edition of Brownell's essays on American writers is *Paul Elmer More's Shelburne Essays on American Literature* (New York, Harcourt, Brace, and World), a Harbinger Book, the essays selected and edited by Daniel Aaron, who also includes a short biographical and bibliographical note and an introduction. More's deepest sympathies were for New England, and, as Aaron points out, he was at his best when dealing with "the winter, spring, and Indian summer of the New England mind," but he was effective as well with writers who were not congenial, Whitman for example. Occasionally his moral outlook led him astray, as when he dismissed Baudelaire as a feeble and degenerate imitator of Poe. While the essays in this volume are not part of the New Humanist ammunition, many readers will welcome their republication all the more for this reason.

Martin Green offers *Reappraisals: Some Commonsense Readings in American Literature* (London, Hugh Evelyn), with chapters on writers from Hawthorne to Nabokov, and Howard Boatwright has edited *Essays before a Sonata and other Writings* (New York: Norton, 1962), with essays on writers of the New England renaissance. See also Alfred Kazin, "The First and the Last: New England in the Novelist's Imagination" (*SatR*, XLVI, 2 Feb., 12-15, 45).

Hamlin Hill in "Modern American Humor, the Janus Laugh" (*CE*, XXV, 170-176) argues that native American humor has not been displaced by the "sophisticated" humor of the *New Yorker* magazine. When it has not been incorporated in the works of writers like Faulkner, it has used the mass media as its outlet. The native streak in American humor can be safely labeled as "sane," and its release is in the hearty guffaw. The other side of modern humor derives from the Genteel Tradition of Charles Dudley Warner, E. C. Stedman, or Thomas Bailey Aldrich. Their descendants concerned themselves with pure nonsense, which tended to peer inward into the world of fantasy, to play with language. Once that urbanity began to encounter a world of harsh reality with which it had no equipment to cope, it turned into neurotic humor, adding the black humor which had been an undercurrent in Poe, Hawthorne, and Melville, and which was seen later in Ambrose Bierce. The retreat from reality is into the delusion, that of Walter Mitty or Balso Snell.

Carl Bode in "The Sound of American Literature a Century Ago" (*PBA*, XLVII, 1961, 97-112, reprinted in *JGE*, XV, 1-17) shows how the tradition of the American lyceum aided American literature. The lyceum augmented the incomes of writers, provided them with a public and a place to test their new works. He points out that Emerson published his essays with practically no changes after their delivery as lectures. Not all writers benefited, but Emerson and Thoreau before the Civil War, Twain and Bayard Taylor after it were great successes.

Henry Nash Smith's "The American Scholar Today" (*SWR*, XLVIII, 191-199), which served in expanded form as an Honor's Day Convocation address at Southern Methodist University in April, 1963, is a provocative restatement of Emerson's attitudes toward American society in "The American Scholar," his Phi Beta Kappa speech delivered at Harvard in August, 1837. Smith compares the Transcendentalists, "the young men with knives in their brains," with many modern American writers who are similarly disenchanted with the "apparently monolithic structure of modern American business."

Smith notes that two works, Paul Goodman's *Growing Up Absurd* and William H. Whyte's *The Organization Man*, show how today's small rejecting minority and large conforming majority parallel, in intenser form perhaps, life in mid-nineteenth-century America. Sensitive observers in both periods have declared the system on the whole unattractive. In nineteenth-century fiction Hawthorne, Melville, James, and Twain added to Emerson's company of Outsiders. Smith separates middle-brow fiction from the serious anti-heroic fiction of Styron, Mailer, Malamud, or Ellison. The rebellious protagonists of popular fiction recognizes finally that society was right all along and comes back into the fold. Although Smith admits that Emerson's doctrine of self-reliance might be somewhat naïve in our more complicated world, he urges us to remember with Emerson that one should honor one's doubts and skepticisms. One should tend to treat attacks on the Establishment with charity and respect.

vi. Contemporary Literary Problems and the Future

Richard Beale Davis in "American Literature in the World Today" (*TSL*, VIII, 119-139, originally the Phi Kappa Phi lecture at the University of Tennessee in 1962) discusses the role of the American professor as an interpreter of the United States. He carries more weight in foreign countries than the professional diplomat because it is felt that he is really unhampered in what he may say and because the foreign intellectual world is more interested in our creative literature than in the nature of our government.

Tracing history of the American image abroad, Davis argues that while in the nineteenth century America symbolized the land where democracy had worked, with Emerson and Whitman contributing to this picture, in our own time the United States is generally seen as the bulwark of capitalism and the major monument of materialism. Largely through the efforts of American professors, however, countries throughout the world have in more recent years become closer acquainted with American literature.

H. Wayne Morgan in *Writers in Transition: Seven Americans* (New York, Hill and Wang) treats Stephen Crane, Edith Wharton, Ellen Glasgow, Willa Cather, Sherwood Anderson, Hart Crane, and Thomas Wolfe in their relation to large cultural shifts and crises. Cather, Glasgow, and Anderson attempted to deal, only Anderson optimistically, with the great shift from agrarian to industrial America. Wharton recorded the profound social change which occurred as the landed aristocracy yielded to the new spokesmen of wealth based on industry and finance. Hart Crane concerned himself with the impact of the machine on society. Both Cranes are viewed as literary innovators, indicative of changes in the concepts of literature, Wolfe as the prime literary spokesman for the American experience. Morgan is frankly interested in these writers as cultural manifestations, and it is as cultural history that his study has value.

The second series of *Writers at Work: The Paris Review Interviews* (New York, Viking) was edited and prepared for publication by George Plimpton, with an introduction by the late Van Wyck Brooks. Of the fourteen writers interviewed, four are now dead, and the interviews recall their vitality and intelligence most vividly. In both of these series (the first was edited by Malcolm Cowley) the interview, skilfully handled, is used as a technique of literary criticism.

Stephen Spender in "Poets and Critics: The Forgotten Difference" (*SatR*, XLVI, Oct. 5, 15-18) stresses the difference between poets and critics. We live, he says, in a critical age in which criticism tends to create its own synthetic kind of poetry and to appreciate only that work which the critical apparatus can deal with.

The critic stands on precedented territory, aware of tradition, which he relates to the work at hand. The poet, according to Spender, is always alone with his experience, "condemned to a life sentence of solitary confinement." Originality is not highly prized in art today, but the poet has to be original. He must be true to the uniqueness of his own vision, if he is to write poetry at all.

Modern American Criticism (Englewood Cliffs, New Jersey, Prentice-Hall, Inc.) by Walter Sutton is part of the series of Princeton Studies of Humanistic Scholarship in America, Richard Schlatter, general editor. The major movements are clearly elucidated and their weaknesses precisely laid bare, but with great objectivity. For example, in dealing with the development of New Criticism, Sutton traces the attitude toward the role of historical considerations from early intolerance to gradual acceptance. Without seeming to diminish in any way the profound importance of the New Critical movement in America, he points out that the current consensus toward a dialectical synthesis of criticism and history has made largely irrelevant the old critical wars. In an essentially fair summary of the neo-Aristotelian Chicago school, he nevertheless points out their too rigid observance of Aristotle's own vocabulary, and while he agrees with Ronald Crane's insistence on the need for true critical pluralism, he reminds us that the Chicago school is in no way humble when it sets up a hierarchy of systems, with its own designated as the most "scientific." In the final chapter, "Criticism as a Social Act," Sutton's own principles shine forth most clearly.

R. W. B. Lewis in "Literary Possibilities of the Next Decade," published in *Trends in Modern American Society* (Philadelphia, Univ. of Pennsylvania Press, 1962), which appeared originally as "American Letters: a Projection" (*YR*, LI, Winter, 1962, 211-226), suggests that the era brought in by the inauguration of President Kennedy may stimulate writers more than did the cultural emptiness of the Eisenhower era.

Herbert Gold, who has edited *First Person Singular: Essays for the Sixties* (New York, Dial), asserts that writers have indeed resumed dealing with general cultural problems in serious essays. The collection contains essays by Saul Bellow, James Baldwin, Paul Goodman, Mary McCarthy, Arthur Miller, William Styron, Gore Vidal, and others, chosen to reflect the writer's comment on contemporary life. With a few exceptions the essays chosen for this collection fail to reveal much significance. Several, however, are exceptionally perceptive: for example, Paul Goodman's "The Devolution of Democracy" and William Styron's "Mrs. Aadland's Little Girl, Beverly."

Approaches to the Study of Twentieth-Century Literature is the published account of the proceedings of a conference held at Michigan State University, East Lansing, on May 2-4, 1961, for the purpose of tracking a path through the wilderness of the academic study of twentieth-century literature. The *Proceedings* print fully the papers presented to the Conference and offer a condensed text of the discussions which followed. The major papers were "Form and Circumstance: A Study of the Study of Modern Literature" by Frederick J. Hoffman; "Synchronic Present: The Academic Future of Modern Literature in America" by Walter J. Ong, S.J., which asserts that scholarly activity and academic interest in modern literature is a positive and helpful influence rather than a detrimental influence on fiction; and "Some Remarks on Programs for Graduate Students in the Field of Recent Literature" by Clarence Gohdes, which raises some tough-minded questions about the study of contemporary literature in the universities. Most of the text of three additional discussion groups is printed: Group I, concerned with bibliographical and textual studies of twentieth-century writers, was led by James B. Meriwether, who spoke of the need of introducing to the study of modern writers systematic principles of bibliography, in the manner of Fredson Bowers. Professor Meriwether outlined some of the work on Cozzens, Fitzgerald, Faulkner, and others that has been done, and in the discussion which followed Roy Harvey Pearce spoke of the new edition of the works of Hawthorne, edited according to Bowers' principles, being prepared for Ohio State University Press; Group II, led by Murray Krieger, dealt with contemporary literary criticism. Group III led by Herbert Weisinger dealt with historical study and comparative literature.

Another symposium, "Individualism in Twentieth-Century America" (*TQ*, VI, ii, 98-176) was held at the University of Texas in December, 1962. The papers presented and the ensuing panel discussions have been edited and introduced by Gordon Mills. The participants were Louis Hartz, Frederick J. Hoffman, David M. Potter, Paul A. Samuelson, and Leslie A. White. Of particular interest for American studies is Hoffman's "Dogmatic Innocence: Self-assertion in Modern American Literature" (*TQ*, VI, ii, 152-161),

which points to Puritanism and Transcendentalism as major historical sources of American individualism.

We have apparently reached a stage of development in this
country in which sophisticated and objective consideration of our
cultural past is thought to be not only possible, but desirable. Tensions and anxieties about the present world may account for the
need to set the record straight. They may also influence our current
urge to relate an unsteady present to a more stable past.

Index

Ching, James C., 105
Chittick, V. L. O., 140
Chivers, Thomas Holley, 215, 216
Christenson, Francis, 89-90
Christman, Henry M., 42
Church, Margaret, 141
Churchill, Winston, 136
Chyet, Stanley F., 104
Clark, Barrett H., 201
Clark, David R., 172, 179-180
Clark, George P., 126
Clark, Robert L., Jr., 70
Clark, Willis Gaylord, 119
Clayton, John, 101
Clement, A. L., 153
Clendenning, John, 172
Cohen, Hennig, 33, 39, 59, 97, 99
Cohn, L. H., 83
Coindreau, Maurice Edgar, 72, 74
Cole, McKelva, 154
Coleridge, S. T., 45, 67
Collins, Carvel, 77
Confucius, 175-176
Connelly, Thomas L., 214
Connolly, Francis X., 142
Connolly, Thomas E., 75, 120-121
Conrad, Joseph, 75
Conway, Moncure, 16
Cook, Captain James, 101
Cook, Reginald L., 11, 169-170
Cooke, Jacob E., 97
Cooke, Rose Terry, 130
Cooper, James Fenimore, 60, 61, 102, 110-111, 114, 117, 218
Cooperman, Stanley, 113, 136
Costello, Donald P., 148
Cotton, John, 99
Covici, Pascal, Jr., 59
Cowley, Malcolm, 72, 132, 212, 221
Cowper, John, 168
Cox, James M., 57-58
Coxe, George C., 44
Cozzens, James Gould, 144, 158, 223
Cranch, Christopher, 3
Crane, Hart, 133, 166, 177-180, 210, 221
Crane, Ronald, 222
Crane, Stephen, 111, 114-117, 133, 198, 221
Cranfill, Thomas M., 70
Creely, Robert, 184, 188, 189, 192
Crèvecoeur, Michel-Guillaume Jean de, 104

Cummings, E. E., 166, 170, 172, 179, 184, 185
Cunningham, J. V., 186
Curley, Daniel, 149
Curley, Thomas F., 141

Dahl, Curtis, 111, 199-200
Dahlberg, Edward, 158, 210
Daiches, David, 49
Dameron, J. Lasley, 25, 121, 123
Daniels, Howell, 66
Daniels, Mabel, 171-172
Dante (Alighieri), 166, 173
Darwin, Charles, 45
Davenport, William H., 201
Davidson, Donald, 187, 213
Davidson, Edward H., 27, 102
Davies, Samuel, 102
Davis, Merrell R., 29, 35
Davis, Richard Beale, 98, 108-109, 220-221
Davis, Robert Gorham, 157, 162-163
Davis, Tom, 147
Davis, Wesley Ford, 145
Day, Douglas, 136
De Falco, Joseph M., 52, 88-89
Defoe, Daniel, 105
De Forest, John William, 112
De Jong, David Cornel, 159
Dekker, George, 173, 174-175
De Koven, Bernard, 51
Dell, Floyd, 137
Dellingham, William B., 116
Dembo, L. S., 174, 175-176
Detweiler, Robert, 45
DeVoto, Bernard, 53, 55, 57, 63
DeVries, Peter, 159
Dewey, Orville, 7
Diaz, Abby Morton, 16
Dickens, Charles, 67
Dickens, Robert S., 11
Dickinson, Emily, 46, 126-128, 129, 169, 183
Dickinson, John, 104
Diggins, John P., 138
Dillon, George, 167, 187
Doolittle, Hilda, 166
Dos Passos, John, 133, 134, 138-139
Dostoievsky, Fëdor, 38
Douglass, James W., 207
Dowell, Bobby Ray, 79
Drake, William, 11
Dreiser, Theodore, 132, 136-137, 212
Drinnon, Richard, 12

Holmes, Oliver Wendell, 13, 126
Hooker, Thomas, 103
Hoole, William Stanley, 109
Hooper, Johnson J., 109
Hopkins, Robert, 109
Hopkins, Samuel, 106
Hopkins, Viola, 68
Horace, 106
Horowitz, Floyd Ross, 159
Horton, Philip, 178
Hosmer, Gladys E. H., 13
Hough, Henry Bettle, 13
Howard, Leon, 30-31, 97, 102
Howard, Sidney, 202, 203
Howe, Irving, 212-213
Howell, Elmo, 79
Howells, William Dean, 54, 56, 67, 70, 112-114, 117
Hudson, Arthur Palmer, 99
Hudson, Benjamin F., 107
Hudspeth, Richard N., 114
Hudspeth, Robert, 136
Hughes, Catherine, 204
Hughes, Hatcher, 214
Hughes, Langston, 198-199, 216
Hughes, Richard, 23 n.
Hull, Raymona E., 10, 26
Humphreys, A. R., 32
Huneker, James Gibbons, 200
Hungerford, Harold R., 116
Hunter, J. Paul, 105, 142
Hunter, Jim, 59
Hutchinson, E. R., 79
Hutchinson, William R., 15
Hutchinson, William T., 98
Hyman, Stanley Edgar, 13
Hynes, Joseph A., 207

Ibsen, Henrik, 200
Ingemar, Bernhard Severin, 43
Irie, Yukio, 6
Irving, Washington, 110, 117
Irwin, W. R., 170
Isaacs, Neil D., 76, 153
Ives, C. B., 70

Jackson, Esther M., 206, 207
Jackson, Joseph Henry, 134-135
Jacobsen, Josephine, 170
Jahn, Erwin, 111
James, Alice, 70
James, Henry, the elder, 36
James, Henry, 59, 64-71, 113, 129, 133, 218, 220

James, Henry, *works*
"Abasement of the Northmores," 71
Ambassadors, The, 65, 66, 68, 69
American, The, 59, 68, 173, 176, 177
"Art of Fiction, The," 67
"Author of Beltraffio," 70
Awkward Age, The, 65, 66, 69
"Beast in the Jungle, The," 70, 71
"Birthplace, The," 71
Daisy Miller, 70
Golden Bowl, The, 66, 67, 69-70
"Great Good Place, The," 71
"In the Cage," 69
"Jolly Corner, The," 70, 71
"Middle Years, The," 70
"New Novel, The," 64
Notebooks, 70
"Patagonia," 69
Portrait of a Lady, The, 66, 67, 68
Princess Casamassima, The, 68
Roderick Hudson, 68
Sacred Fount, The, 66, 68-69
Sense of the Past, The, 70
Spoils of Poynton, The, 64, 66, 69-70
Tragic Muse, The, 64
"Turn of the Screw, The," 66, 70
"Velvet Glove, The," 68
Watch and Word, 67
What Maisie Knew, 66
James, William, 168, 169, 171, 183
Jarrell, Randall, 184-185, 187
Jeffers, Robinson, 48, 167, 184, 192
Jefferson, Thomas, 95, 100, 104-105, 106, 215
Jessop, G. H., 198
Jewett, Sarah Orne, 111
Jocelyn, Sister M., 150
Johnson, Andrew, 126
Johnson, George W., 111, 115
Johnson, Thomas H., 126
Jonas, Maurice, 205
Jones, Alun R., 153
Jones, George F., 98
Jones, Gordon W., 101
Jones, Granville H., 160
Jones, Howard Mumford, 106, 218
Jones, James, 160, 163
Jones, Joseph, 109
Jones, LeRoi, 188, 216-217
Jones, Madison, 152
Jones, Robert Edmond, 208
Jones, Sir William, 35
Jonson, Ben, 178

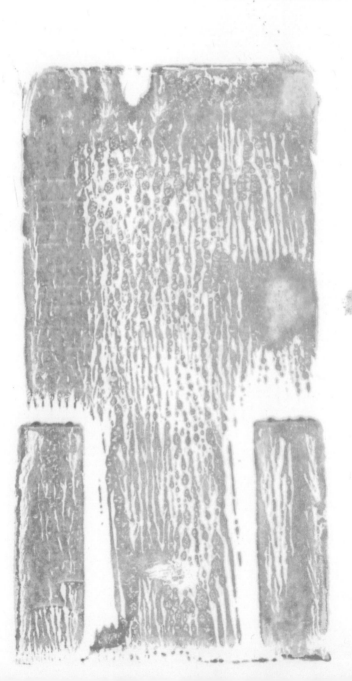